I THOUGHT I WAS DOING WELL UNTIL ...

A PERSONAL TESTIMONY

MIAH WILLIAMS

WESTBOW
PRESS®
A DIVISION OF THOMAS NELSON
& ZONDERVAN

Copyright © 2021 Maha Termanini Williams.

All rights reserved. No part of this book may be used or reproduced by any means, graphic, electronic, or mechanical, including photocopying, recording, taping or by any information storage retrieval system without the written permission of the author except in the case of brief quotations embodied in critical articles and reviews.

This book is a work of non-fiction. Unless otherwise noted, the author and the publisher make no explicit guarantees as to the accuracy of the information contained in this book and in some cases, names of people and places have been altered to protect their privacy.

WestBow Press books may be ordered through booksellers or by contacting:

WestBow Press
A Division of Thomas Nelson & Zondervan
1663 Liberty Drive
Bloomington, IN 47403
www.westbowpress.com
844-714-3454

Because of the dynamic nature of the Internet, any web addresses or links contained in this book may have changed since publication and may no longer be valid. The views expressed in this work are solely those of the author and do not necessarily reflect the views of the publisher, and the publisher hereby disclaims any responsibility for them.

Any people depicted in stock imagery provided by Getty Images are models, and such images are being used for illustrative purposes only. Certain stock imagery © Getty Images.

ISBN: 978-1-6642-2815-3 (sc)
ISBN: 978-1-6642-2817-7 (hc)
ISBN: 978-1-6642-2816-0 (e)

Library of Congress Control Number: 2021906202

Print information available on the last page.

WestBow Press rev. date: 4/12/2021

All Scripture quotations, unless otherwise indicated, are taken from the Holy Bible, New International Version®, NIV®. Copyright ©1973, 1978, 1984, 2011 by Biblica, Inc.® Used by permission of Zondervan. All rights reserved worldwide. www.zondervan.com The "NIV" and "New International Version" are trademarks registered in the United States Patent and Trademark Office by Biblica, Inc.®

Scripture quotations marked (AMP) taken from the Amplified® Bible (AMP), Copyright © 2015 by The Lockman Foundation. Used by permission. www.lockman.org

Scripture quotations marked (ESV) are from The ESV® Bible (The Holy Bible, English Standard Version®), copyright © 2001 by Crossway, a publishing ministry of Good News Publishers. Used by permission. All rights reserved.

Scripture quotations marked (KJV) are taken from the King James Version of the Bible.

Scripture marked (NKJV) taken from the New King James Version®. Copyright © 1982 by Thomas Nelson. Used by permission. All rights reserved.

Scripture quotations marked (NLT) are taken from the Holy Bible, New Living Translation, copyright ©1996, 2004, 2015 by Tyndale House Foundation. Used by permission of Tyndale House Publishers, a Division of Tyndale House Ministries, Carol Stream, Illinois 60188. All rights reserved.

Scripture marked Phillips is from the Phillips New Testament in Modern English.

Scripture quotations marked (TLB) are taken from The Living Bible copyright © 1971. Used by permission of Tyndale House Publishers, a Division of Tyndale House Ministries, Carol Stream, Illinois 60188. All rights reserved.

Scripture quotations marked (GNT) are from the Good News Translation—Second Edition. © 1992 by American Bible Society. Used by permission.

Glory to God,
who
"called me by His grace" (Galatians 1:15).

CONTENTS

Foreword xi
Preface xiii
Acknowledgments xix
Introduction xxiii

PART I   HE TRIED ME 1
Chapter 1   First Strike 3
Chapter 2   Second Strike 14
Chapter 3   Seigneur Dieu 18
Chapter 4   The Dream—First Time 22
Chapter 5   Madame Rita 25
Chapter 6   Financial Adviser 28
Chapter 7   The Dream—Again and Again 29
Chapter 8   Doctor's Rounds 34
Chapter 9   Mari 37
Chapter 10   Easter Sunday 43
Chapter 11   Praying for a Miracle 47

PART II   HE CALLED ME 51
Chapter 12   Westminster Chapel—First Visit 53
Chapter 13   Dr. Kendall 60

PART III   HE TOUCHED ME, OH, HE TOUCHED ME 69
Chapter 14   The Healing Prayer 71

PART IV   HE HEALED ME 75
Chapter 15   God Had a Different Plan from the Doctors' 77
Chapter 16   He Healed Me! End of Strike One 84

| Chapter 17 | Doesn't God Heal Everyone? Mari's Impromptu Sermon | 87 |

PART V	HE PROVIDED FOR ME	95
Chapter 18	Divine Promotion	97
Chapter 19	Divine Testing	101
Chapter 20	Divine Family	111
Chapter 21	Divine Instrument—End of the Second Strike	115

PART VI	HE CONFIRMED ME	121
Chapter 22	Dr. R. T. Kendall, What's Next?	123
Chapter 23	Divine Confirmation—the Baptism in the Holy Spirit	130
Chapter 24	Divine Prophecies—Out of the Mouths of Babes	134

PART VII	HE DISCIPLED ME	143
Chapter 25	Discovery Journey to the Trinity	151
Chapter 26	Discovery Journey to God the Father	172
Chapter 27	Discovery Journey to God the Son	213
Chapter 28	Discovery Journey to God the Holy Spirit	245

| PART VIII | HE REGENERATED ME | 263 |
| Chapter 29 | And He Regenerated Me | 265 |

Sources 277
Appendices 281
Appendix A Diversity-in-Unity within the Godhead 283
Appendix B Three Hundred Fifty-Six Prophecies Fulfilled by Jesus Christ 289

FOREWORD

I could not put down Miah's book *I Thought I Was Doing Well Until*.... I was not prepared for what I was reading. It far exceeded my greatest expectations.

I will admit to getting many requests to write endorsements for books, whether a foreword or a blurb for a dust jacket. I will also admit to asking my wife Louise to read the manuscripts for me—to vet them, to test them, or to give me a synopsis of the book in order to save me time.

Because I was writing a book of my own and was rushing to meet a deadline, I asked Louise to read this first. But when I noticed how excited she was as she read the manuscript, I put everything aside to start reading it immediately. And, as I said, I could not put it down.

I kept thinking of the verse, "For whoever has despised the day of small things shall rejoice" (Zechariah 4:10 ESV). When this Arab woman came to me after one Sunday morning service and said, "How do you convert? I want to convert to Christianity; I am a Muslim," I honestly did not take her seriously. I told her to see me during the prayer time before the evening service, thinking to myself that I would never see her again. But there she was, first in the queue. What is more, I could see in a minute that I was looking at a genuinely converted woman. I felt a bit guilty for having virtually dismissed her that morning. And yet I was very glad to have gotten it wrong.

Maha Termanini (as I knew her in those days) is an example of pure sovereign grace. God did it without my knowing it—whether it be Maha's salvation or her miraculous healing. I absolutely had nothing whatever to do with either. It is what God and God alone did. Her conversion to Christ is the most spectacular I have seen during my entire ministry of sixty-five years, including my twenty-five years at Westminster Chapel.

It was a year or so after her conversion that she invited Louise and me to lunch in a London Turkish restaurant. What impressed me most was at least twenty cassette tapes of my preaching on the floor of her car. She apologized for the mess, but believe me, any pastor would forgive a mess like that! It was at that lunch that she told her story about hearing "Kendall" in a dream, thinking it was *candle*. It was at that lunch I learned more about her healing from thyroid cancer. I learned later that she is the Turkish equivalent of royalty; her mother belonged to the end of the Ottoman Empire, and her father was a prominent government leader of Syria.

What I remember about praying for her and anointing her with oil is singularly nothing. What I mean is this: I felt utterly nothing when a deacon joined me in anointing her with oil. There was no manifestation, no sense of the Holy Spirit's presence—nothing. It goes to show that God can do something amazing and one may not realize it. As Jacob put it, "Surely the Lord is in this place, and I did not know it" (Genesis 28:16 ESV).

There is one thing that worries me a lot about Miah's book: she praises me too highly. It is rather embarrassing, to be honest. I hope the reader will take her opinion of me with a grain of salt. I've said for years that those I began to admire a bit too much sooner or later always disappoint me. That will come to Miah too.

That said, this book is bound to be a great blessing to those who read it. I guarantee it.

R. T. Kendall

PREFACE

It was 5:00 a.m. when the phone rang. An angry voice shouted in my sleepy ear, "Have you become Christian?"

My eyes flew wide open while my heart skipped a beat. I sprang straight up in bed. I recognized the voice; it was my dad. He sounded as if he was fuming in anger.

"Dad, please calm down," I begged him.

Dad's voice went to a crescendo: "Have you become Christian? Answer me right now."

"Dad," I softly replied, "this is not a topic to discuss on the phone."

"I gather from your answer that it is true!"

"Dad, please, let's not talk about this on the phone."

Three times my dad asked me if I had converted, and each time I remained quiet. No words came out. When I did not respond, my dad's voice tone escalated to a threat: "Listen to me carefully, girl. Because you have become Christian, I now disown you. You are no longer my daughter, and I am no longer your father. I will cut you off totally from the family and your inheritance. I will pour Allah's wrath and curse upon you." And he hung up the phone.

The dial tone kept ringing in my ears for a while until it switched to a busy tone. Then, I put the receiver down. I pulled the covers over my head and replayed in my mind Dad's threats. I regretted my silence, but what could I have told him?

Dad must have detected my conversion from the letter I had sent him in which I subtly hinted of my gratitude to Jesus for healing me from a cancerous nodule on my thyroid gland. Knowing my dad to be a highly educated and open-minded man, I believed that he would rejoice that Jesus had healed me. Besides, I grew up in an environment where religion and race created no division or hatred. So, what had changed?

I shared with my friend June the conversation with my dad. "What troubles me most," I said, "is that I answered Dad's questions with complete silence. I am concerned that I may have grieved the Holy Spirit for not confessing Jesus to my dad."

"No, no, no," June interjected. "No, you did not grieve the Holy Spirit." She reminded me of the passages where Jesus did not reply to all the charges when the Roman officials questioned Him about the accusations the Jewish leaders had brought against Him. The only response Jesus gave was His silence (Matthew 27:14; Luke 23:8–9). June's answer comforted me; sometimes silence may be the best response in a critical situation.

Yes, on Sunday, April 28, 1996, I converted from Islam to Christianity.

Nothing in the world would have prepared me for Sunday, April 28, 1996, when the course of my life took a sharp 180° turn and changed me forever. On that day, at 9:30 a.m., something woke me up—actually, almost pushed me out of bed with an inexplicable urge to get up and get dressed. One minute my body was begging me for a couple more hours of sleep, and the next minute, I had found myself on the steps of a big church I'd never seen before. To this day, I don't recall getting dressed, leaving the flat, getting in the car, or driving, or having any rational explanation as to how I had gotten to the church. Shocked— to say the least—I stood at the steps as if I had fallen from the sky, but that sort of thing happened only in movies! A big sign read "Westminster Chapel."[1] *A church? Where am I? What am I doing here? How did I get here?* The mystery of how had I gotten

---

[1] For ease of reading, I refer to Westminster Chapel as "the Chapel."

to the church—the last thing I recalled I was being at home—agonized me. I was sure that I was not dreaming (to this day, the church testifies of my presence on that day). I was awake with full awareness with a mystifying expectation of something about to happen. But what?

At the Chapel, I encountered Jesus! Why would Jesus appear to me, a Muslim, when I did not worship Him? I don't know. The encounter was unexpected, and the way it happened was supernatural and dramatic. Intellectually or mentally, I can't explain how the Holy Spirit transported me from my home to a church seven miles away, faster than a blink of an eye. I witnessed that nothing is impossible for God!

However, the main subject of *I Thought I Was Doing Well Until …* is my conversion, not about being transported. This book relates to the radical decision that instantaneously transformed me from within with a new heart. Undoubtedly, my conversion was the best thing that ever happened to me.

Around the time when Jesus called me to follow Him, my life was a total mess. The year 1996 started on a sour note with a series of disasters raiding my life at every turn. In February, cancer threatened my health. My boyfriend's extravagant spending led me to considerable debt and near-bankruptcy. And bullying endangered my health and career.

Unlike the previous collection of tragedies that came my way throughout the years, these three problems came in like a wrecking ball and hit me *simultaneously*. Fear paralyzed me and plunged me into the worst sort of suffering and frustration. In a matter of a few days, I found myself alone, sick, penniless, and emotionally distraught, unable to bear my problems—as I used to do in the past. A severe depression engulfed me. I became an absolute train wreck! I reached the end of my strength and gave up on the last shred of hope. Suicide started playing Russian roulette with my mind. I was desperate for a miracle to keep me alive. So, as a last resort, I called Allah for help—and Jesus showed up.

Looking back at that Sunday, I see that the Holy Spirit of God prepared my heart to yield to God's authority and will. He supernaturally carried me to the Chapel, where Jesus called me to follow Him. How did I know that the tiny whisper in my ears was the Holy Spirit of God? I don't know. It was then and there that I instantaneously received Jesus in my heart and confessed Him as my God, Lord, and Savior. How did I know that Jesus is God and a "Savior"? I can't answer any of these questions. My experience showed me that God does not do anything accidentally or spontaneously. I firmly believe that God planned my conversion before the creation of the world and scheduled the event to occur on a particular date. I am convinced that God planted seeds of faith in my heart many decades ago. On the Sunday I'm now speaking of, the seeds of faith germinated with a lifetime commitment to follow Jesus. It was then and there that I gave my life to Jesus. And I never looked back.

At the Chapel, people called me the *convert*, which did not amuse me, simply because I never saw myself fitting the definition. The *Oxford Dictionary* defines a convert as "a person who has been persuaded to change his/her religious faith or other belief." I want to make it clear that no one persuaded me, evangelized to me, or brainwashed me. I categorically refute my family's allegation that my then boyfriend influenced me. Besides, becoming a follower of Jesus is God's calling through the Holy Spirit; it is never humankind's work. That's why Jesus said in John 6:44, "No one can come to me unless the Father who sent me draws them."

Some readers may ask if my family is talking to me now. I can answer: "Absolutely!" Our relationship got closer and stronger than ever before. I have changed; the Lord replaced my heart of stone with a heart of flesh—He gave me a new heart pumping His love. My affections and feelings for my family are set on my love to glorify God. My love for my family is motivated by Jesus's teaching/commands and is empowered by the Holy Spirit. I admit that at first, my family was puzzled by my conversion. But the more they noticed the changes in me, the more they became drawn to God's love that reigns in my heart. Now, they ask me to pray for them in times of need. I unconditionally love my family with all my heart.

The reader may also ask if and how I resolved the problems, which I call strikes, that hit me around the time I met Jesus. I shout, "Praise God!" Jesus ran to my mess, miraculously got me out of it, and ushered onto the path He established for me. Jesus took me from the desert of confusion and despair to the shore of hope and life. One thing I learned is that while problems may knock at my door, I will not be alone, for God has promised throughout the Bible that He would never leave us or forsake us (this includes me). And while I cannot change my past, I can change my future with God's help and direction. I stand on God's promise for me: "I know the plans I have for you ... plans to give you hope and a future" (Jeremiah 29:11).

The purpose of *I Thought I Was Doing Well Until ...* is not to compare religions; far from it. I am *not* a theologian or a scholar, nor did I ever intend to be. This book describes the journey of my new Christian faith. It is my testimony of how I have become a believer in Christ. I am sharing a collection of passages from my journals, describing in my own words, my thoughts, understanding, challenges, and discoveries of God while studying the Bible. It's my testimony witnessing the grace of Jesus Christ, the love of God, and the fellowship of the Holy Spirit.

I wanted to share with you the aha moments I had while discovering the heart of the Godhead and the mysteries of the Trinity. O the precious Word of God that enriched and transformed my life! I loved researching, digging through, and studying the scriptures through the lens of the Holy Spirit and asking questions of why and how. I can say that God never got upset with my inquisitiveness and questions, some of which were quite daring. I learned that God never misses the opportunity to answer prayers in two ways: either directly or through a Word given to someone else. In the latter case, Dr. Kendall recommended that I test the spirit of the message to ensure compliance with the scripture. It took me time to get used to God's silence as His answer to some prayers. My journey led me to discover and know a loving God intimately with an everlasting love. One of the most significant discoveries was the knowledge that God loves me (and you) so much that He laid down His life for you and me. He died on the cross for our sins so we could have eternal fellowship with Him in heaven. O the grace of God! By His grace, He offered me the gift of salvation; this is my sure hope and confident expectation for an eternal presence with the Lord when I die.

I celebrate April 28, 1996, as my new birthday, the day Jesus Christ touched me, enriched my life, and gave me eternal life.

I pray that my journey gives you the desire to open your heart and mind to know Jesus Christ personally and sincerely and jump-start your walk with Him. I am confident that He will renew you and empower you in your life as He did to me—if you allow Him.

ACKNOWLEDGMENTS

First and foremost, I would like to thank God for His unfailing guidance and wisdom that He lavished upon me. Thank You, Father God, for Your gift of my salvation. Thank You, Lord Jesus, for giving me the passion for loving You and writing about You and the power to pursue my childhood dream to follow You! Thank You, Holy Spirit, for counseling me and teaching me through the years. I could never have finished *I Thought I Was Doing Well Until* ... without the faith I have in God, who "has rescued [me] from the dominion of darkness and brought [me] into the kingdom of the Son he loves, in whom [I] have redemption, the forgiveness of sins" (Colossians 1:13–14).

It is with immense gratitude that I acknowledge the support of my dear husband, Michael. This book would have remained a dream had it not been for Michael's affection, inspiration, and patience. Michael, I thank God for having you in my life. You were a constant source of support and encouragement, demonstrating understanding during my long solitary writing period.

Leah Tekie. Thank you, dearest Leah, my dear and loyal friend of all time. You stood by me in my darkest moments. I still feel the power of your prayers over me.

My most profound appreciation goes to Dr. R. T. Kendall, senior pastor of Westminster Chapel (1977–2002). I thank God for sending me to Westminster Chapel and putting me under the pastorship of Dr. Kendall. Dr. Kendall's book *God Meant It for Good* was instrumental in leading me to forgive myself and those who hurt me and causing me to start a new life.

I am also indebted to my dear friend Isabel Espindola Pollard for taking the time to review the chapters and walking with me from vision to reality. Isabel's support of this book was pivotal in my moving forward. I am grateful for her valuable comments and advice.

In his sovereign providence, God used Carol Honodel's prayer to send me a message to write my testimony of faith. On that day, Carol rushed to my house to tell me that she had heard the Holy Spirit saying, "Tell Miah that she has a book to write. She knows which one, not the novel she is currently writing." No one, including Carol, had previous knowledge that I was interested in writing, let alone writing my testimony of faith. I could not contain my joy at the privilege the Lord had bestowed on me by wanting me to write about my spiritual journey. From that moment on, I started writing *I Thought I Was Doing Well Until* …. Thank you, Lord, for the divine inspiration.

My fondest gratitude goes to my dear Ofelia Hernandez for her nonceasing prayers, and to Sally McDaniel for her constant encouragement to write my testimony.

My sincere appreciation goes to my friends[2] Mrs. Summons, Anwar, Gretchen, Jacob, June, Marita, Mervet, and Nabil, who have shown interest in my conversion. They wanted to know why and how I converted. Thank you for your support, dear friends! Your inquisitive questions, the debates that we had over many dinners, and your comments motivated me to further my research on the scriptures and read the works of numerous theologians. You helped me to study the Word more in-depth and expand my knowledge. I reconstructed your questions, our conversations, and our debates from memory and my journals in the form of meetings called Core Friend Group Meetings. What I present herein is very close to what we discussed and said. Thank you for walking with me throughout my journey. I mourned at the news

---

[2] Fictitious names.

that Mrs. Summons went to heaven; she was a great teacher, a friend, and a great moderator in our debates.

Special thanks to my dear friend Mrs. Lois Miller O'Neal for her words of encouragement, complimenting my writing and the depth of the analysis and research I've covered. Lois's encouraging words boosted my morale and motivated me to complete my book. Thank you, Lois. Your dear father, Dr. Miller (RIP), was the first person I told about my conversion. We rejoiced. I loved our time together in London and in Dallas. I cherish his teaching of the scriptures and photography. I considered Dr. Miller my spiritual father. Also, I hold on to Mrs. Miller's faith in Jesus in the face of her illness.

I am also grateful to the people and deacons at Westminster Chapel for their warm welcome to the Chapel. Special thanks to Brian Reed, Bill Reynolds, and Benjamin Chan for their advice and explanations to my endless questions, which I used to bring to them on Sunday. Thank you for not running away from me or hiding when I came to the Chapel! Benjamin, I cherish the prayer meetings on Saturday mornings with Mrs. Louise Kendall. I loved those meetings and listening to your prayers. I was in awe of how simple they were, and yet they shook every fiber in me. The other reason I loved those meetings was because of the visions I had. I used to get two to three visions at a time with specific messages. Thank you, Brian, for taking the time after working hours to meet with me and disciple me! I cherish those moments and your precious advice. I coveted your deep understanding of the scriptures and wanted so much to reach your level of knowledge!

A big and sincere thanks to my dear friends Jennifer and David Olson, who shepherded me in my walk with fresh streams of teaching and knowledge. Jennifer and David are my spiritual family. My gratitude for their friendship is beyond words!

I would like to express my deep and sincere gratitude to my siblings for their exceptional love. Although my siblings disagreed with the new way of life I had selected, they nevertheless remained faithful to their love for me and the unity of the family. I am fortunate to have a loving relationship with them. I pray that the publication of *I Thought I Was Doing Well Until* ... will not change their hearts. I want to make it clear that I have the highest regard for my family's culture and superior reputation. Special thanks to my brother Rocky, with whom I have a special, close bond. Stirred with compassion, Rocky continually inspired, motivated, and challenged me to widen my intellectual horizons. Our conversations were a great source of learning. Thank you, Rocky, for your patience when editing my letters and memos (and, boy, there were many!). Thank you for teaching me your writing methods to improve my English language, which has enabled me to write this book. You have played a big part in my life to get me where I am right now. Zafer and Radwan, I will never forget your love and support. Thank you!

As always, I am indebted to my father (RIP) for his unconditional and unprecedented love, guiding me through life to be a positive person, even in the darkest hours. My dad was my inspiration. From a young age, I witnessed my dad demonstrate by example his wisdom, knowledge, discipline, trust, moral values, respect, and great intellect. I am eternally grateful to my dad, who lavished on me valuable guidance, teaching me everything I needed to succeed in life; any good traits within me, I owe them to Dad. I believe I inherited my dad's passion for writing and the determination to reach the stars. Thanks, Dad! You were the greatest of God's blessing! I miss you loads!

I Thought I Was Doing Well Until ... would not have been possible without all the people mentioned here.

INTRODUCTION

Everyone has a story. My story started on April 28, 1996, when, unexpectedly, Jesus appeared to me and touched me! Why would Jesus show Himself to me, a Muslim, when I did not worship Him? I don't know. All I knew was that when Jesus said to me "Follow Me," I followed Him with firm conviction. I never looked back. It was then and there that I converted from Islam to Christianity.

My conversion inspired me to write my story, even though English is not my native language. By reading my testimony, you will travel with me through the supernatural conversion and find out how Jesus delivered me. He gave me the courage to come out of the spiritual and emotional dungeon in which I had lived for years. Jesus helped me to remove the many and different masks from my face. He tore down the brick walls behind which I had hidden the broken child within me for decades, and He liberated me to become a thriving woman!

My story is a story of freedom. With the pages you are about to read, you will walk into my journey of healing from the deep wounds caused by sexual abuse that started on my fifth birthday and lasted five years.

The horrific experience of my childhood abuse turned my heart to stone. Fueled with passionate rage, I distrusted everyone. As a traumatized child, and paralyzed by pain, I turned my back on Islam and sailed away from its mirage shores.

And yet, in the depth of my child's heart, I fantasized of the divine power of my Christian friends' God, whom I called

"Seigneur Dieu."[3] I don't know why I believed that He was the only one who could give me the courage to survive the horrific ordeal that lasted five years, which seemed like an eternity. And He did give me courage. The proof is that I am still alive today. Once the abuse ceased, I ended Seigneur Dieu's mission for help and put Him on the shelf.

When the abuse stopped, I did not go free; I remained in bondage. The repercussions of the abuse haunted me throughout my adult life, no matter how well I suppressed the memories or secretly hid them. The abuse plagued my life with intense emotional struggles that turned me into a walking time bomb sort of person. Still, I managed to move on. I surfed on my own through the glassy waves of life, aiming for those perfect waves that might bring success, peace, and joy into my life. While I found success, I lacked peace and joy.

My quest for peace and joy led me to dabble in man-made religions. I moved from one temple to another and chanted prayers in foreign languages I did not understand. I prayed to powerless and mute statues, joined secret societies, and adopted the New Age philosophy. After many years of being involved in various spiritual systems, I found that none of them had satisfied my hunger for genuine and lasting inner peace and joy. I became more frustrated than ever before. What struck me most was that I had found many gods and many contradictions. And each religion or faith system claimed *the* true God. What is the meaning of "true God"? How does one identify the true God? Is Allah the true God? Is Jesus the true God? How does one choose the true God?

A friend asked me how I would recognize the true God. I answered, "*If* there is a true God, *He* will come to me. He will draw me to Himself. I have had it with chasing a rainbow of spiritualism."

---

[3] French for "Lord my God." I imitated my Christian friends at my Catholic French school.

"Still," she said, "how would you know that He who is drawing you to Himself is the true God?"

I replied, "If His presence is magnetizing and He performs a unique supernatural miracle that transforms me instantaneously into a believing person, only then will I know that He is the real and true God—and I will follow Him." In my mind, I had laid down not only a bold condition but also an impossible one.

With this thought in mind, I aborted my quest of searching for the true God and fought with all my might all calls of spirituality and all isms. *Who wants religion?* I concluded. I praised the 'me' generation movement and embraced it. Without my realizing it, idolatry crept into my life. It led me to focus on myself and to honor the divine spark within me.

I worshipped my "almighty self" and idolized my professional victories. While I had the financial means to enjoy everything that life might offer, a feeling of loss continually gnawed at me. Despite my career successes, which fulfilled my madness of materialism, I remained discontented. I felt empty and stuck in a rut. Outwardly I looked happy, but inwardly my emotional struggles continued. My deepest longings were for genuine love. My heart, mind, and soul craved for something, but what? Nothing satisfied me. Nothing was able to put out the fire in my heart. *What is the purpose of my life in this world? What is the reason for my being?* I started wondering.

I filled the emptiness in my soul with work. Little did I know, I had become trapped in the abyss of workaholism. My job dominated my life and put me on a wild race of blind ambition. My life seemed like being on a merry-go-round, going faster and faster until it was too fast to stop it or get off. But suddenly, one day, the merry-go-round abruptly stopped, and I collided unexpectedly with two tragedies. The collision was so intense that I lost balance and fell off the merry-go-round, landing flat on my face. In a matter of one week, my life turned upside down, confronting me with a life-threatening illness and unforeseen financial challenges. In one week, the doctors diagnosed a lump in my thyroid that, unless removed, could damage my vocal cords and hinder my speech for life. In the same week, the manager of my bank called me to say that my account was in serious arrears, which could result in collection and possible default. If that was not enough, the abuse I had endured as a child had made me unconsciously susceptible to being enslaved by bullying.

My disastrous circumstances had dropped a millstone over my head. No conventional bomb would have an effect on me like these three strikes that life had thrown at me. Thinking about my health issue led me to ponder on death. I had never thought of death. Why should I? I was young, and I believed in the world's scientific evolution of an end to aging. The question that occupied my mind was where I would go after I died. Not knowing what would happen after I died was the epicenter of my anxiety. Would I go to Jannah[4] or Jahannam?[5] A Christian family friend, Mrs. Miller, once told me that she wasn't afraid of dying. Death would usher her into the presence of Jesus Christ, who would, in turn, shepherd her to a new phase that she called the beginning of eternal life in heaven. My friend's confidence in eternal life in heaven agonized me as I did not have a similar assurance of eternal life in Jannah. I mourned my ill-stricken luck.

I was desperate for a miracle. One night, I started crying out to Allah for help, but my prayer stuck in my throat. I had not prayed to Allah for years, so why now? Frustrated, I yelled aloud, "Which God shall I call now for help? Is there a true God in this universe who can help me? Let Him show up!" I wept for a long time, lamenting the sudden and sharp turn in my fate. Suddenly, my cries and pleas came to an abrupt halt when I heard myself

---

[4] Arabic for "heaven" and "paradise." Both the Qu'ran and the Injil (Arabic Bible) use *Jannah* for "heaven" and "paradise."
[5] Arabic for "hell." Both the Qu'ran and the Injil use *Jehannam* for "hell."

whispering, "Seigneur Dieu,[6] my Christian friends' God, I need You. Would You please come back again to my aid?"

I had not called on Seigneur Dieu for decades. Would He help me again as He had when I was a child? Would He help me although He was not my God? Would He help me, a Muslim? I stretched my arms up in the air and cried out loud, "Seigneur Dieu, my Lord! I am calling You again. If You genuinely exist and have not forgotten me, show Yourself to me again, as You did when I was a child, and come to my rescue as You did before."

And He did!

On April 28, 1996, I was supernaturally transported from my home to Westminster Chapel to meet the Lord Jesus. To this day, I do not recall how I moved from my bedroom to the steps of Westminster Chapel faster than the blink of an eye. The church was seven miles away from my home. I had never been to this church; actually, I did not know its existence. I had no clue how I had gotten there or why I was at a church, more so at that particular church. All I knew was that I was awake with full awareness. For years, and to this day, people from the church talk about my supernatural conversion.

During the service, I felt a divine presence around me! Immediately, and without any shadow of a doubt, I recognized that He was the Lord Jesus, the true God. How? Jesus fulfilled my condition to believe in Him. Jesus's presence was magnetizing. He had performed a miracle by transporting me to the church, and He transformed me instantaneously into a believing person. I felt in my heart a still soft whisper: "Follow Me. You did not choose Me; I chose you. You are Mine." Wow! Does God really speak?[7] [8]

---

[6] French for "God, my Lord."

[7] I learned later that God often speaks to people by the inner witness of the Holy Spirit to our spirits (John 10:27). Jesus said that His sheep listen to His voice.

[8] After my conversion, I found that the words I had heard in my spirit complied with the Word of God (specifically, Matthew 4:19 and John 15:16).

How? Why did Jesus reveal Himself to me when I had not sought Him? I do not know. But the moment I heard the gentle whisper, I believed, as if a switch had been turned on inside me, birthing a new faith with power. I believed because I heard His voice and did not harden my heart with disbelief (Hebrews 3:7).

Then and there, I confessed Jesus as my Lord and my God. My heart leapt with joy; it was hard to hush the drumming of the beats. A sudden longing grew in my heart, not only to become a follower believer in Jesus, but also to be adopted into His family of believers and to have eternal life with Him in heaven, just like Mrs. Miller said.

On that day at the Chapel, the Lord revealed to me the meaning of one of the dreams that I had had a few weeks before my conversion. I had had the same dream three times in which I heard a voice calling, "Candle." Wait until you read chapter 13 about my biggest surprise, when I found out that the name of the senior pastor of Westminster Chapel was Dr. R. T. Kendall! Following my conversion, the Lord has performed other miracles in my life, notably, the miraculous disappearance of the lump on my thyroid weeks before the surgery to remove it and the provision to pay off my debts in full. Also, by grace of God, the bullying that I had endured ended in victory. Since my confession of Jesus, I have never looked back regretfully or moved forward fearfully.

My journal entries testify to the birth of my new faith from seeds that God had planted decades ago. One of the mysteries of my faith is that I believed in Jesus as God since I was a child.

I Thought I Was Doing Well Until ... is far too short compared to the mass of knowledge I learned along my journey that started on April 28, 1996. Being a professional systems analyst, I used my analytical expertise in analyzing and studying the scriptures and researching history and sciences for facts. All pointed to the authentication of the Bible, proving that the Bible is indeed the Word of God. Through the pages that cover years of studying, you will join me in my walk with Jesus and God's transforming power through His Holy Spirit, who changed me into His child. I will also share with you my humble understanding of the Trinity.

The scriptures were (and still are) my source of learning. In addition to the Bible, I thank God for placing me in the Westminster Chapel under the pastorship of Dr. R. T. Kendall, who was the senior pastor there (1977–2002). Dr. Kendall's teaching was solidly biblical, nourishing my soul and my spirit "with real meat." I had the privilege to build a solid foundation with his teaching.

My story is my case for Christ, the foundation of my life and the pillar of my faith.

I divided my story into eight parts, as follows:

Part I—He Tried Me, a chronicle of real-life trials—"strikes"—that preceded my conversion.

Part II—He Called Me. The call started with the Holy Spirit of God, when He supernaturally transported me to Westminster Chapel to receive Jesus's calling to follow Him.

Part III—He Touched Me. I attended my first prayer meeting at Westminster Chapel—a short prayer with a lifelong effect.

Part IV—He Healed Me. God had a different plan from the doctors' plans. God won!

Part V—He Provided for Me, discussing another divine miracle that paid off my debts.

Part VI—He Confirmed Me. God confirmed His calling when I was baptized in the Holy Spirit. I include a chapter of events that occurred while I was a child, only to be fulfilled decades later after my conversion.

Part VII—He Discipled Me, a synthesis of my personal journey of discovering the Trinity, the Godhead. In this section, I reveal how my study of the Bible took me to knowing God as a Father, knowing the divinity of Jesus as God and man, and knowing the fellowship of the Holy Spirit. One of the significant outcomes of my studies is the shifting of my perspective, from seeing life through my own human finite microscopic lens to seeing it through God's infinite telescopic lens.

Part VIII—He Regenerated Me is a description of how God regenerated me. Like peeling an onion, God peeled off my old self, including the sadness that dwelled within me for decades, and replaced it with the joy of finding true love, His everlasting love.

My conversion has generated interesting debates with various friends and family on critical topics that represent the core differences between Christianity and other religions. In these chapters, you will listen to our discussions about the divinity of Jesus, salvation, and Jesus's death and crucifixion.

I sincerely say that I was not persuaded by anyone to change my birth religion, nor had anyone witnessed to me about Jesus. Period! Additionally, I did not believe in any ritual-driven religious faith. I emptied myself of all religious beliefs and girded the void throughout the years with thick protective walls against any trespassing religious influences. I purposely shied away from all discussions about any religion. While I was skeptical about religion, I did not profess atheism.

I thought I was doing well in life.

Finally, this is not a typical storybook with an ending clause or chapter. Instead, my journey is ongoing and unfurling.

PART I
HE TRIED ME

Bring to an end the violence of the wicked and make the righteous secure—you, the righteous God who probes minds and hearts.
—Psalm 7:9

1
FIRST STRIKE

February 5, 1996

It was a beautiful sunny winter morning when I drove to County Hospital. I had an appointment with an ENT specialist at 9:30. On regular days, I would already be at work. I found it sheer torture being at home waiting for the clock to give me the go-ahead. I thought of postponing the appointment, but my boyfriend Victor reminded me that I had changed the date twice already. My GP, Dr. Smith, had noticed a progressive and stubborn change in the tone of my voice and a lump on my thyroid gland. Immediately he referred me to an otolaryngologist/endocrinologist at County Hospital.

Being a workaholic, I gave my job a higher priority than my personal needs, including my health! While driving to the hospital, I entertained some painful thoughts that were swinging around in my mind: *What happens if my clients call me and do not find me in the office? What happens if no one in the office is able to assist them? What if the doctor found nothing alarming? I will have taken time off for nothing!* These thoughts were suddenly hijacked by a more sinister notion: *What if the doctor found a dangerous disease that will require me to take time off from work?!* This thought suddenly opened the door for an avalanche of guilt, which struck me hard.

I postponed the matter for many months, until the GP's nagging became a nuisance and forced me to see a specialist.

Waiting in the waiting room was brutal. The room was small, taken up mostly by the large desk where a nurse was transcribing from recorded dictation. I was checking my watch every second, repeatedly asking the nurse if I could jump ahead of others' appointments. At one point, the nurse was close to losing her temper with me. She was annoyed by my constant interruptions, as she had to play back the recording for her dictation. When I persisted in jumping ahead, she asked me in a very authoritative tone to sit down and wait for my turn. Otherwise, she said, she would have to ask me to leave and reschedule my appointment when I had some free time!

"Free time? Hah!" I exclaimed. "You don't understand," I said. "I don't have free time. I have a critical job, and I can't take any time off.

But neither she nor the other patients were interested in my story or my job. Instead of showing any sympathy, she asked me to take my seat and silently wait for my turn. While waiting, I bombarded Peggy, my secretary at the office, with calls, loading her up with endless instructions! When I was not on the phone, I was on my Dictaphone recording letters and notes.

Finally, the phone rang. The nurse called my name, and I raced to the doctor's office. Dr. Ashok was a young Indian man in his midthirties. After a casual greeting, the doctor mentioned that he had received a letter from my GP, Dr. Smith. The letter reported the fast progression of my voice hoarseness and the presence of a lump on my thyroid. Consequently, Dr. Ashok barraged me with a great many questions, some of which I had a hard time understanding. I found his English Indian accent challenging. His head wobbling, which was a cross between a nod and a shake, distracted me a great deal. *Is he okay?* I wondered. I struggled to decipher what he was saying to me or asking me, also struggling to understand the mysterious body language behind the wobbling of his head. The worst was when the wobbling accompanied a total silence, giving no clues to what he was thinking. Consequently, my answers were just shots in the dark, limited to "I don't know," "I guess so," and "Something like that."

I thought of leaving because of his annoying silence. But then I remembered Dr. Smith's high recommendation and the confidence he had in him. I convinced myself to remain calm and be amused by his accent. It worked like magic! So I smiled instead of giving answers.

Following the comic interrogation (which was a one-way conversation), Dr. Ashok wrote two pages' worth of notes. When I asked what he was writing, he responded, "Your answers." My answers?! Are you kidding me? What had I told him that was worthy of two pages?! I almost choked on the laughter I was holding in. Then he pressed a buzzer for a nurse and asked me to follow the nurse to the examination room. Guess who showed up? The nurse whom I had annoyed! She walked in, pushing a machine on wheels. My heart dropped in embarrassment.

The nurse ushered me into the examination chair. The moment I sat, and without any advance notice, she pulled the back of the seat down and the footrest up. My back flew backward while my legs shot up in the air, and my head landed between her knees! "Madam, are you comfortable?" she asked.

"No!" I yelled, for fear of falling off the chair. "You should have warned me before transforming the chair." I was not pleased at all. Suddenly, the little comfort I'd had just flew away. I felt agitated.

This is it! my mind shouted. *I must leave.* But the nurse moved swiftly, stuffing my mouth with an enormous mouth guard that held it open. She then sprayed some cold medicine into the cavity of my throat that froze my jaws open. Shoot! She had trapped me as a child stuck in a high chair! Anger mounted inside me for losing control. Seconds later, Dr. Ashok joined the nurse and connected me to more machines that he had pulled from the wall cabinets behind the examination chair. In seconds, the room was transformed into an operating room! The nurse handed the doctor a pair of surgical gloves, and the two of them mumbled words I couldn't make out. Suddenly, I heard the word *laryngoscopy*.

"What's that?" I mumbled, using my tongue to push the gadgets to the side. Immediately, I regretted having asked. I did not understand a word the doctor said in reply! I wondered if a laryngoscopy was similar to a colonoscopy. Sure, it must be—from the opposite end!

The laryngoscopy and scan examination lasted forty-five minutes, during which Dr. Ashok exhausted a series of instruments, neatly displayed on a beaten-up tray that probably dated to the last century. With my eyes open to their full extent, I followed every tool going in and coming out of my mouth. For the grand finale, he inserted a tiny camera hooked to a tube into my mouth and took several photos of my throat and thyroid from different angles. The camera clicked and clicked for a few minutes.

"I am taking pictures of your throat and thyroid," he said.

"Shall I smile?" I mumbled, trying to disguise my fear with a bit of humor.

At first, I followed the procedure on the screen in front of me, until I noticed all eyes were on the gory things displayed. I closed my eyes and diverted my mind to my work. In the end, Dr. Ashok removed the tubes and freed my throat and mouth. He straightened the chair (with advance notice this time!) and ushered me into the chair opposite his desk. The nurse picked up a stack of photos printed on a nearby printer and hung them on an x-ray reading machine on the wall. They surely looked gory. After he checked each one of them, Dr. Ashok walked over to his desk, picked up his phone, dialed a number, and started dictating his notes. My heart went out to the person who would have to decode his accent!

And I waited for his verdict. My jaws and lips were still sedated and numb; they were uncontrollably moving in all directions. The aftertaste of the Novocain was nauseating. *How am I going to the office like this? Will I be able to speak? How long will I stutter?*

Finally, the doctor finished dictating. He moved his chair around the desk and faced me. Again, with a gentle nodding and shaking of his head, he said that he had found a very peculiar lump on my thyroid in my throat pressing on the vocal cords.

"Peculiar?" I stuttered.

"Yes," he said. "The lump is most likely hypopharyngeal cancer given its shape. Also, the thyroid looks abnormally large." He pulled a book from his high stack of papers and put it in front of me. He showed me colored photos of healthy thyroids compared to ones with hypopharyngeal cancerous lumps. Great fear fell upon me when he explained the pictures of my thyroid. My heartbeats started drumming a military tune in my temples.

Dr. Ashok used an anatomical model of a larynx to show me the location of the lump that was pressing on my vocal cords. He explained that the peculiarity of my case would be my voice loss, which would happen rapidly—even in its most benign condition. In the end, he stressed, "The voice loss is also irreversible." At these words, my heart dropped with a big bang to my feet. When I finally was able to grasp the bomb that had just hit me, my mind shut down and refused to accept the verdict. I found myself staring at the doctor, totally absentminded—probably hypnotized by the swinging of his head like the pendulum of a clock. Behold, my head was also swinging while lip-synching every word he was saying. I felt lost in the translation of the accent from Indian to English. At one point, my ears blocked out the rest of his explanation.

When he finished his deliberation, he moved to the back of his seat and looked at me. "Are you okay?" he asked. I blushed, embarrassed for looking lost. I remained silent; my words were frozen in my throat. My silence annoyed him. He got up, and my eyes followed him. He walked to his desk, sat in his chair, turned to his computer, and said, "I will send my report to your GP, Dr. Smith, with my recommendation for surgery." Suddenly, I snapped at the word *surgery*.

Did he say surgery? I cleared my throat and stuttered, "Did you say surgery?" Dr. Ashok stopped typing and turned to me. He explained his recommendation for a second opinion from a specialist to investigate the lump, saying that he was confident that the specialist most probably would agree with his diagnosis and his suggestion for surgery to remove the disease before it spread. My world stopped.

I pulled my head from the fog and stuttered, "I agree that the lump must go." Without looking at the doctor, I stood up, grabbed my briefcase, purse, and coat, and walked in slow steps toward the door. I turned the doorknob and stopped to collect my lost thoughts. Before stepping out of the office, I turned to Dr. Ashok and said, "I agree to the surgery. Make sure that it is ASAP." After a brief pause, I added in an almost authoritative voice, "But I cannot—no, I must not—lose my voice."

What did I just say?! my mind screamed inside me. *You want surgery? Are you out of your mind? How can you agree to it without even thinking about it or, worse, when you did not even listen to most of what the doctor was saying? What about work? Can you take time off? No, no, no, you cannot take time off! Take back what you just said.* The debate went on in my mind for a while. Work was my primary concern; not a single thought addressed my health and well-being!

I was surprised about my unexpected decision for surgery without thoroughly assessing its scope and implications. From the look on the doctor's face, I gathered that he was equally surprised by my immediate decision.

"Mrs. Termanini, are you sure?" he asked. "Don't you want to investigate the lump further, think about the surgery, and discuss it with your family and with Dr. Smith?"

"No. I am sure," I interrupted. "I've made up my mind. The

thing must go. My answer is final." I refused to accept the presence of a lump, which I referred to as "the thing." I quickly glanced at my watch. "Oh my word, I am extremely late for work. I must leave now."

Aiming to walk out of the office, I suddenly heard Dr. Ashok saying, "Dr. Smith mentioned that you are workaholic; you must take it easy. I have never seen anyone taking such news with similar calmness." He was speaking as he walked to join me at the door.

Displeased with Dr. Smith's gossip and his remark, I looked him in the eye and asked, "What else did Dr. Smith say?"

Dr. Ashok realized that I was displeased with his comment. "Nothing." He nodded with an apologetic voice and quickly barged into the adjacent room. The secretary was on the phone; she rapidly put the caller on hold. Dr. Ashok gave her my folder with instructions in medical jargon. Then he turned to me, saying that Lora, the secretary at whom he was now pointing, would take care of me. The moment the doctor left the room, Lora asked me to take a seat and returned to her call.

The wait was excruciating. Lora's phone conversation seemed interminable. I ran out of patience; seeing her scrambling over a pile of forms with the telephone receiver sandwiched between her tilted head and her shoulder had hit my nerves. I felt an urge to run away from that place. The secretary's office suddenly seemed very small, as if the walls and the ceiling were closing in on me. Gasping for air, I signaled to the secretary to mail me the information, then I quickly got up and left the room. I walked as fast as I could, when suddenly I heard someone calling me: "Mrs. Termanini, please stop."

I turned back and saw Lora running and waving an envelope in her hand. By the time she reached me, her face was red and she was panting as if she had just run a marathon. Her office was just a stone's throw away. She took a deep breath and said, panting, "You left so quickly, before I had the chance to give you all the application forms you need to complete and send for your surgery."

"I am in a hurry; I have a meeting to attend," I said with a stern voice.

She handed me the envelope and said, "Please review, sign, and return the enclosed forms to the hospital's admissions office to schedule your surgery as soon as possible. The office will contact you when a bed becomes available."

"Excuse me?" The last sentence thunderstruck me.

Suddenly, the panting stopped. A half smile appeared on Lora's face with its polished makeup. She leaned forward, closer to my ear, and whispered with a faint giggle, "As you may know, Mrs. Termanini, County Hospital is not a private hospital. Patients' priority admission is dependent on the severity of their health issues and bed availability." Rolling her eyes upward, she said, "It could be mixed-sex with multibed wards."

My heart dropped to my feet, throwing a five-foot stream of burning lava up into my cheeks.

"What?" I protested. "You must be joking. I insist on having a private room. I will talk to my GP who sent me here." Lora raised both eyebrows for a couple of seconds while biting her lips hard enough to hide a smile. Her facial expression annoyed me. *Is she making fun of me?* With an aggressive voice, I said, "Oh, you think it's funny, do you? We'll see about that."

I snatched the envelope from her hand, picked up my briefcase, and turned on my heel to take flight. I ran as fast as I could.

A loud and authoritative voice reverberated behind me and exploded in my ears: "Madam, stop. I have not finished yet."

By then, I was fuming with impatience and frustration. I stopped and turned around, shouting angrily, "What is it now?"

She ran toward me and handed me a Post-it Note that read, "Extended leave for forty days."

"What is this?" I asked.

"Well, this is very important," she said. "Dr. Ashok wants you to know that you may need to take an extended medical leave after the surgery because you will not be able to talk for at least forty days."

"What?!" I screamed. She began repeating Dr. Ashok's instruction, and I quickly interrupted her, saying, "I heard you the first time. Forty days! Young lady, I cannot miss forty days from work! You have *no* idea how critical a job I have and—"

She interrupted me. "Yes, I know," she said. "Everybody says that before their surgery."

I quickly realized that it was no use discussing the matter any further with her. I thanked her and resumed my race through the hallway to the parking lot.

"Hah!" I exclaimed as I entered my car. "Forty days? In your dreams!" I planned to call Dr. Smith to schedule the surgery on a Saturday so that I could resume work on Monday without any interruption.

I left the hospital very agitated and raced to the office, driving absentmindedly. One driver shouted at me so loud that I snapped and quickly swerved my car to the other side of the road. I was driving on the wrong side of the road! I snaked through the heavy traffic until I reached the office.

I asked my secretary to hold my phone calls and messages, telling her that I needed a private moment. I closed the door behind me, dropped my briefcase and coat on the desk, and threw myself into my chair. I covered my face with my hands and replayed the entire appointment in my head over and over. How does one process such unbearable news? Dr. Ashok's words drummed in my ears. In just one hour, my world had turned upside down. Not only did I need to face surgery, but also I needed to manage the impact of the operation and the recovery period of forty days. Suddenly the future looked pretty grim. Doubt and uncertainty crept into my thoughts. The dark shadow of insecurity threatened me. I felt trapped. To escape my mind and my anxiety, I called denial to speak to me. Sure enough, denial emerged and silenced my fear, saying, "No, no, the diagnosis was not correct. It could not be. It could not happen to you. The doctor misdiagnosed your condition. You misunderstood the doctor." Denial finished its lengthy discourse by distracting me with positive thoughts I needed to hear, at least for the moment.

As I regained a few streaks of hope, composure returned to my mind. I took a deep breath. I heard the familiar beep telling me a new email had arrived. Saved by the bell! The faint sound of the beep had dissipated the dark cloud of fear that had fallen over me, bringing me back to reality. In slow motion, I corrected my position in my chair and rolled the chair forward, toward my desk. Like a pianist, I raised my finger and pressed the enter key. A flood of emails jumped up on the screen. I plunged into work and forgot about my appointment at the hospital. The shadow of Dr. Ashok's diagnosis, as well as the forty-day extended leave, fell from my mind. I did not think about the whole matter until my boyfriend called me in the evening to check on how my doctor's appointment went. I shared with him the diagnosis, except for the ridiculous request for extended medical leave.

"So, what are you going to do?" he asked.

"I agreed to have the thing removed as soon as possible," I said. "Tomorrow, I will call Dr. Smith and demand to have the operation done in a private hospital." While I did not mind the surgery, the extended leave consumed my mind throughout the evening and kept me awake all night.

February 6, 1996
At 4:00 a.m., the alarm went off. I jumped out of bed, took a shower, and left the flat for work around 5:15 a.m. Mari, my housekeeper, was still sleeping.

I spent the day with my team, planning the next business trips and following up on projects. As I did every day, I buried myself in my work (which I loved) and forgot about the outside world entirely. Above all, I forgot about my health issue.

I stayed in the office until 9:00 p.m., when the cleaners started vacuuming. The moment I stepped outside the building, the reality of my health issue, which had been waiting for me, struck me. Doubt, uncertainty, fear, and all the feelings that I had bottled up throughout the day exploded out of their jars. Suddenly, I felt a mass of lead plummet on my shoulder and crush my spirit. I burst into tears in a dramatic exit and covered my face. I indulged in self-pity and cried my heart out until I reached the parking lot.

I drove with the window rolled down, hoping that the icy-cold air would numb the battle of grief and self-pity raging in my head. By the time I got home, my bones were shivering and rattling. My hands and feet were frozen, and my fingers were so numb that I could not turn the house key in the lock to open the door. I kicked the door with my foot until Mari opened the door. I was freezing and exhausted. Mari asked me a couple of times if I was okay. I had no desire to talk. I wondered if Victor had told her about "the thing." I excused myself and went to bed. All I wanted was to be alone and nurse my feelings.

I could not sleep a wink.

2
SECOND STRIKE

Wednesday, February 7, 1996

My typical workday was 5:00 a.m. to 9:00 p.m., not "9 to 5" as the Dolly Parton song goes. While at work, I did not think of "the thing" since I had adopted denial and muted truth and reality. My passion for my job had instilled in me the belief that somehow miraculous healing would happen and the thing would one day disappear by itself!

On the way home, I also made every effort to divert my mind from thinking about my health issue. I put in a cassette of Charles Aznavour and turned the sound up high. I sang loudly, hoping to override the little voice creeping into my ear and shouting, *What about me? How can you ignore me? When are you going to face reality and think seriously about me? Okay, consider me as a new business and deal with my case as a project. Above all, you must not imprison your emotions.* The tiny voice triggered fear and guilt, but I was determined to resist it. So, I sang even louder until I reached home. The moment I switched off the car engine, the thing broke loose and swung a hammer throw ball a couple of times before hurling it at me and hitting me on the head, releasing a dam of tears. All colors of emotions battled in my mind; loneliness was the weakest and got beaten up very severely.

Facing illness alone scared me the most. The independent person in me suddenly needed more robust support, but who? And how? The glittery assets of being a successful businesswoman suddenly faded in the face of the illness. Who would be my support group? I scanned my family and friends and found no one other than Mari. Mari alone was not enough. What about Victor? I shook my head as I thought of him. Victor is the only person I know whose life motto is "Me, me!"

The devastating reality started to sink in. What did I know of a life storm like this one? Nothing! With that grim thought, I went home.

Victor and Mari were waiting for me. I joined them for dinner but could not eat. Instead, I had a couple of shots of Glenmorangie to relax myself and put me to sleep. After dinner, Mari followed me to my bedroom, handed me the box where she keeps my mail, and whispered, "It is important."

"Mari, I am too tired now; I need to sleep. Please leave it for tomorrow."

Having pushed her head out of the door to make sure that we were alone, she whispered, "Please, open it."

"Why are you whispering?"

She pointed at the box and quickly left the room.

Usually, I read my mail in the morning. But Mari's persistence and whisper alerted me to something serious. I opened the box. The first letter was from the bank. The envelope had large printed letters in red: "Urgent—Final Notice." I quickly opened it and read the letter over and over. I gasped for air. My knees caved in, and I fell into the nearby chair. As if my throat disaster were not enough, the bank was pressuring me to pay my credit card arrears balance of £6,000![9]

"What? What?" I yelled. I quickly checked the addressee's information, hoping for misdelivered mail. But, no, the letter

---

[9] Approximately $10,000 USD given the conversion rate of the time.

was correctly addressed to me. "Oh my word, how could it be?" I cried. The shocking news smacked my sleepy eyes and forced them wide open. Anxiety pressed on my head and blew all the fuses in my overloaded and exhausted brain.

The letter made reference to several previous letters and past statements, which I had not seen. I summoned Mari, who told me that Victor had been checking my mail during my absence. I roared for Victor, who showed up with a pile of opened envelopes—past bank statements and correspondence. Victor admittedly looked guilty and troubled. How could he have neglected to tell me of such an important matter? I snatched the letters from his hands and asked him to leave me alone. He left the room without saying a word, while Mari stood by the bedroom door. She was mumbling prayers; that alone warned me of the severity of the matter.

I quickly opened the statements and laid them on the bed. Skimming the transactions, I froze, stunned at the sight of a set of unpaid bills. An extravagant spending spree had taken place when I was away on business trips. Tears flooded my face. "I can't believe it," I repeatedly yelled. The debt news had dropped a millstone onto my head. I had never been in debt in my whole life.

I ran to Victor and threw the statements in his face, "How dare you?" I shouted. Under different circumstances, I would have waged war on him and ended our relationship then and there. But not tonight. Dr. Ashok's news had already turned my life upside down. I felt lost, spiraling quickly down into a dark abyss. The thought of my impending surgery and the fear of facing the unknown alone led me to believe that I needed Victor. So, I refrained from breaking off the relationship, although it would have been the right opportunity to end our asymmetric relationship. Victor left the flat without saying a word.

I had met Victor in 1973 while spending the summer vacation in Dorset, UK. My parents knew his family. After several meetings on different occasions, he and I had become good friends. What attracted me to Victor was his charm and his flamboyant fashion style. His passion was bespoke three-piece custom suits and matching shoes. He looked like a Hollywood star. (I was young, naive, and hopelessly looking for someone to love me!) But in my heart, I had one reservation: Victor was not interested in working. He had grown up in a wealthy family who had provided him with a luxurious lifestyle.

At the end of the summer of 1976, I moved to the States to build a new life, while Victor moved to France. We maintained a long-distance relationship through the years, visiting each other a couple times annually. In 1989, my job moved me to London. There I found Victor, as always, living in one of his parents' mansions in the South of France. He shared with me that he had been diagnosed with ADHD, which did not bother me. A few months later, he moved to London, and we renewed our relationship.

My job required travel, and there was a time I was traveling a lot. During that period, I trusted Victor to manage my bills. What a horrendous mistake! I kicked myself for having added Victor as an authorized person on my bank accounts and payment cards. I should have known better as I worked in a bank. In addition to pay my utility bills, Victor had used my cards for himself. His expensive tastes led him to burn through my credit cards and reduced my savings to ashes. Although I was angry at him, I blamed myself. I had no doubt in my mind (though I do not like to admit it) that Victor had *no* malicious intention in using my cards. I learned later that Victor never had managed his own money or paid bills. His butler managed his bills and the bank statements and accounts.

A dreadful sense of hopelessness shrouded me. I was filled with a gripping fear. In this mood, I went to bed.

Now I understood the meaning of the proverb "When it rains, it pours!"

3
SEIGNEUR DIEU

February 8, 1996

Although I was exhausted beyond measure, I could not sleep. As soon as my head hit the pillow, my brain exploded, blasting horizontally dark thoughts like shrapnel, shattering the walls of denial and exposing the reality. The devastating fact of my illness started to sink in. But I was more afraid about my financial situation than about my health condition. Being in debt hit me like a ton of bricks. "I am not only sick but also broke!" I lamented. Surely, when it rains, it pours.

My temples drummed military marches, vibrating the cold sweat from my forehead onto the sides of my face. Catastrophic thinking clung to my mind and spiraled into a worst-case scenario. The letter *c* flashed before my eyes, swinging back and forth. The thought of cancer terrorized me. I jumped out of bed, went to the kitchen, and sat at the table by the window. I lifted my head and gazed into the midnight expanse. O my word! A multitude of stars covered the sky while the moon played peekaboo between the silver clouds. The stars were shining brightly like diamonds on black velvet. It was the most beautiful sight I had ever seen. It was majestic! The beauty of the sky moved me, stirred the depth of my emotions, and zoomed my attention onto my fear of the imminent surgery. Suddenly, a dam broke inside me and burst in an torrent of fresh tears that buried the slopes of my cheeks and rolled down my neck onto my chest. Massive lava of black terror snaked through my body and consumed every fiber in me. With both hands, I covered my mouth to muffle my cries. Quietly, I wept and wept for a long time that seemed like hours. No conventional bomb would have had an effect on me like the two strikes that life had recently thrown at me. I wanted to scream, *This cannot happen to me!* but my throat had closed off tight and choked my words. The pain in my heart had no words. I had never felt as lonely, hopeless, and helpless as I felt that moment. Facing illness alone was bad enough; the financial crisis made it even worse.

Thinking of my health issue led me to think of death. What *is* death? I had never thought about death. Why should I? I was young, and I believed in the world's scientific evolution of an end to aging. Which is more painful, the journey to death or death itself? What would I feel before and after I died? And where would I go? Would I go to Jannah[10] or to Jahannam?[11] Not knowing what will happen after I die was the epicenter of my anxiety. The thought of Jannah vs. Jehannam tormented me even more.

I recalled a conversation I had had years ago with Mrs. Miller (RIP—a close friend of the family) when she told me that she had terminal cancer. I asked her if she was afraid of death. Her response surprised me. She said that she was not scared because she knew what would happen to her after she died. Her physical death on earth would usher her into the presence of Christ. *That is absurd,* I thought. Then again, she was a devout Christian. Although Mrs. Miller and I never talked about her Christian belief, her response resonated within me for a long time. Her description of

---

[10] Islam uses the term *Jannah* to refer to paradise and heaven.
[11] Islamic concept of eternal punishment in hell.

death reflected an extraordinary anticipation of a joyful reunion with her God, Christ, who would usher her to what she called the beginning of eternal life in heaven. Mrs. Miller's confidence in a guaranteed eternal life puzzled me. How could she be sure of things she had not seen or experienced? How had she gained that level of confidence? I coveted her positive attitude toward death and her faith in Christ, who removed the perplexity of death, which most people, including me, feared. I wished my mother (RIP) or Mrs. Miller would come back from death so I could ask them about their death experience. I wondered what my mother's experience was when she died. Had she had a similar assurance of eternal life in Jannah? Did I have the confidence of eternal life in heaven? Was there anything I could do to guarantee my final resting place would be in Jannah? What did it cost, and how to earn the certainty of eternal life in heaven? The absence of such assurance agonized me.

I mourned my ill-stricken luck. I lamented the futility of life. The more I contemplated my life, the more I found it to be lacking a sense of purpose. *What is the purpose of my life?* I asked myself. Surely there ought to be something worthwhile other than work. What had I done with my life? What had I achieved, and for what? What was the legacy I am leaving behind? Suddenly what I had regarded important in life was no longer important. Even work and successful career seemed petty and futile compared to the enormity of death, let alone its mystery. Nothing stood equal to death.

Suddenly, my hand flew up in the air, only to race back onto the table with a big bang, followed by a shout that tore the silence of the night as I cried out loud to Allah, "I don't know what to do. I do not know how to break the news to my dear dad. He just lost Mom to cancer, and now cancer is claiming his child." I sobbed and pleaded to Allah for help. Minutes later, the name of Allah caught my attention, and straightaway I stopped, shocked. *Behold, am I calling on Allah? I have not prayed to Allah for years. So why now?* I had turned my back on him after he had failed to help me during my childhood trauma. I looked up to the sky and cried, "Which God shall I call on now for help? If there is a true God in this universe, let Him show up." I rested my head on the table with my arms wrapped around it, and I wept for a long time, lamenting the sudden and sharp turn in my fate. Suddenly, my cries and pleas came to an abrupt halt when I heard myself whispering, "Seigneur Dieu,[12] I need you. Would you please come back to my aid?"

What? I'm calling whom? Seigneur Dieu? I slowly lifted my head and sighed. "O Seigneur Dieu!" A shiver ran up my spine as I remembered the time when I was a child calling on Seigneur Dieu, the Christian God, for help. O how I missed that name! How I missed the peace He used to provide me with each communication. I had not called on Seigneur Dieu for years. The thought of Him made me cry even harder. Would He help me again as He had done when I was a child? Would He help me although He was not my God? Would He help Muslims?

An inexplicable force stretched my arms into the air and interrupted my thoughts. I cried out loud, "Seigneur Dieu, my Lord! I am calling You again. If You truly exist and have not forgotten me, show Yourself to me again as You did when I was a child. Come to my rescue as You did before. Not only am I battling illness, but also I am drowning in a financial crisis. I have no one to help me but You. So please, Seigneur Dieu, come to my aid again, please." I poured my heart out, telling Him of my ill-preparation to face the life storms that had hit me, let alone death. I found myself talking to Seigneur Dieu as if He were sitting in front of me. I cried out to Him until I felt sleepy, at which point I went to bed.

Not only did I sleep well, but also I had an extraordinary dream.

---

[12] French for "God, my Lord." I used this term as a child, referring to my Christian friends' God.

4
THE DREAM—FIRST TIME

February 8, 1996

In my dream, I heard a voice calling, "Candle." I looked for the caller, but there was no one around. The voice grew louder in the air and repeated the word *candle* three times.

When I woke up in the morning, the word *candle* was still ringing in my ears. *What does it mean?* I wondered. I pondered on this question all the way to work. *Is the voice asking me to light up a candle in a church?* The dream revived my childhood memories of my older sisters lighting candles and offering up prayers to Saint Mary. Usually, praying to any Christian saint is forbidden to Muslims, but it was allowed in my family only in times of need.[13] *Surely, this is a time of need,* I assured myself, deciding to light up a candle. And so I did. I spent my lunchtime at the church, Santa Catalina, located across the street from the bank. I lit a candle at the foot of the statue of Saint Mary holding baby Jesus and another candle at the foot of Jesus on the cross. I prayed for healing and a solution to my financial disaster.

After praying, I sat in the last row, watching people; some lit a candle at the feet of Saint Mary and left the church, while others

---

[13] See chapter 5.

lit a candle and stayed to pray. My eyes traveled from baby Jesus sleeping in His mother's bosom to the adult Jesus crucified on the cross. I wondered why Christians worship Saint Mary when Jesus is *the* God. There were two candles at the foot of the cross, compared to rows of candles lit for Saint Mary.

Moments later, a side door opened and a group of teachers entered, leading preschool children into the church and walking to the front of the altar. One of the teachers reminded the children that they were to rehearse a play for Easter. Children's cheers filled the church before the priest led them to quietness. I watched the entire rehearsal with laughter and awe. I marveled at the freedom the children had while acting out passages from the Bible. They asked many questions about Jesus and God, some of which I found pretty daring. I admired the way the church brought Jesus as God down to the children's level in informal teaching. Yet, the children showed unpretentious respect and love to Jesus, Saint Mary, and other Bible personalities.

I sighed as I thought of my experience learning about my religion as compared to these children. I wished I had had similar freedom to create songs and simple stories of Allah and the Prophet when I was a child. I would not have dared to put the Qur'an on the floor as the children put their Bibles on the floor or to ask challenging and curiosity-driven questions about Islam. My parents were diligent in teaching my siblings and me the Islamic etiquette of reading the Qur'an. "None touch it except the purified" (al-Waqi'ah 56:79[14]).

Once the rehearsal was over, two young students of the Royal Academy of Music played a duet, one on piano and the other on cello, rehearsing for the Easter concert. The deep sound of the cello, beautifully accentuated by the piano, filled my heart with an awe-inspiring mystical sense. The cello played my sorrow as if

---

[14] *The Qur'an: Arabic Text with Corresponding English Meanings* (Singapore: Abul-Qasim, 1997), 773.

my grief were printed on the music sheets, while the piano tunes shined rays of hope. I left the church energized with hope. My spirit felt very light as if I were walking on air, and all my worries flew away.

The days following the candle dream (as I called it) and my visit to the church were amazingly peaceful. Although my financial and physical problems were not solved, the sting had supernaturally disappeared.

5
MADAME RITA

The visit to the church reminded me of my mom's secret visits to Madame Rita's house for prayers. I was ten years old when I accompanied my mother, my older sister, and my Christian governess Tikin Anahit[15] to visit Madame Rita.

For years, Madame Rita had been a French resident of my hometown. Allegedly, Madame Rita had severe arthritis in her deformed bowlegs. The pain had grown to paralyze her movement, and yet she refused to have surgery, holding onto her faith in Saint Mary for healing. For fifteen years, Madame Rita offered daily prayers to Saint Mary, a marble statue placed on the fireplace mantle in her living room next to a crucifix statue of Jesus.

Madame Rita claimed that one day while praying to the Virgin Mary, she heard a tiny voice whispering in her spirit. The voice asked her to address her healing prayers directly to Jesus. The request startled her as that was the first time she had received a demand to lift her prayers to Jesus, not Saint Mary. Madame Rita mentioned that in the past, the Virgin Mary had spoken to her on different occasions.

---

[15] Armenian for "madame."

Following the voice, Madame Rita pushed her wheelchair to the front of Jesus's crucifix. As she started to pray, the voice interrupted her with a demand to kneel. Kneel? She thought of laughing. "Ha-ha, I hardly can walk from pain; my knees have been locked for years." Suddenly, she saw her body sliding down from the chair. She fell to the floor on her knees. Madame Rita could not believe her eyes. She was stunned because she hadn't been in that position once for the last fifteen years. Despite the excruciating pain, she managed to remain for a few seconds on her knees, before she collapsed on her face and landed on her rosary. The rosary broke loose, and the beads rolled in all directions. Madame Rita burst into tears and anger after seeing her precious rosary broken. While on the floor, she felt an unusual electric sensation racing up and down her spine that jolted her body and caused her knees to shake uncontrollably. Stunned at the movement of her knees, she prostrated herself before Jesus, lifting her arms in praise, speaking in a passionate voice, and crying bitterly. She poured out her soul before the Lord Jesus, pleading for healing. Madame Rita said that the story of Hannah[16] in the Bible came to her mind. So, like Hannah, she vowed that if the Lord Jesus were to heal her, she would dedicate all the days of her life to serving Him. Madame Rita remained facedown on the floor, praying, for a long time, until her husband entered the room and helped to her feet.

In a few months, Madame Rita became the talk of the city. Her house turned into a shrine upon the people's seeing her miraculous healing. She was free of arthritis and free of pain!

Since then, a multitude of people from all over the country have come to visit Madame Rita's home for prayers and petitions. Young girls would go to her house to pray for marriage. I am sure that back then my sister prayed for her then boyfriend to propose to her (and he did! Currently, he is her husband of fifty-five years).

---

[16] 1 Samuel 1:1–13.

My mother did not want my sisters to be seen in public visiting Madame Rita, so my Christian governess, Tikin Anahit, had to go with us. She would go first, alone, into the house while we waited in the car to make us look as if we were waiting for Tikin Anahit. We would stay in the car until all visitors praying in the prayer room had left. Then, we would race inside, at which time Madame Rita would lock the main door so no one would come in while we were at her house.

As a child, I found my family's visits to Madame Rita's home for prayer very confusing because Mom used to ask us to recite Qur'anic verses before entering the house (as well as after leaving) for protection from the Christian Spirit. On the one hand, Mom believed in Saint Mary's divine power to answer prayers. On the other hand, she wanted protection from the Christian Spirit. But the question that puzzled me most was why people continued praying to Saint Mary when Jesus was the one who had performed the miraculous healing of Madame Rita.

The frequency of our visits to Madame Rita depended on the urgency and the nature of our family's issues. We had to have *severe* problems or be in desperate need to justify a visit to Madame Rita for prayers to Saint Mary. I found this approach hypocritical because, while Mom and my siblings vowed and offered prayers to Saint Mary, Allah received all the credit for the answered prayers. Furthermore, for each answered prayer lifted up to Saint Mary, one or more lambs would be sacrificed in gratitude to Allah. I do not recall any celebratory thanksgiving festivities offered to Saint Mary or Jesus.

6
FINANCIAL ADVISER

My visit to Santa Catalina Church gave me the courage to call Mr. Louis, my financial adviser. I thought he should know of my financial disaster. He was not surprised. However, he was extremely displeased. *Who wouldn't be?* I thought.

The conversation with Mr. Louis threw me into the depression abyss; the weight of the debt completely crushed me all over again. We agreed to meet tomorrow at my lawyer's office, to get legal advice. Just before hanging up the phone, Mr. Louis rushed: "Mrs. Termanini, one last thing, eh … uh, I strongly suggest you take immediate action concerning, eh … uh."

I interrupted Mr. Louis because I was too embarrassed to hear his concern again. I knew that he was referring to my boyfriend. I said in an embarrassed whisper, "I canceled both my credit and debit cards and removed his name from my accounts," and quickly ended the conversation.

Following my call to Mr. Louis, I called the bank and scheduled an appointment with the branch manager and Mr. Louis. After a prolonged discussion on the phone, the manager agreed to halt the collection proceedings until we met and prepared a remedial repayment plan. What a relief! Streaks of hope and peace dabbled in my heart throughout the evening.

The power of the candle dream seemed to be working!

7
THE DREAM—AGAIN AND AGAIN

Friday, February 9, 1996

For the second time, I had the dream where I heard a voice calling "candle," reverberating in a large room with a high vaulted ceiling. I looked around, searching for the caller, but there was no one there. I woke up shaking and drenched in sweat. I pulled the covers over my head; my nerves were on high alert. *What in the world does the dream mean? Why a candle? Why is the caller hiding and not showing up? What is the dream telling me?* I kept thinking about these questions all morning as I was preparing my suitcase for my business trip to Kazakhstan. When Jimmy, the driver, arrived to take me to the airport, I asked him to stop at Santa Catalina Church. I quickly went in, lit candles to both Saint Mary and Jesus, whispered a quick prayer, and left.

Saturday, February 17, 1996

The dream returned a third time! I was in a hotel in Kazakhstan. This time, the voice sounded so powerful that it woke me up, shaking. My heartbeat was pounding and felt heavy in my chest. The voice in the dream was so loud and clear that it felt as if the caller was in the room. My eyes jumped at the alarm clock; it was

3:35 a.m. I quickly turned the light on and shouted, "Anybody here?" I raced out of bed to the front door. It was locked; the deadbolt lock and the chain were in place. *Wow! What was that?* My heartbeat reached a new high, setting off alarm bells. I checked under the bed, in the closets, behind the shower curtain, and even in the vents. Nothing. I ran back to the bed and hid under the covers. The caller's voice was still ringing in my ears long after I had awakened. I pondered on the dream until the alarm went off at 5:00 a.m. for my eight o'clock flight back home. I was thrilled to go home. I felt an urge to return to Santa Catalina Church as soon as I got home. In the interim, I took a few minutes, closed my eyes, and visualized lighting a couple of candles at the feet of Saint Mary and Jesus's cross. I felt a need to do so before boarding the plane.

Throughout the flight, I thought of the three dreams; they captivated my mind. I knew in my heart that because I had had the same dream three times, the word *candle* must carry a strong message. But what?

When the plane finally landed in London, I rushed out of the airport. Jimmy, my good old driver, was waiting for me. I was steaming with impatience to go back to the church.

"Jimmy," I said while walking toward the car, "before we go home, I need to stop at Santa Catalina Church."

"Again?" The grimace on Jimmy's face indicated that my plan did not amuse him. Making a long detour and driving through the busy streets of London on Saturday morning can be a nightmare.

We drove to the church, which was closed off to the public for a wedding preparation. I managed to sneak in through the back door with the florists and entered the main hall. Wow! The wedding decorations had transformed the church into a scene of magical and mystic bliss. I stood breathless, utterly transfixed by the beauty before me. The altar was covered with vintage cream lace interwoven with sparkling silver threads that gracefully caressed the floor. A large centerpiece adorned the altar, decorated with candles wrapped in vintage lace and an ensemble of blue orchids and white roses. Matching rose petals decorated the pews, adding a gentle aroma to the air. Softer yellow and white lights were shining on the statue of the Virgin Mary and the crucifix. There was such a sweet glow in the face and eyes of Saint Mary, as if a sunburst light had softly embraced her. The dark polished wood of the cross shone like glass. The decorations were breathtaking.

Ignoring the florist's request to leave, I zigzagged my way between the workers until I reached the candle stands, where I lit three candles. I took one step back and stood in awe! The beautiful light projected on the Virgin Mary's face spoke volumes of love that I had never seen before. It was the crucifix that grabbed my attention. The soft yellow lights contrasted with the fiery agony shining from Jesus's face, which spoke of a divine reality. I moved closer and stared at the large drops of crystal-like sweat illuminating the rivulets of blood running from His head, down His forehead, and onto His beaten and cut cheeks. His face, though disfigured, shone with humility. His eyes blazed with a fiery call for hope. The projector above His arms spread an intense light around the statue and embraced me in warmth, while the brilliance almost blinded and made me jump one step back. The nails in His hands and feet gave me a chill. Out of the deep sorrow that welled up inside me, a whisper flew from my mouth, blowing away the teardrops that had gathered on my lips: "Wow, who would do such a barbaric thing to Jesus?"

Looking at Jesus reminded me of Tikin Anahit's words when I had asked her about the cross she wore all the time. She explained that the crucifix pendant was a constant reminder of Jesus's torturous and excruciating death when He willingly sacrificed Himself on the cross to save her and all people. "Everyone? Me too?" I asked her. I recall that she hugged me and said, "You too." When I asked her what she meant by her being saved, she explained that Jesus, the God-man, died so that we could live in heaven because He loves us with an everlasting love. Huh? Why would God die for me when no one would sacrifice anything for me? Would my family make sacrifices for me? The sacrifice and the agony that Tikin Anahit described, which I did not understand then, was visibly displayed before me, and touched me profoundly. The physical suffering echoing from the cross was beyond my comprehension. The more I looked at Jesus's agony, the more I thought of Tikin Anahit's words about His sacrifice. I pondered with sadness on the world's glamorization of the cross. In recent years, I had noticed people wearing gaudy golden crucifix pendants and tattoos. I wondered if they honored the story of the Crucifixion in their lives or if they were showcasing their lifestyle and wealth.

Involuntarily, my head dropped to my chest as a sign of respect. I slowly and shyly raised my eyes to Jesus's face. When I met His eyes, a floodgate of tears exploded within me. Suddenly, I realized that I was standing in front of Seigneur Dieu, the God of Tikin Anahit, Madame Rita, the nuns at school, and my Christian friends. The thought froze me. *Is that Him?* I kept asking myself. I stood in front of the crucifix in complete awe. I wanted to talk to Seigneur Dieu—I had so much to share with Him—but I could not unlock my lips. Everything in me stopped in awe.

I do not know how long I stood there before, suddenly, a tap on my shoulder startled me and brought me back to reality. The priest, standing next to the wedding planner, asked me to leave the church at once; he escorted me to the door. I walked backward while my eyes remained fixed on Jesus.

On the way home, Jimmy quizzed me about my recent obsession with Santa Catalina Church, but he got nothing more than a big smile flashed behind a curtain of tears. How could I explain my emotions? I needed a bigger heart to contain all the emotions that had poured onto me. I leaned on the headrest and gazed out the window into the clouds, reliving the experience I'd had at the church.

I thought of Tikin Anahit's explanation of the crucifix. I tried to connect the dots between her words and the Easter scenes that the children had rehearsed during my visit to the church a few weeks ago. While I was thinking of the crucifix, an avalanche of questions bombarded my brain: What did Jesus's crucifixion represent? Why are some crosses bare while some others include an image of Jesus's body? If the crucifix symbolizes the Christian faith, then why do people treat it so lightly as to have it tattooed on their bodies? No Muslim would dare of having a Qur'an tattoo on their bodies. That would be considered blasphemy.

I also pondered on the contrasting views of Muslims and Christians about wearing religious jewelry. I recalled my Christian classmates wearing their crosses all the time, while I had to remove my Qur'an necklace every time I entered the toilet. My mother repeatedly warned me that it is haram to go to the bathroom carrying or wearing anything bearing the name of Allah. I never understood the wisdom of honoring a physical book or a piece of jewelry of the cross that can be easily damaged or destroyed. What is more important, the spiritual essence of the words, the Author, or the physical book?

My joy did not last long, as guilt peeked in and hijacked my thoughts. Why was I thinking of Jesus? Why did I not have the same emotions of comfort and peace whenever I thought of Islam? My guilt infused my heart with a sense of shame, and suddenly my mood changed to gloomy.

8
DOCTOR'S ROUNDS

Dr. Smith—February 19, 1996

To this day, I had not mentioned my health problem to anyone in the office. Therefore, taking time off for a doctor's appointment would not go unnoticed. I managed to escape during my lunchtime to see Dr. Smith. It was the first time I was seeing him after my last visit to Dr. Ashok, who had discovered the thing, as I called it, in my throat/thyroid. I was anxious to learn about the two doctors' discussions of my case and to hear Dr. Smith's recommendation. I jumped in a cab and urged the taxi driver to drive as fast as he could. I ran into the building to Dr. Smith's office. Once the receptionist announced my arrival, Dr. Smith walked to the reception area to greet me with his posh English accent and ushered me into his consultation room.

Dr. Smith read aloud Dr. Ashok's report. His serious voice caused alarm bells to ring in my heart. I was not pleased to be reminded again of my throat condition when I had managed to forget it on my work and business trips. Dr. Smith agreed with Dr. Ashok's diagnosis and his recommendation to remove the lump as soon as possible, before I lost my voice. And yet he suggested getting a second opinion, which I gladly welcomed, hoping to prove that both doctors were wrong. Also, this suggestion raised my hope of having more time to complete urgent projects. Dr. Smith referred me to Dr. Sign, a renowned specialist whom he trusted.

Instead of rushing back to the office, I strolled down the street, lamenting my luck with a rain of tears. Dr. Smith's serious tone had alarmed me. Fear of death haunted me. I dreaded my fate. Suddenly I lost my desire for everything. Streams of tears rolled from beneath my sunglasses down my face and soaked my turtleneck. Suddenly I felt very small and insignificant, facing a Goliath problem. I wished I had someone to lean on. But who? Mari? I wondered how she would take the news.

I walked all the way to the office. On the way, I stopped by a hotel and went to the ladies' lounge to wash my face and refresh my makeup. That afternoon, I stayed in my office behind a closed door. With blank eyes, I stared at the papers covering my desk. I could not work. It was as if my brain had shut off completely.

Dr. Sign—February 22, 1996
Dr. Sign looked to be in his late sixties, and that comforted me because I wanted an experienced specialist to deal with my throat (vocal cords and thyroid). The doctor invited me into his consultation office and ushered me to the armchair facing his desk. The room was dark; thick half-drawn velvet drapes covered the closed shutters. A single desk lamp brightened his desk area and my chair. Diplomas from various universities, doctorate frames, and achievement trophies decorated the walls of his office. I sat down quietly, trembling inside, praying that his verdict would override that of the other doctors.

Dr. Sign had already received detailed information from both doctors, Smith and Ashok. In a separate small room crowded with machines, Dr. Sign examined my neck, head, and throat while referring to Dr. Ashok's report. After thirty minutes of examination, Dr. Sign ushered me back to his office and gave me his verdict; unfortunately, he agreed with Dr. Ashok's diagnosis and recommendation. In the end, he told me that I had no other choice but to do the surgery to remove the lump to save my vocal cords. I left his office speechless and depressed, feeling sorry for myself and hopelessly lonely. At the end of the day, I called my GP to inform him that I had agreed to have the surgery at County Hospital and insisted on having a private room. Meanwhile, he suggested experimental medication and treatment, to which I agreed.

The following day, I flew out of town on a business trip. I knew it would be my last trip for a while. Soon I would be delegating my business trips and projects to my staff.

March–April 1996
Jimmy, my faithful driver, was understanding and supportive. For weeks, he picked me up at 5:30 p.m. from work and drove through the congested streets of London to various medical appointments, where he waited for me to drive me back home. I could not have done it without Jimmy. The experimental treatments drained all my strength and made me vomit all night. I lost my appetite, and my weight loss was visible. For every compliment I received about my weight loss, my heart screamed and sobbed, *If only you knew the truth!*

9
MARI

One evening when I came home after a round of doctors' appointments, I found Mari wiping her tears from her face. When I asked her why she was crying, she hugged me and started sobbing.

"Mari, are you okay?" I anxiously asked.

When she did not stop crying, I became even more worried. "Did you receive bad news from your family back home? Please tell me."

I wondered if she had received bad news about her eighty-year-old mother living in Sudan. In the last few months, Mari had learned that the rebels in her village were burning churches and had killed some Christians, including one of her brothers. When I started consoling her, she burst out, saying, "No, madam, it is not my family. It is *you*! I am crying because I know that you are sick. You have lost lots of weight, you go to doctors, and you look pale."

I unwrapped her arms from my shoulders, although I needed a hug, and moved one step back. "How do you know that I am sick?" I asked.

"I know," she said.

"But how? Who told you? Did Jimmy say something?" Quickly she jumped to his defense.

"No, madam, Jimmy said nothing."

I held her hands and looked her in the eye. "So, how do you know that I am sick?" I stood there waiting for an answer. "Well, tell me," I pressed.

In a whisper, she said, "God told me."

Well, how about that answer! Mari's response shocked me so much that my hands flew open and I dropped her hands. After a few seconds of staring into her eyes, I blew out a deep breath and asked her to repeat what she had said. And she did. God had told Mari that I was sick!

"Hmm," I mumbled, swaying my head slowly and squinting my eyes in confusion. "So, God told you. How interesting!" I walked to my bedroom, laughing in my head.

"So, God told you, yeah?" I shouted from my bedroom. No reply. "What else did God tell you?" I laughingly continued. "How did God speak to you?"

The idea of God speaking to Mari and telling her about me amused me and worried me at the same time. Didn't God have more pressing issues to solve in the world than my thyroid? How could God be mindful of me, an insignificant person, compared to the plight of innocent people dying in civil wars, poverty, and natural disasters? Most importantly, was Mari mentally sober?

While preparing dinner, I kept teasing Mari about God speaking to her. When we sat at the table, Mari was unusually quiet. I felt I should apologize to her for making fun of her God talking to her. So, I did, and I ignored her questions about my health.

Before retiring to bed, Mari asked me if I would allow her to pray for me. It was past my bedtime, and yet, not wanting to hurt her feelings again, I agreed to a short prayer. Mari flew to her bedroom and reappeared with a tiny bottle in her hand. When I asked her about the bottle, she said, "Holy oil." *Hmm, this is getting more interesting. What is next?* I thought. I laughed even harder in my head but forced a straight face to show respect to her. Mari waited until I had changed and made myself comfortable in bed. She knelt on her knees next to me beside the bed. As she dabbed a few drops of oil on my forehead and my neck, she softly said, "Madam, God speaks in prayers. All you do is ask God to speak to you, then you listen and agree. You do this by faith."

"Okay, Mari," I said, "you pray and ask God. God speaks to you. Then you tell me what God told you, okay?" Mari giggled and started to pray, applying small drops of the oil on my forehead. I do not know how long she prayed. The moment I closed my eyes, I fell into a deep sleep.

Every night that week, Mari dabbed her oil on my forehead and neck and prayed until I fell asleep. Not bad, huh! I learned from Mari that God not only speaks in prayers but also has a language called "tongues." Oh really? Mari never ceased to amaze me with her God.

One evening, I was about to doze off while Mari was praying, when suddenly the tone of her voice changed. She sounded agitated, praying aloud in an incomprehensible mumbo-jumbo language. From the corner of my eye, I saw her punching her fists in the air as if fighting a mighty ghost. I was taken aback by this unusual sight and sound. I was scared, but I could not stop her or even slow her down. She was going full speed! What would the neighbors think if they were to hear her shouting? The language she was praying in did not sound like her native language. Could this be the tongues that she had spoken about? *Wow, she surely prays differently from Tikin Anahit and my Christian friends.*

Troubled by the sound, I held Mari's arms and asked her to stop. I told her in a stern voice that I was not pleased with the gibberish language she was shouting and that her animated prayer was out of line. I'd never seen Tikin Anahit, any of the Christian nuns, or any of my Christian friends praying the way she did.

What concerned me most was that I hadn't seen Mari praying

this way before. Had she joined a cult that led her astray from her Christian faith? That thought disturbed me and drove my mind to think of unpleasant scenarios. I even contemplated asking her not to pray in that manner in the house.

In the morning, while having breakfast, I asked Mari about her prayer.

"I prayed in tongues," she said. "It is a language to use to speak to God alone. The devil can't understand it."

I choked and started coughing violently. Nothing could have prepared me for this discovery! She had most definitely joined a cult, I concluded.

"In-ter-es-ting!" I tried to keep a straight face. "Sooo, God has a special language that the devil can't understand."

"Yes, madam," she said in a serious tone, looking straight into my eyes.

"But, Mari, if I may say, it did not sound like any human language. It sounded more like gibberish. Allah doesn't have a special prayer language other than Arabic. What language is your God's? Why does God need a special language for prayers? Does Saint Mary have a special language?"

"No, madam, I only pray to God, not Saint Mary!" Her response almost blew my mind.

"What?! You do not pray to Saint Mary?"

"No, madam. I pray to God directly in the name of Jesus. I am not a Catholic."

"Oh my word! You have joined a cult."

"Cult? What is that? No cult."

"Mari, please look straight into my eyes and answer me honestly: Are you Christian or not?"

Mari's serious face broke out into laughter. "Of course I am a Christian. I am a devout Christian but not Catholic."

"*Good*," I said. "So, you are Protestant?"

Mari shook her head and said, "No."

"Orthodox?"

"No, not anymore. I was Orthodox when I was living in Sudan."

When I ran out of possibilities, I shouted, "What kind of a Christian are you?"

She leaned toward me and held my hand. In a soft and loving voice, she said, "Dear madam, I am a Christian. I believe in Jesus, my God. In the Bible, there is no Catholic, Protestant, or Orthodox—only Christian! I follow Jesus and the Bible. I pray to Jesus, who is God—God alone, and no one else."

I was lost and confused. At that critical moment, Jimmy buzzed; he was waiting for me to take me to work. On the way, I asked Jimmy what kind of a Christian he was. Laughingly, he replied, "A nonpracticing Catholic."

"Do you know what type of church Mari attends?" I asked.

"I think she goes to a Christian church; they call it a nondenominational church."

"Huh?" I regretted having asked the question because now I was more confused and doubtful about her Christianity. My concern grew when I thought of a Christian cult worshipper living in my house.

A few days later, I recalled my Christian friend's comments about Mari's faith. He assured me that she was a devout Christian and "the best," as he put it. What a relief. That was all I wanted to know.

I must admit that I sometimes felt Mari's prayers touched me in ways I cannot describe. I cannot forget the day I left on a business trip. As a nervous flyer, I noticed that the plane was taxiing longer than usual. Finally, the captain announced that our plane was returning to the gate to investigate an electrical problem with the main door.

While waiting for the technicians to complete their work, the captain allowed us to use our electronic devices. I called Mari. Before I told her about the door problem, she cried, "Madam, the plane, madam … big problem," and she started in praying in tongues again.

"Mari," I interrupted her. Mari's cries put me on high alert. "How did you know the plane had a problem? Are we going to be okay? Are we going to crash?" I almost panicked.

She said, "God told me to pray Psalm 91 for your protection."

Wow! Wow! Why had I not thought of such a response?

I sank in my seat, stunned. I continued to be blown away until the captain announced that the technicians had fixed the problem and the plane was ready to take off. I quickly called Mari and asked her if it was safe now to fly. She giggled and said, "Yes, madam." The mystery of God speaking in prayers remained on my mind throughout the trip (as it has remained to this day). Whenever I think of that incident, I get goose bumps.

10
EASTER SUNDAY

Sunday, April 7, 1996—Easter

Home alone! Mari had gone to church and would not be back until late in the evening. I had offered to drive her, but she declined, claiming that I might be tempted to go to my office, which was close to her church. So, I commissioned Jimmy, the driver, to take her to church and bring her back home.

When they left, I went back to bed and brought along the box in which Mari kept the mail. I scanned the pile and found two letters from County Hospital and Dr. Ashok. My heartbeat began a frantic race. With a trembling hand, I pulled the letters out and moved the box to the side of the bed. Mari had drawn a smiley face with a nose in the shape of a question mark on the envelopes. Her scribbles warmed my heart and stilled my trembling and fear. Thank goodness for her presence in my life. We had been together for five years, and yet she had never pried or meddled in my personal affairs. Unless I shared something with her, she never asked or questioned. I always admired her strong Christian faith, notably, her faithful and cheerful tithing to God despite her poverty. She reminded me very much of Tikin Anahit.

I held the letters in my hands and gazed at Mari's drawing.

Her gentle way of asking for more information about my ever-increasing trips to doctors and coming home sick touched me. I realized that I had been quiet and withdrawn when I got home. Lack of sleep and appetite loss started to show on my face and sent alarming signals when my body displayed a rapid loss of weight. My clothes got baggy. I could tell how concerned she was; her eyes spoke of mountains of anxiety.

I summoned my courage and opened the letters. The first letter was from the County Hospital's administration office, informing me of my surgery date of June 11.

The second envelope held a copy of the letter from Dr. Ashok to my employer informing them of my surgery and the need for a medical leave of forty days following the operation. There was a note attached to the letter asking for my authorization to mail the letter to my employer. In the letter, Dr. Ashok also reminded me to refrain from using my vocal cords for at least forty days, for example, no speaking, whispering, or murmuring. The letters and Dr. Ashok outraged me! Grr!

I lamented my misfortune. What scared me most was the extended medical leave. To date, I had not informed my boss about my health condition or the surgery, let alone the extended medical leave of several weeks. It was this last that tormented me most. I cried myself to sleep, remaining asleep until the phone woke me up. It was Victor calling from London. I invited him to share the Easter turkey that I had purchased from Harrods. I had not seen him since he had gone to France to visit his family.

I quickly glanced at the clock. It was 4:00 p.m. Holy moly, I had slept for almost eight hours. I pulled myself out of bed, took a shower, and got dressed. While waiting for Victor, I made coffee and went to the lounge. I stood in front of the bay window, sipping my coffee. I could see the London skyline spread out for miles, zigzagging around the River Thames, from my window. It was the time of the day when the sky displays spectacular twilight hues on the horizon before bringing the sunset to a complete rest.

As the sleepy sun slowly crawled toward the western horizon, the lights of the East London skyline emerged in the distance like sparkling jewels. The buildings came alive and showed off their adornment with flashing lights. The Canary Wharf Tower stood majestically tall, towering over and illuminating the entire area with its pyramid-shape crown adorned with laser beams. The view was breathtaking. An unusual quietness in the air accented the sunset. The streets looked deserted with no people or cars. It was Easter Sunday after all.

The stillness of the air was contagious. It silenced my brain, which was exhausted from ruminating on the past and worrying about the future. It defused the bomb of worries that had been ticking in my head. My body went limp in total surrender and bowed onto the couch.

For a long time, I did not move. Suddenly, something prompted me to turn on the TV. I stretched my arm with a mechanical gesture, reached the TV remote next to my coffee cup, and clicked the power button. Behold, an angelic voice filled the room. I turned my head toward the TV, where I saw a young boy in front of a choir of boys his age, probably no older than ten years of age, in a white robe singing in an angelic voice. The lyrics of the hymn "Be Still, My Soul,"[17] printed on the screen, gripped me like a magnet. A chill ran down my spine and sprang me up straight on the couch. I embraced every word. Nothing could have defined my personal needs better than the lyrics of this hymn, as if the author knew of my current situation. With trembling lips and voice, I sang along with the young boy. The lyrics that touched me most were these:

---

[17] The Christian hymn "Be Still, My Soul," written in German ("Stille meine Wille, dein Jesus hilft siegen"), in 1752 by Katharina Amalia Dorothea von Schlegel (1697–1768), was translated into English in 1855 by Jane Laurie Borthwick (1813–1897).

Be still, my soul; the Lord is on thy side.
Bear patiently the cross of grief or pain.
Leave to thy God to order and provide.
In every change, He faithful will remain.

Be still, my soul; thy God doth undertake
To guide the future as He has the past.
Thy hope, thy confidence, let nothing shake;
All now mysterious shall be bright at last.

When the program finished, I turned the TV off and crawled back onto the sofa, curling my legs up to my chest. The echo of the hymn lingered in my ears. I pondered on the words "The Lord is on thy side" for a long time; it took me back to my childhood Seigneur Dieu. *Where are You, Seigneur Dieu?* I cried in my head.

11
PRAYING FOR A MIRACLE

I shared with a Christian friend, Kelly, my health and financial issues. "I want a miracle to heal me and solve my problems," I said.

"If you were Christian, I would have suggested that you visit a church and attend a healing prayer," he said.

What? How could an educated person suggest such a naive and superstitious thing? I thought. I felt like scolding him for taking my problems lightly, but I held my tongue.

He told me about the pastor of a church in Victoria known for his superior teaching and the church's prayers for healing. "If you are interested, I will take you there," he said.

"Will the pastor pray for Muslims?" I skeptically asked.

"I think he will," he hesitantly said, adding quickly, "but you need to believe." I sensed reluctance in his reply. *Believe in what?* I thought.

Kelly would not tell me which church or its location for fear that I would go by myself. "I need to take you because I know the pastor. I want *him* to pray for you, not anybody else," he said. And he reiterated the importance of believing.

"Believe in what?" I curiously asked.

Then he told me a story his uncle told him about the young

son of his Muslim friend who was losing his sight rapidly because of a rare genetic disorder. The father had traveled with his son from the Middle East to the United States and consulted with the top ophthalmologists there. Unfortunately, all the doctors told the father that there was nothing they could do; the child would gradually go blind. The father, hugely disappointed and heartbroken, decided to return home. One week before his departure, he visited a friend whom he knew from back home, a Christian man living in the city. The friend suggested that the father take the boy to a Christian healing center where he had witnessed miraculous healings. The father got angry at his friend and rebuked him for his suggestion. He stormed out, saying that he would prefer his son to be blind, even dead, than to be healed by Christian prayers.

Only when the child's condition deteriorated, with great pain, did the father's desperation take him back to his Christian friend. Together, they took the child to the healing center. While the pastor prayed over the child, the father stood at the door, reciting Qur'anic verses. The deacons joined the pastor and prayed together over the child for a long time.

The father spent his last week in the city taking his child to the healing center for prayers. The pastor and the deacons continued pleading to God to heal the child's eyes, while the father stood by the door praying. At one point, suddenly, the child shouted that he was seeing faint shadows of people around him. The prayers intensified even more, pleading in the name of Jesus for the child's complete healing. When the father heard the name of Jesus and saw one of the deacons anointing the child with oil, with the third one reading from the Bible, he ran to his son, grabbed him by the hand, and dragged him out of the center. He shouted that he would prefer to have a blind Muslim son than to have him healed by Jesus!

I was appalled by the father's stand. Wow! I wondered, *Are the two religions that different? Isn't Jesus mentioned in the Qur'an?*

Doesn't the Qur'an declare Jesus as a son born to the Virgin Mary by way of Immaculate Conception by the Holy Spirit? Doesn't the Qur'an state that Jesus performed unique miracles ranging from healing the sick to raising the dead? So, why did the father refuse Jesus's healing of his son? What was in the name of Jesus that the father feared?

The story of the child touched me profoundly. I felt sad for the child. The father's reaction reminded me of Ibn Rushd's (Averroes's) quote "Ignorance leads to fear, fear leads to hatred, hatred leads to violence. This is the equation."

PART II
HE CALLED ME

You did not choose me, but I chose you and appointed you so that you might go and bear fruit—fruit that will last—and so that whatever you ask in my name the Father will give you.
—John 15:16

12
WESTMINSTER CHAPEL—FIRST VISIT

April 28, 1996

It was the last Sunday in April. The sunrays filtering through the shutters caressed my cheeks and woke me up. It was 10:30 a.m. I never slept that late, but my body was aching from a long transatlantic flight. A screaming headache begged me for just a couple more hours of sleep. And yet I felt an inexplicable urge to get up; it almost pushed me out of bed. With hesitating steps, I got out of the bed and opened the bedroom door. Mari had already left for her church.

Even today, I do not recall getting dressed, leaving the flat, getting in the car, or driving. I do not have any rational explanation for how I got to Buckingham Gate Street. Suddenly, I found myself standing on the steps of a large building, staring at a plaque on the brick wall: "Westminster Chapel." My lips uttered the two words several times. A church? In slow motion, I moved my head around to examine my surroundings. I did not recognize the area. *Where am I? How did I get here?* The mystery of how I got to the church, fully dressed, agonized me. The last thing I recalled was being at home in my pajamas. I felt as if I had fallen from the sky, but that happens only in movies!

Children with joyous voices galloped up the steps, undisturbed by my frozen position on the staircase. The adults zigzagged around me to enter the church. A young man standing by the main front door walked toward me and greeted me, saying, "Welcome to the Chapel." I did not know what to say. My face flushed crimson. "Is this your first visit?" he asked. Giving no reply, I only smiled. I summoned my mind for an answer but got none. Everything in me had gone silent. The young man extended one hand to shake my hand as he said, "Please come in." Without any hesitation, my legs walked up the steps, while my eyes remained fixated on the plaque. He handed me a leaflet, which I quickly shoved into my pocket without even reading it. I doubted if I answered any of his questions or listened to anything he said. As I approached the double door in front of me, my heartbeats raced to a sudden crescendo as if I were approaching an unexpected significant encounter. I quickly walked through the double glass door and froze. Wow. I was standing at the back of a big hall. It was a church! *It is a church, right? But why am I at a church?*

For a second, I wondered what kind of a church it was. Surely, it looked different from all the churches I had visited in the past. It was a bare church. I was taken aback by its bareness. What, no statues of Saint Mary? No crucifix of Jesus? No cross? No icons of saints? No basin or vessel of holy water? My eyes, alone, moved around and scanned the hall.

Another thing that struck me was the brightness of the hall as if it were illuminated by fire. The brilliance of the light at one point felt like blinding, though it cheered me up and wrapped me in a blanket of peace, a unique peace I had never felt before. Although I had never been in that place, I felt a strange sense of belonging and fully grounded. For the first time in my life, I experienced the feeling and meaning of being at home. It was such an amazing and warm feeling. Yes, I even sighed. "I am home at last!" I was completely surprised by my declaration.

Although there were no statues of Saint Mary or Jesus, I did what Tikin Anahit and my Christian classmates at the Franciscan school would have done: I bowed my head, knelt on one knee, and made the sign of the cross on my forehead and chest. Then, I raced my way to the front and sat in the third row on the church's left side. I pulled the collar of my coat up high, letting my bangs fall down over my eyes. I dropped my head to my chest. *If only the people knew that I am a Muslim attending their church, they would kick me out.* From the corner of my eye, I skimmed my surroundings, checking if people were watching me. I must admit that the moment I sat down, all questions about my being there had ceased. A sweet sensation that surpassed all my intellectual understanding enveloped me and guarded my heart and mind, leaving me in total peace.

Seconds later, my stomach started growling and roaring as if a flood had gushed inside me, splashing me and wetting me. *What?* I at once crossed my legs, thinking that I had peed in my pants. Slowly, I slid my hand under my coat and checked the wooden bench under me. What a relief when I found it dry. So what was that water gushing inside me? In spite of its roaring, it felt soothing. My fear of being noticed by those surrounding me disappeared. An extraordinary peace enveloped me. Never before had I known such peace.

When the singing started, I was stunned by the simplicity of the lyrics. The hymn described a loving, forgiving God, so close to people and very real as if alive. Following the last song, a gentleman with salt-and-pepper hair went up the podium to announce news related to the church.[18] I kept my head down and my eyes closed, focusing on the peace that had embraced me. He closed his announcements by saying that Dr. R. T. *Candle* would be preaching the sermon. What?! My ears perked up. My head and back shot straight up, and my eyelids flew wide open. I quickly checked the leaflet the usher had given me. My

---

[18] I learned later that he was Deacon Bill Reynolds.

eyes shot high beams of light as they fell on the line "Dr. R. T. Kendall preaching the 11:00 a.m. and 6:00 p.m. services." I froze in awe. My heart plummeted to my feet. The voice that had called "Candle!" drummed again in my ears. I gasped for air. I needed an extra pair of lungs and a new heart to hold the sudden avalanche of emotions that swept over me.

When Dr. Kendall went up onto the altar, I must have stared at him like a deer caught in the headlights. He took notice of my strange staring at him. He turned to me with curious eyes for a split of second before resuming his teaching. Perhaps he wondered why I was looking at him that way. I pulled my head down to my chest and went deep into my thoughts.

Throughout the service, I pinned my eyes on Dr. Kendall. I replayed in my mind the three dreams, over and over. Suddenly, I believed without any shadow of a doubt that the caller in my dreams had been referring to Pastor Kendall, not a physical candle! But why? What was the connection between the dreams, Dr. Kendall, and my presence in this church? My mind was jammed with a zillion questions.

As I debated these thoughts in my mind, I suddenly heard a change in Dr. Kendall's voice, as if someone else had taken his place. He spoke in a very faint and soft voice, almost a gentle whisper that flew over the pews and entered my ears. The still whisper was talking to me alone! My whole body jolted forward. I closed my eyes and inclined my head so my good ear could focus on the voice. Oh my word! I recognized that voice. It was the same voice I had heard in my dreams. It was also the same voice and tone that had spoken to me as a child when I prayed to Seigneur Dieu. Wow. With a trembling voice, I whispered, "Seigneur Dieu, Jesus, it is You, isn't it?" Before receiving a response, I instantaneously believed without any shadow of a doubt that the voice was that of Seigneur Dieu, Jesus. Why? His presence magnetized me and electrified me.[19] Every fiber within me started trembling. My tears erupted at the knowledge that Seigneur Dieu, Jesus, was beside me and talking to me and me alone: "Follow Me. You did not choose Me; I chose you. You are Mine." The moment I heard the gentle whisper, I believed. I did not doubt or harden my heart; I just believed. "As the Holy Spirit says: 'Today, if you hear his voice, do not harden your hearts'" (Hebrews 3:7–8).

The echo of Jesus's whispers grew gracefully in my spirit. My eyes beheld a vision of chains breaking from around my feet (I can still hear the clattering sound of the metal chains). Released, I crossed over the shackles, jumped in the air with arms wide open, and roared with shouts of joy, "Yes, Lord Jesus, my God! I will follow You! I am Yours!" I confessed Jesus as God—the belief I had had as a child but that had gone dormant for decades. My body shook and felt weightless. I had never experienced a similar shaking.

Then, I saw myself holding Jesus's hand, and together we walked through the tapestry of my life. In the vision, I was a child of five years. Without looking at His face, I walked silently with Him on a narrow road overlooking a deep valley on one side and a high mountain on the other. The Lord walked on the open valley side, while I walked on the inside. The fear that paralyzed me as a child had gone. Deep peace enveloped me like a second skin, and I walked with Jesus in complete trust. Seconds later, the vision transitioned me from childhood to my current adult age, living under the shadow of my painful past. Then, faster than the blink of an eye, Jesus pulled me out from under the shadow. Freed at last! Except, my bones were so weak that my steps were

---

[19] Having been agnostic about prophets in general and about the true God in particular, I once mentioned to a friend that I would only believe in God if, and only if, His presence were to magnetize me and if He were to perform a unique supernatural miracle and electrify me, instantaneously turning my heart into that of a strong believer and follower.

slow, almost crawling. The Lord told me that I needed to work my muscles. I moaned from the pain and complained that I did not have the strength. He said that His grace was enough for me.

Then, the vision gave me a brief glimpse of various events in the future, one of which lasted longer than the others. Here is one of them: Walking on a dirt field in a place that looked like the Middle East, I was shouting, "There is not enough time;! There is not enough time!" The sky turned red, woven with rainbow colors. A sense of reverence mixed with urgency filled the air. Slowly, the sky started moving closer to the ground. I knew in my heart that I needed to let people know that the end was near. The terrain was dry, covered with briars and thorns; hence, it was not easy for me to run. Yet I ran through the field, anxious to warn the people and rescue them. But my voice was not loud enough for all the people to hear me. I knew in my heart that there was an urgent need for all these people to listen to my message, so I climbed a minaret and called through the microphone.

I went through a timeless experience of different periods, feelings, and emotions—hard to put into words—in such a short time. The encounter with Jesus ended with the instruction that I would soon have a vision that would confirm my calling. It was the most supernatural and magical moment of my entire life! I remained in awe until I heard the congregation saying "Amen."

From the corner of my eye, I looked at my surroundings. I was sad that my encounter with Seigneur Dieu, Jesus, had ended and that I was back in my seat in the Chapel. Slowly, Dr. Kendall's voice popped back into my ears and got my attention. He was asking people to do something behind the pulpit. Even though I did not understand his instruction or know what the pulpit was, I found myself on my feet. I walked forward, almost running, toward two men standing behind the podium. I recognized one of them; he was the announcer.[20] They surrounded me as I

---

[20] Deacons Bill Reynolds and Benjamin Chan.

approached them. The announcer asked me, "What is your name, and how can we pray for you, and—?"

I interrupted him by saying, "My parents are Muslims. You may ask me to leave the church, but I want to become a Christian and follow Jesus. I must see Dr. Kendall." I could not believe my boldness. Shyness had suddenly deserted me. What had prompted to say these words? I had never planned to come to this church, let alone request to become a Christian. I was extremely sure of myself and of my decision to follow Jesus. The words flowed out of my lips. I did not think of anything else. It was as if the world had stopped at this moment. My voice was clear, and my mind was made up to follow Jesus. Jesus had brought me to this church to receive Him as my God. And I committed to doing so. Nothing else mattered.

I stood there between the two men, waiting for their responses. Why in the world were they looking at me in total shock? It took them a few seconds before they told me that they were gobsmacked by what I had said as they had never received such a request.

Then, the one on my right said, "Are you sure you want to convert?"

Without any hesitation, I replied, "Of course I am sure. The Lord instructed me to follow Him. And I want to follow Him. For this, I must see Dr. Kendall."

The announcer said, "Let us pray." And they prayed.

When they finished, I said at once, "Please excuse my naive question. Is the pastor's name really Kendall?"

"Yes," the announcer replied. "He is the senior pastor."

"Then, in this case, I must see him now. Please lead me to him," I said.

The two men left to check with Dr. Kendall. I did not move from my spot as I waited impatiently for their return. While I was waiting, waves of peace transmitted hope; indescribable joy and comfort bubbled in my heart. A few seconds later, the two men returned and ushered me into Dr. Kendall's office.

13
DR. KENDALL

When I entered the vestry office, Dr. Kendall was standing behind his desk. He shook my hand, greeted me with ultimate politeness, and asked me to sit on the large couch facing him. Then he sat at his chair behind his desk. From his accent, I realized that Dr. Kendall was American. He was in his fifties, very handsome with bushy eyebrows that covered his beautiful deep blue eyes.

"How may I help you, young lady?" he asked.

In a few words, I reiterated my request by saying, "Sir, I want to follow Jesus. That is all I want to do. So please, sir, tell me what I should do and how to do it, and I will do it."

Unlike the two gentlemen I had spoken to earlier, Dr. Kendall seemed doubtful and cautious about what I had said. After a short pause, staring at me, he said, "Would you please tell me a little bit about you, your background, and where you're from? Is this your first visit to the Chapel? Do you live in London? And what brought you to the Chapel?"

Wow! I had not expected such an inquisition! I guessed Dr. Kendall wanted to know if I was a genuine person. So, I shared with him a little bit about my Muslim family background and the reason for my being in London. I finished my discourse by recounting that I had come to the church to follow Jesus. I did not volunteer too many details, keeping my focus on learning what I needed to do to follow Jesus. Dr. Kendall moved forward in his chair, put his elbows on the desk, clasped his hands together, looked me in the eye with his piercing eyes, and asked, "What would you ask God if you were standing before Him?"

Startled by the unexpected question, I felt a surge of heat on my face—I blush when nervous. "Well," I said, "I would ask God why He waited many long years before calling me. I wish He had made it clear to me when I was a child that He wanted me to follow Him. He surely would have protected me better than Allah from the horrific trauma I experienced in my childhood. And more importantly, I would thank Jesus for ending that trauma when I called His name." My own words alarmed me; why was I sharing my private life with a total stranger? I scolded myself.

"What do you mean?" Dr. Kendall asked inquisitively.

I regretted bringing up the unrelated subject and feared that it would move the conversation away from the original purpose of my visit.

"Well, suffice it to say that I experienced trauma in my childhood. But this is not the point of our meeting or the reason for my being in your church." With a stern voice, I quickly added, "Sir, I came here to follow Jesus. Today, the Lord Jesus unexpectedly brought me here to your church and called me to follow Him. So please tell me what I need to do to."

After few seconds of silence, Dr. Kendall smiled and said, "Remarkable, but here is my other question: Do you know for sure that if you were to die today, you would go to heaven? Let me put it in other words: If you were to stand before God—which you will do one day when you die—what would you say to Him to let you in His heaven? What is your hope for going to heaven?"

Huh? What kind of questions are these? What do these questions have to do with my request to follow Jesus? my mind shouted. I turned red; Dr. Kendall's questions had caught me by surprise. I paused, searching for an answer. I cleared my throat and said, "Well, I hope that God will not judge me based on what I have done in my life."

"What do you mean?" he asked.

My nervousness started to show as I squirmed in my seat. "What I mean is this," I said. "If God were to judge me on who I am as a person, my morality, my values, or what I've done during my life, I would most definitely be eternally punished in hell. However ..." I paused for a second. A tiny voice grew in my ear as if dictating to me. "However," I continued, "my hope is in Jesus. By accepting His calling, believing Him, putting my trust in Him, and following Him in this world, He will guide me to heaven for He lives in heaven."

By then, Dr. Kendall's inquisitive frown had gotten deeper. "This is extremely remarkable," he said, quickly throwing another question at me: "And *why* should you go to heaven?"

Wow, the complexity of the questions was at a peak. I had never thought of this question! I nervously smiled and wondered if Dr. Kendall would ever get back to my original request.

"*Why?*" I said with a trembling voice. "Well, because I don't want to go to hell!" I took a deep breath to refresh my strength. "I believe that I am a decent, good person with good morals and values." I continued, "I never intentionally did any terrible things like stealing, hurting a person, or killing. Also, I believe that I have done more good deeds than bad, and for this I feel that I am good enough to go paradise." I went on, stressing that since Jesus had called me to follow Him, I believed that somehow He would take me to heaven to be with Him there. I concluded by saying, "Following Jesus is my hope. And this is why I am here meeting with you, so can you tell me how to follow Jesus." I straightened my back and showed an upset face, wondering about his questions, which were unrelated to the original purpose for my visit.

After a short silence, Dr. Kendall smiled and said, "Praise God. I am speechless." He paused for a long while. Dr. Kendall's silence did not amuse me. *Will he ever respond to my question?* I wondered. Suddenly, he said, "One last question: What brought you to the Chapel? Who brought you to the Chapel?"

My shoulders dropped and my chest caved in from the weight of my disappointment. *Will Dr. Kendall ever understand my question and answer it?* Tears of sadness dampened my eyes. *Will he ever tell me how to follow Jesus?* I paused to reflect on his last question. That was a tough one. How could I explain my memory gap and my mysterious journey to this church? For a second, I earnestly searched my memory bank for a clue about the incredible trip from my home to the church, but I found none. *O Seigneur Dieu, Lord Jesus, help me to remember how I got here, for I do not recall driving. I did not even know the location of this church. Lord, how did I get here?*

I swallowed to moisten my dry throat as I murmured, "Frankly, sir, I don't know. The strange thing is that I do not even recall driving or taking a taxi, a bus, or the Tube. I don't know if someone drove me here. I have never heard of this church; I do not know its location or its address."

"So, you don't know how you got here," he said. "Where were you before coming to church? Do you live in the neighborhood?"

"Sir," I said, not knowing how to address a pastor, "I do not have an intelligent answer to give you. Even I cannot believe what happened."

"What happened?"

"I woke up this morning with an inexplicable urge to get up quickly as if someone had pushed me out of bed and ordered me to get dressed and to leave the flat. One minute I was in my bedroom at home getting dressed, and the next minute I was standing on the steps of the church. It is unbelievable, isn't it? But this is what happened."

Suddenly, a thought flashed into my mind: *Could I have been zapped as seen in alien movies?* I shouted in my head, *What? Be serious, girl!* If only Dr. Kendall knew about the irrational ideas I was entertaining in my mind, he probably would have asked me to leave not only his office but also the church. So, I quickly veered off the topic, saying that perhaps my dreams had led me to the church.

"Your dreams?" Dr. Kendall asked with a voice full of curiosity.

Oh, man! Would he believe another unusual dream? I regretted having mentioned my three dreams.

"Yes. My dreams," I said, and went on sharing the three dreams I had in which I heard a voice calling "Candle," mentioning how I interpreted the dreams by lighting candles at Santa Catalina Church. "But," I said, "it was only in this church that I discovered that your name is Kendall, and I now believe that the voice in my dreams foretold me about you, not physical candles. During the service, the Lord Jesus spoke to me, telling me to follow Him, and I instantaneously received Him in my heart. I do not doubt that the Lord directed me to this church so I could meet you and give my life to the Lord. So, please, sir, will you tell me how to follow Jesus? I believe this is the sole reason for my coming here."

By then, Dr. Kendall had moved to the back of his chair. He looked at me. I could not tell from his smile and frown what his deliberation might be. Dr. Kendall shared that he had been pastor of this church for more than nineteen years, during which time he had witnessed not one single conversion from Islam and had never heard such testimony.

Did he say conversion? What was that? Will he ever reply to my question? I repeated my question, asking him if he would teach me how to follow Jesus, quickly adding, "I now have a mission to follow Jesus." In my heart, I asked the Lord Jesus to help me and for Dr. Kendall to believe my story, though unusual.

While I was talking, a gentle breeze brushed my right cheek when I mentioned the name of Jesus. My head slowly turned to the right side. Soft waves of chills swept up and down my spine while goose bumps covered my legs. Could the Lord be here? My heart leaped in reverence; I took a deep breath. My head rolled onto my chest. A peaceful tune serenaded my heart. I knew then and there that I had taken my first step in following Him; I was standing on the threshold of my real destiny. All I wanted was to be with Jesus.

Dr. Kendall asked if I was okay. "Never better," I replied with a big smile. After a few minutes of silence, Dr. Kendall reiterated that my testimony was exceptionally astounding. He then asked if he could pray for me, and I accepted gladly. Dr. Kendall moved to the armchair next to the sofa, where I was sitting, and prayed.

"Well?" I said after he had finished praying. "Will you teach me how to follow Jesus?"

"Young lady," he said with his beautiful smile, "your commitment to following Jesus is remarkably unique. But I cannot teach you now in one session how to follow Jesus. It is a lifetime commitment and a serious one. May I suggest that you come back next week? We can talk more then." He stood up, hinting that he needed to leave. Dr. Kendall's invitation to return to the church encouraged me. But what had happened to my question?

As he ushered me to the door, he said, "Reading the Bible and asking the Holy Spirit to reveal God's Word to you is the best and only way to know God."

Ah! Finally, I had found my answer: *I will ask Jesus's Holy Spirit Himself to teach me.*

As we stood at his office door to say goodbye, Dr. Kendall mentioned that he and the deacons would pray for me. I took this opportunity to share with him the recommendation that Kelly, my Christian friend, had made to ask him pray for my illness. With a charming smile, Dr. Kendall suggested that I return to the church at 5:00 p.m. and attend the healing prayer meeting. I promised that I would return. With a beaming smile on my face, I left his office and ran out of the church. I did not feel my feet touch the ground!

When I got out of the church, I wanted to shout for joy from the top of my lungs that I was following Jesus. Standing on the same church steps where I had stood that morning, I closed my eyes and took a deep breath to breathe in the first breeze of my new life. When I opened my eyes and looked at the cars parked on the street, reality hit me. *Where is my car?* Panic stole my joy. I paced the blocks around the Chapel, hoping to find my car, but it was to no avail. One hour later, I was exhausted. I got angry at myself for not having written down the location where I had parked the car, when suddenly I remembered that I had not driven there! The mystery of how I had gotten to the church rechallenged me. My sore feet had ignited a violent headache that left me no choice but to jump in a cab and go home. During the taxi ride, I recalled the events of the morning.

It was close to 2:00 p.m. when I entered my flat. I called my Christian friend Kelly to say that I had great news to share with him. When he arrived, I took him by his hand to the living room and asked him to sit and listen to my good news. I stood in front of him, threw my arms in the air, and shouted, "I became a Christian. I am now following Jesus!"

My news gave Kelly a great shock; his eyes popped out of their sockets. He went dead silent for a few long seconds before he burst into laughter that almost caused him to choke on his cigarette. "What?" he shouted, coughing again for a few seconds. "Come again, what did you say?"

"I am a Christian now," I calmly said. "You are looking at a Christian woman and a follower of Jesus."

He stared at me with curious eyes. In a serious tone, he said, "Please don't make fun of Christianity. Christianity is not something you *become*; it is a *calling*. And a serious one, I may add."

"Okay," I said. "Today, Jesus called me to follow Him, and I accepted the calling." Then I jumped into the seat facing him and told him about the whole journey, starting with the dreams about the candle and moving on to my entering the church and my encounter with Jesus. Kelly was stunned and speechless. His jaw dropped to the floor as he gasped for air.

"Unbelievable! Unbelievable!" he repeated a few times. "To which church did you go?" he asked. "And what is the name of the pastor?"

"I went to Westminster Chapel, and the pastor I talked to is Dr. R. T. Kendall."

Suddenly he choked on his cigarette again and started coughing violently. I quickly put my hand in my pocket and pulled out a Kleenex to give him. With it, the leaflet the greeter had given me fell on the floor. When my friend calmed down, he shouted even louder, "No, it can't be. No. No. No."

I kept nodding my head. "Yes, yes, yes."

"But how? You do not even know the location of the church. I don't believe you."

I handed him the church flyer and said, "I hope you believe me now." He pulled the paper from my hand, read it, and went through my notes from my meeting with Dr. Kendall. "I can't believe it," he said, his eyes filled with surprise and awe. "This is the church I wanted to take you to and introduce you to Dr. Kendall, as I know him personally. He is an authority on teaching the Bible."

I was so excited that I repeated several times the entire journey, until I reached complete exhaustion. After a short pause, I saw that Kelly was still in shock.

"Do you *really* understand what happened to you?" he questioned my intention. "Do you *really, really* understand the meaning of following Jesus? Are you ready to face the costs of following Jesus? How can you explain it?"

"Kelly, I can't explain it, but I wholeheartedly believe it. It was a miracle. And, yes, I am ready to follow Jesus at all costs."

I could not tell from Kelly's comments if he believed me. After a few minutes of silence, he said, "Indeed, the Lord works in mysterious ways."

I looked at my watch and jumped to my feet. "Well, we have forty-five minutes before we return to the Chapel for the healing prayer." I left in a hurry to go to my room, where I locked the door. I wrote down the entire journey in detail in my journal, which you are now reading.

A few seconds later, Kelly knocked on my bedroom door and said, "But your car seemed to be parked here all morning; the windshield is still covered with ice. How did you get to the church when you did not know the name or the address?"

"Ah, that!" I shouted.

What shall I say? How to explain the inexplicable transportation to the church when I, myself, did not comprehend it, let alone have the ability to describe it.

"Oh yeah. The car," I said. "Well, uh, uh, how I got to the Chapel is another miracle. Kelly, you must believe in God's miracles!" I shouted from across the room with a smile that filled my heart with joy. Then I resumed writing.

PART III

HE TOUCHED ME, OH, HE TOUCHED ME

Don't be afraid; just believe, and she will be healed.
—Luke 8:50

Shackled by a heavy burden,
'Neath a load of guilt and shame.
Then the hand of Jesus touched me,
And now I am no longer the same.
He touched me, oh, He touched me
And oh, the joy that floods my soul!
Something happened, and now I know
He touched me and made me whole.
—Bill Gaither (1963)

14
THE HEALING PRAYER

At 4:30 p.m., my friend and I drove back to Westminster Chapel.

A young man ushered us to the prayer room on the first floor of the Chapel. Kelly and I sat in the last row. There were about ten to fifteen people there.

Dr. Kendall asked who wanted prayer for healing. I raised my hand.

"You are back," he said with a smile. Surely, he had a different smile from the one he'd had that morning; this one was a welcoming smile.

He asked me to move to the front. While I was walking to the front row, Dr. Kendall told the attendees about our morning meeting and my miraculous conversion to follow Jesus. "Praise to God" filled the room.

I sat in the designated chair. Before starting, Dr. Kendall asked, "What is your name again?"

"Maha," I replied.

"Maha, may I lay my hand on your head?" he asked.

"Yes. What shall I do?" I asked.

"Nothing; you sit still. There is nothing for you to do. The deacons and I are going to pray."

I adjusted my position in the chair and closed my eyes. As Dr. Kendall started to pray, he stopped as if he had just remembered something important.

"Maha," he said. "I want you to know that although we pray for healing, we *do not* heal. We are human, just like you. The healing, *if any*, is done by the Lord Jesus and Jesus alone. He is *the* only healer, and it is done by *faith*. You must believe. Is this understood?" he asked.

I gently nodded my head and said, "I believe." I shut my eyes, bowed my head, and rested my hands on my knees. I clenched my fists while repeatedly reciting in my head, *I believe, I believe.* Prayers flowed over me and bathed me in complete tranquility. A few minutes later, the praying ended. I thanked Dr. Kendall and the deacons. Other people moved forward for prayers. I took my seat next to my friend in the last row.

My friend asked me if I wanted to leave. I shook my head no. I was mesmerized by the casual manner in which the people had prayed. The prayers were not recitals of memorized verses from the Bible. Instead, they were informal, unconstrained by rigid rituals, and spoken in a simple language. Yet, they sounded like sincere cries from the heart to God. There was a sense of reverence in the room. I never had felt such a feeling before. What shocked me most was the freedom to approach God as a Father, hold the Bible, and pray without the cleansing ritual in Islam called Wudu.[21]

The thought that God accepted me just the way I was without my going through the cleansing ritual (Wudu) overwhelmed me. I thought of my beloved nana who performed the Wudu five

---

[21] The Wudu is nullified in case of bodily discharge, including urination, vomiting, defecation, excessive bleeding, and gas. Sleep also nullifies the Wudu. In such cases, Muslims must repeat the Wudu. The Wudu involves washing the hands, mouth, nostrils, arms, head, and feet with water. The Wudu is considered an integral part of ritual purity in Islam, mandated before the five-times-a-day salat, holding and reading the Qur'an.

times a day in spite of her advanced age. Poor Nana, she'd fallen several times while attempting to wash her feet. I wished Nana had known that God would have accepted her anytime of the day or night without the Wudu. If Nana were alive, I would have asked her if she ever had felt God's love.

My visit to the Chapel's upper room and attending the prayer time made me realize that God does not look at the cleanliness of the body's exterior. He looks at our interior motives and the cleanliness of our hearts, minds, and souls.[22]

When the prayer meeting ended, my friend and I followed the crowd to the main hall for the evening service. I led him to the place where I had sat that morning. "This is the place where I met the Lord," I whispered in his ear. During the sermon, I closed my eyes to reminisce about the events that had happened that morning. Never had I felt so ecstatically happy. Never had I felt so high, high above the clouds.

---

[22] Later on, I learned that the cleanness of the tongue (our speech) is very important (James 1:26; Matthew 12:36–37).

PART IV
HE HEALED ME

And when Jesus went out He saw a great multitude; and He was moved with compassion for them, and healed their sick.
—Matthew 14:14 (NKJV)

15
GOD HAD A DIFFERENT PLAN FROM THE DOCTORS'

Monday, April 29, 1996

Dr. Sign called me early in the morning, suggesting that I get another opinion from one of his best university students, a renowned ENT, Dr. Pierres. Dr. Pierres had moved from the States to London and brought with him the latest in medical technology. Dr. Sign's request caught me by surprise because the date of my operation was set. Besides, I had no desire to see different doctors—not even for a second or third opinion. I was about to decline Dr. Sign's offer, when he said that he had mentioned my case to Dr. Pierres while playing golf with him yesterday, and Dr. Pierres had agreed to see me.

Bummer! I felt too embarrassed to decline. I was curious to know what had made Dr. Sign think of me during his weekend and discuss my case while playing golf! He had aroused my curiosity. Reluctantly, I agreed to see Dr. Pierres during my lunch break on Thursday, May 2. I asked Mari to go with me.

On Thursday, at 11:30, Mari came to the office, and together we took a taxi to Dr. Pierres's clinic. I was still annoyed about Dr. Sign's request. "I should have declined; I have no time for doctors," I angrily muttered to myself, feeling compelled to see Dr. Pierres.

We arrived at my appointment on time. Mari stayed in the waiting room while I followed the nurse to a changing room. After I'd put on a short disposable cape, the nurse led me into Dr. Pierres's examination room, adjoining his consultation room. I stood at the door examining the room, which was as big as a basketball stadium. A Victorian-style vaulted ceiling with ornate decorations crowned the room. The original opulent artistry was still visible beneath years of black smoke and dust. Large shipping crates occupied the room's perimeter; the doctor was moving his practice from Boston to London. The room was bare of furniture except the examination table, which was placed in the center, surrounded by computers, large screens, and various pieces of medical equipment.

Dr. Pierres walked in and greeted me. "Mrs. Termanini, please come in." After a brief introduction, he ushered me into the examination area. Dr. Pierres was much younger than I had expected. His young age did not impress me, but I trusted Dr. Sign's seasoned-age opinion. The tapping of my high heels on the wooden floor echoed in the room. My discomfort was visible by my shaking legs. The closer I got to the examination table, the louder my heartbeats drummed in my chest. The sight of the examination table, which was hooked to many screens and machines, overwhelmed me. *If this is his examination room, I wonder what his surgery room looks like,* I thought.

The nurse helped me into the examination chair and covered me with a warm blanket. In one synchronized movement, Dr. Pierres and his nurses put on surgical gloves. "Mrs. Termanini, are you comfortable?" Dr. Pierres asked.

"Yes, but scared," I nervously stuttered. "Are you sure you aren't operating on me?" I jokingly added, pointing to the numerous machines and the massive light above me that looked like those found in operating rooms. The nurse laughed. I needed this laughter to ease my anxiety.

"No surgery. No pain. Don't worry," he said with a big smile as he adjusted his chair. "The examination shouldn't take long," he said. What a relief! To distract myself, I engaged in small talk.

"Dr. Sign mentioned that you brought the latest technology from the States. You seem to be the first surgeon to acquire this in the UK," I said.

"Yes," he said, "but I am not sure about the first in the UK. I can see that you are well-informed."

"Yes," I said. "Dr. Sign spoke highly of you and told me about your new machines."

"Thank you." A polite smile softened the seriousness of his face. He lowered the headrest horizontally to the floor. All went quiet, and the examination started. I closed my eyes and opened my mouth. Dr. Pierres secured my jaw with mouth guards and inserted a tube into my throat, followed by one that almost choked me. A few minutes into the examination, I heard Dr. Pierres mumble, "Huh? Hmm. Interesting." From the corner of my eye, I saw all the organs in my throat displayed in color on a big screen and Dr. Pierres frowning, his eyes traveling back and forth from the screen to some photos he held in his hand. He looked nervous. The expression of seriousness on his face alarmed me. He inserted another tube with a larger camera that pressed hard against the organs in my throat. The examination became painful; I gagged. I signaled to stop and wiggled in the chair. "Mrs. Termanini," the doctor shouted with a threatening tone that startled me. "Please don't move." I shut my eyes to block my tears. I lost count of how many tubes he inserted into my mouth. The pressure in my throat and jaw became unbearable. My tears escaped and rolled down my cheeks. "Tissues," he ordered. Instantly, tissues covered my cheeks and brushed away my tears. Minutes later, an unusual commotion went on in the room. Footsteps and whispering emerged in the background. But it was Dr. Pierres's mumbling "Hmm, hmm" that alarmed me the most. His tone grew stern as he spoke with his nurses. He exchanged the machine he was using for another one and repeated the examination process all over again. At one point, Dr. Pierres shouted, "Incredible."

Oh my word, the cancer had spread all over! I screamed in my head. The doctor's comments injected more adrenaline into my heartbeat throughout the remaining of the examination, until the nurses removed all the tubes from my mouth and readjusted the chair. I opened my eyes and saw Dr. Pierres walking out of the room without saying a word. The nurses looked dismayed. One of them walked with me back to the dressing room and told me that the doctor would like to see me after I got dressed. Fear of imminent tragic news paralyzed my hands; my fingers were trembling so much that they were useless to button my shirt while I was dressing. I shoved my bra and tights into my purse and left the dressing room half dressed. I ran to the doctor's office.

Dr. Pierres was on the phone. "Please have Dr. Sign call me as soon as possible. It *is* an urgent matter," he stressed. "It is about his patient Mrs. Termanini." I stood before his desk like an innocent person waiting for the judge's deliberation. The thought that the cancer had spread was biting my nerves. After a few minutes of silence, which seemed an eternity, Dr. Pierres closed my file and moved back into his chair.

"Mrs. Termanini," he said, "if I did not know Dr. Sign and trust his high expertise, I wouldn't have agreed to see you. But …" He paused and flipped through a few pages in my folder. His stern voice and frowning face alarmed me and shook me.

"But?" I fearfully stuttered.

"But"—he paused and took a deep breath—"the previous tests confirmed the presence of a medium-sized lump on your thyroid that would affect your vocal cords. But—"

"But?" I nervously asked. The suspense was killing me.

"But I am facing a dilemma now," he resumed.

"A dilemma?" I quickly interrupted.

"Yes. A dilemma. The tests I just conducted came with negative results. I was unable to locate the lump that Dr. Sign wanted me to check. Instead, I found a tiny nodule on your thyroid next to your vocal cords, not as per the tests." He paused, reviewing his test results again. "I am left to face an inexplicable deliberation," he said.

"Which is?" I nervously asked, seeking more information.

In a hesitant voice, the doctor said, "The lump has shrunk to a very tiny nodule—almost an insignificant trace by itself. The good news is that the tests I have done on the nodule show it is benign. Given its small size, it does not merit surgery because it is no longer pressing on your vocal cords." He reclined in his chair.

"But I have a surgery scheduled in June," I said.

"Look for yourself," he said, handing me two pictures. I looked at the before-and-after pictures; on one, the lump was visible, while on the other, there was a tiny dot highlighted in yellow. I handed the pictures back to him.

"I don't have a logical explanation," he said. "The lump has taken an incomprehensible course of change; it has shrunk so much that you can hardly see it. You have nothing to worry about, Mrs. Termanini." He shouted, "It is inexplicable!"

After a short pause, he said, "I just don't understand what happened. How could a lump shrink in such a short time and change its form and nature without any medical intervention? I am sorry, Mrs. Termanini; I don't have any medical explanation to give you." He put the photos back in the folder. "I am waiting for a call from Dr. Sign to share my findings," he said.

"So, in your opinion, I don't need surgery?" I asked to confirm my understanding.

"No. You don't need surgery," Dr. Pierres said.

While the conclusion that I wouldn't need the surgery thrilled me, my head labored to understand how my case had changed to "inexplicable." Suddenly, my mind flew to the healing prayer in the upper room at Westminster Chapel. Wow, God must have answered Dr. Kendall's prayer! *Lord Jesus healed me! There is no other answer.* Dr. Kendall said that I must believe, and I believed with all my heart while praying. Nothing is impossible for the Lord; God had answered the upper-room prayers and healed me.

"Okay. No surgery?" I asked again for confirmation.

"No, you don't need surgery," he repeated. "If it were my wife, I would tell her the same thing."

I smiled at his comment. Why had he mentioned his wife? I looked him in the eye, and with a big smile, I asked, "What would you do if it were you? Would you have the operation? (*He might not like his wife,* I thought.) My question amused Dr. Pierres. He laughed.

"No, I would not have the surgery," he replied. "But again," he added, "I don't understand what happened to the lump. I will send the scan, the biopsy, and all examination results to Dr. Sign, and I am sure that he will advise you of the same conclusion. Mrs. Termanini, your case is difficult to explain." He stood up and ushered me to the door, saying, "I am sorry, I don't know what else to say. Medically it is impossible. I do not understand what happened. Your results are utterly puzzling to me."

While standing before him, witnessing his desperation for an intelligent answer, a current of chilled air ran through my spine. Goose bumps rose up my skin with tingles. Under normal circumstances, these would be signs that my heart wanted me to say something. *Should I say what happened and how the results changed? Will he ever believe me? Or will he recommend that I have my head examined instead of my throat?* I summoned my courage, cleared my throat, and said in a soft voice, "Dr. Pierres, I know what happened. While you and Dr. Sign plan the basis of your prognosis on physical evidence, God has a different plan than you doctors. The Lord Jesus touched me and healed me. You see, sir, I went to the church for a—"

Dr. Pierres jutted his neck forward as he interrupted me, saying, "Excuse me?"

"The Lord Jesus answered prayers and healed me," I said.

Dr. Pierres's eyes flew open. "What?" he shouted.

"Last Sunday, I had a prayer at church for healing. God honored the prayer, touched me, and healed me."

My response caught Dr. Pierres off guard. He was displeased by my declaration.

"Well, if you believe that, then I have nothing else to say," he said.

"Oh yes, I believe!" I quickly added, "I strongly believe that Jesus heals."

Without a word, Dr. Pierres turned on his heel and reentered his office.

I ran back to the dressing room to get my coat and handbag. I went on my knees and bowed my head, praying, "Lord Jesus, I believe with all my heart and mind that You healed me. You are truly God and a miracle maker. Thank You for answering Dr. Kendall's and his team's prayers. I confirm my commitment to serve You for the rest of my life. I am Yours." I ran to the waiting room, grabbed Mari by the hand, and shouted, "Mari, quickly, let's run before the doctor changes his mind!" Hurriedly, we left the office. That was the last time I saw Dr. Pierres.

Once in the street, I told Mari what had happened and how the Lord Jesus had touched me and healed me. We hugged and cried with joy. We praised God while walking to the underground station. On the train, I revisited in my mind Dr. Kendall's remark when he and the deacons had laid hands on me in the upper room: "Maha," he said. "I want you to know that although we pray for healing, we *do not* heal. We are human, just like you. The healing, *if any*, is done by the Lord Jesus and Jesus alone. He is *the* only healer, and it is done by *faith*. You must believe. Is this understood?" "I believe," I replied. *Wow, the power of prayer,* I thought.

When I returned to the office, a colleague stopped me in the hall, saying that I was glowing and my face looked radiant. "Praise the Lord," I said, running up the stairs to my office. My heart was also glowing!

16
HE HEALED ME! END OF STRIKE ONE

On Tuesday, May 28, 1996, Dr. Sign's secretary called me for a same-day appointment; she stressed that it was urgent. I was eager to know Dr. Sign's reaction to Dr. Pierres's test results. When I entered Dr. Sign's office, I saw Dr. Pierres's images of my thyroid gland and the tissues of my vocal cords displayed on his desk. Unlike previous visits, Dr. Sign's greeting this time was somber. I sat in the chair opposite his desk, and quietly I watched him shuffle through the images and examine some under a magnifier. When he had gone through all of them, he put the magnifier to the side and gazed at me while shaking his head. His sheepish smile reflected an uneasiness in his mind. I wondered if he ever regretted sending me to Dr. Pierres. Minutes later, a span that felt like hours, he broke his silence and said in a deep voice, "Mrs. Termanini, I received Dr. Pierres's report and test results. I consider his diagnosis final, and I concur with his recommendation. Therefore, my final decision is to do nothing and close your case. I will send Dr. Smith Dr. Pierres's test results and report along with my recommendation. I am sure that you are pleased to know that you will no longer need surgery. My secretary will do what is necessary on your behalf to advise the hospital and cancel the operation. Do you have any questions?"

He stood on his feet and extended his hand for a handshake, gesturing that we had reached the end of the appointment. Stunned by his brief and speedy speech, I wondered, *Is he dismissing me without explanation?* I remained in my seat. Seeing me seated, he repeated, "Do you have any questions?"

"Yes. I do have a few questions," I said.

Dr. Sign sat down, crossed his arms on the desk, and looked at me with a question mark on his face. "Yes?"

Although my healing was an undeniable reality for me, I found myself seeking information to satisfy my intellect. I wanted to know if the nodule would ever grow back again and become malignant and/or threaten my vocal cords. While I was thinking of these critical issues, a debate ignited in my mind: Would my questions annul my faith?

"Yes? What are your questions?" Dr. Sign asked impatiently.

Instead of addressing my issue—fear of losing faith—directly, I pointed to the images of my throat on his desk and said, "Aren't they interesting?" He reached for the photos and spread them out facing me. He said, "I am speechless. Utterly speechless. A complete mystery." Streaks of disbelief mixed with anger echoed in his voice.

"I understand," I said. "However, I would appreciate some details or at least your suggestions on the way forward."

My insistence on discussing details did not amuse Dr. Sign; he wanted to end the appointment as soon as possible as if my case suddenly had become a threat.

"Explain? Explain what?" he said with his low, tenor-like voice. "Mrs. Termanini, I can't explain what I don't understand." He went on, sharing the lengthy discussion he had had with Dr. Pierres and their debate on how to explain medically the lump's sudden change in size and nature in a short time without any medical or surgical intervention. He purposely and repeatedly pointed out that medically speaking, the lump's transformation was impossible to re-create and prove.

"Praise the Lord! I exclaimed. "I believe that the Lord Jesus touched me and healed me. He is the miracle maker." With a big smile, I added, "Dr. Sign, would you say it's a miracle?"

"Oh yes," he said. "Dr. Pierres shared with me the strange story of your healing prayer. It is unfortunate for those sick people whom God did not choose to receive similar divine healing. Right?" He quickly ushered me to the door.

Ouch! Another mystery of God. Suddenly, I ran out of words. I shook his hand, thanked him, and left his office. That was the last time I saw Dr. Sign.

A week later, I received a letter from County Hospital's administration office confirming the surgery's cancelation. The section "Reason for cancelation" was left blank.

Wow, what does it take for humankind to acknowledge Jesus's miracles? I bet the doctors and the hospital management deliberately left the section blank. They did not want to admit divine healing from Jesus for reasons of political correctness.

With a red marker pen, I wrote in the blank section, "Miraculously healed by the Lord Jesus, the Divine Physician! 'By his wounds we are healed' (Isaiah 53:5)." In the evening, I called British Airways and purchased a ticket to Dubai to visit my dad and my sister. I left on the same date as my canceled surgery.

With the Lord's help, I had overcome my first strike. Praise the Lord.

17
DOESN'T GOD HEAL EVERYONE? MARI'S IMPROMPTU SERMON

Consecutive business trips that took a couple of months made me miss going to the Chapel. I was eager to return to London and the Chapel, the place that had changed my life, the place where I had accepted the Lord's calling to follow Him. Also, I was equally excited to share with Dr. Kendall Jesus's healing miracle. My joy was high until I looked at Mari's face. She was unusually quiet and appeared anxious. She hardly had touched her breakfast. Instead, she squeezed her lips tight—a sign that she was holding something in.

"Mari, what's wrong?" I asked. Mari looked at me and kept quiet. When her silence lasted an even longer time, I knew she was holding back something serious.

"Maybe we should not go to church until we talk about what is bothering you," I said, hoping that a little bit of reverse psychology might work.

"No, madam." She quickly said, "We should go."

"Then what's wrong? I know that you have something to tell me."

After much hesitation, she spilled the beans. She explained that I should not be disappointed if people did not believe that the Lord Jesus had healed me, adding that some may be angry and upset. Her comments caught me by surprise. The thought that she might have some doubts that Jesus had healed me struck me hard. How could she doubt when she had witnessed the doctors' final verdict? I looked her in the eye and asked her, "Mari, do *you* have any doubts that Jesus healed me?"

"Of course I don't," she said. "Jesus's healing power through His Holy Spirit healed you. Of course, I believe."

I sighed. What a relief!

"Then," I said, "why are you saying that people won't believe? I am planning to share my healing only with the people who attend the Chapel, who are Christians."

Her next response shocked even more. She explained that not all Christians who attended the church were believers and followed the Bible word for word, adding that not all believers believed in Jesus's supernatural healing and the manifestation of the power of the Holy Spirit. She warned me that I should not be disappointed if I did not get an enthusiastic response.

Wow! Mari's comment was too confusing for my new Christian mind. "But why?" I asked.

"Well," she said, "some may doubt you or not believe you because they do not know you. Some may get upset wondering why the Lord Jesus healed you and not others, or perhaps them."

"Wow," I exclaimed, pausing to think about what she had said. I had never thought of that. I believed that Jesus's healing was for everyone.

While I was lost in my thoughts, Mari surprised me with another bomb comment. She said, "Even some pastors, priests, and other Christians who believe in Jesus's healing in His time don't believe in the manifestation of the power of the Holy Spirit today."

"What?! What? What you are saying is absurd! What kind of Christians are they? But why?" I asked. Immediately, my mind went to Dr. Kendall. I anxiously asked, "What about Dr. Kendall?

I am sure he believes in Jesus's healing and the power of the Holy Spirit. Isn't it? Otherwise, he would not have prayed. Isn't it?"

She smiled because she knew that I had already put Dr. Kendall on a high pedestal.

"Isn't it?" I repeatedly asked her, hoping that she would confirm that Dr. Kendall believed in God's divine healing and miracles as it happened in Jesus's time and after, as in the book of Acts. My persistence to obtain her approval and confirmation did not change her stance.

With a soft and loving voice, she said, "Madam, I don't know Dr. Kendall. I don't want you to be upset if Dr. Kendall questions your healing because he doesn't know you and for the sake of those who were prayed for and not healed."

What did she mean? Jesus's random healing challenged me. Why had Jesus healed me and not others? As if Mari had read my mind, she quickly said, "You will learn from the scriptures that Jesus healed *many*, but He did not heal *all* sick people."

"Why?" My inquisitiveness expanded.

"I don't know why; God alone knows why," she said. "But this is what I do know: One day, He will remove all pain, sickness, and grief from all sick people. Until that day, God gives us the grace to endure all things."

Mari's words sounded comforting. However, her mention of "one day" seemed far and excruciating for sick people who needed healing as soon as possible. This thought dampened my mood with sadness. I did not want to continue with this sad topic. I walked out of the room, mumbling, "I wish all sick people would get healed."

Mari threw an "amen" into the air and said, "Madam, God does not allow anything to happen to us without reason and purpose—even if we don't understand it. And I believe there is a reason for suffering and being sick; sometimes these things are trials."

O how I wished she had not said that. She had piqued my

curiosity. I turned on my heel to face her and asked, "Trials? And why are there trials?"

"Trials strengthen our faith and put our trust in God. Trials draw us closer to God," she said.

I had run out of words. My mind was churning at full speed, processing every word she had said. My mind shifted from healing to faith. Contemplating that thought, I left the room and got ready for church. We were running late.

While driving to the Chapel, I kept quiet for a while; my mind seemed intrigued by the thought that God seemed to desire our faith and trust in Him more than our healing. So, it takes faith and trust to heal. I broke the silence by asking, "Mari, what about those sick believers who have a strong faith in Jesus and yet are not healed, like, uh, Mrs. Miller, for example? And what about those good people, like my mother, who died of cancer?"

Mari pulled her Bible from her bag, flipped through the pages, and said, "Listen to what the apostle Paul said when he was afflicted." She read the following:

> I was given a thorn in my flesh, a messenger of Satan, to torment me. Three times I pleaded with the Lord to take it away from me. But he said to me, "My grace is sufficient for you, for my power is made perfect in weakness." Therefore I will boast all the more gladly about my weaknesses, so that Christ's power may rest on me. That is why, for Christ's sake, I delight in weaknesses, in insults, in hardships, in persecutions, in difficulties. For when I am weak, then I am strong. (2 Corinthians 12:7–10)

She closed the Bible, turned to me, and said, "Do you think Paul lacked faith? No, he surely did not! And yet, for some reason that God alone knows, God did not answer Paul's request; instead,

He poured grace and power upon him that strengthened him in all circumstances. God also used other apostles such as Paul and Peter as a tool to heal other people. And God continues to do so today."

"So?" I interrupted Mari, hoping to conclude this discussion before we arrived at the Chapel.

Mari went quiet and looked pensive. She suddenly started praying in tongues, a few words at a time, as if she were listening and receiving. I slowed down to prolong our drive. When she had finished praying, she shifted her position to face me and said, "Yes, God desires our heart and our faith more than anything else, even our health. Yes, God heals, and yes, there are times when God does not heal for a reason He alone knows; we cannot and must not question Him. God has a plan and purpose for everything He does, including sickness. And, yes, God tests our faith to find out whether we love Him with all our heart, soul, and mind always, in health and sickness, and even when facing death. It is important to put our trust in God, to trust Him, believing that He has a reason and a plan for every aspect of our lives, even in sickness and death. Faith cannot be shaped or weighted based on what is visible but rather on what is invisible. God works behind the scenes and does things that we cannot fathom or understand—unless He reveals His reasons to us. Jesus's command is to love God with all our hearts, souls, and minds, irrespective of our health condition. It was not for lack of faith that God did not heal the apostle Paul. And the same is true for believers today who are stricken with infirmities. Paul accepted his condition and continued to serve the Lord with all his heart, soul, and mind. And so should we."

Thank God we arrived at the Chapel; I could not drive any longer. A surge of tears flooded my eyes and blurred my vision. I turned off the engine of the car to listen to Mari. I would not dare to interrupt her. I was utterly in shock. Mari's perfect command of the English language struck me; she seamlessly articulated words whose meanings I wondered if she knew. Mari's English ordinarily was poor and extremely limited to a few words. So, what had happened to her now? Had I just witnessed a miracle? My mind immediately recalled Romans 8:26,[23] which explains that the Holy Spirit at the right time helps us say the right words. I believed that the scripture had just been applied to Mari in front of my eyes; the Word of God came alive!

After a short pause, Mari held my hand and said, "As far as you, madam, you must guard your faith very closely. Yes, the Lord Jesus had healed you, and you must rejoice, but do not expect everyone to do so. Always remember that Jesus's mission on earth and the purpose of His death on the cross is to heal us, save our souls from sin, and redeem us to God, not to heal our mortal bodies. Also, you must always remember that the Lord called you *first before He healed you.* The Lord healed you for a specific reason. What is more important is that He called you for a mission: to bear witness to our Lord Jesus Christ by telling people around the world about Him!"

She stopped. She turned her head toward the window and prayed in tongues. I watched her as she soaked in the Holy Spirit and communed with Him. I realized then and there that the Holy Spirit was the source of the comments and words she had shared with me since that morning—and in perfect English! I immediately pulled out my notebook and wrote down every word she said. We stayed in the car until she had finished praying. We were both tired but were soaked in peace. Sweat covered Mari's face. She looked as if she had run a marathon

Finally, we summoned our strength, pulled ourselves from the car, and walked to the Chapel very quietly. Just before entering the Chapel, I asked Mari if God speaks to us through other people.

"Of course, madam; how can I say it in …?" She paused as if searching for words. She raised her shoulders and said with her

---

[23] The Spirit helps us in our weakness. We do not know what we ought to pray for, but the Spirit Himself intercedes for us through wordless groans.

usual beautiful smile, "I don't know how to say it in English. Madam, you know my English is no good." She giggled—her usual musical giggles!

I put my arm around her shoulder. "Don't worry, Mari; I got it."

Mari did not have to say anything; she had conveyed the message the Lord wanted me to hear. Indeed, God had spoken to me through Mari in a mysterious way. Mari's good English language was a miracle!

PART V
HE PROVIDED FOR ME

The Lord is my shepherd, I lack nothing.
—Psalm 23:1

18
DIVINE PROMOTION

My Turkish friend Ismet called me from Istanbul airport before boarding his flight to London.

"What a wonderful surprise!" I exclaimed. Looking at my schedule, I added, "I thought you were coming next Friday, not this week, weren't you?"

"A sudden change of plan," he said. "Will you be in town this weekend? Any plans for tomorrow?"

"Yes and no to both questions," I replied.

"Great! Then let's have lunch tomorrow," he said.

"Sure. I'll look forward to seeing you!"

"I'll pick you up at 10 a.m. tomorrow, and we'll drive to Oxford for lunch. I'll make a reservation at your favorite restaurant."

"Great! Can't wait to see you!" I shouted. "Oh, by the way, I have great news to tell you."

"What? You got promoted *again*?" he teasingly asked.

I paused for a second, thinking of promotion.

"Yes," I replied, drawing out the word. "You may call it a promotion, uh … but it's not a job promotion."

"What then? What? Please tell me!" he shouted over the airport announcements.

"I will tell you tomorrow," I said laughingly.

"Girl," he said in a playful voice, "you tell me right now or—"

"Or I won't see you," I quickly interrupted. "No, you have to be patient." I laughed.

"It had better be worth waiting for."

"Oh yes!"

"Just give me a hint. What kind of promotion is this?" he said.

My mind searched for an answer, but I could not come up with anything other than "A divine promotion," which I said by way of reply.

"What?" he shouted. "A divine promotion? What's that? You must tell me now."

"See you tomorrow, Ismet!" I mumbled with a soft giggle. "I am swamped with work now. I have a meeting in fifteen minutes and must prepare for it. I've got to go. Have a safe flight." I quickly ended the conversation to keep the surprise intact.

The thought of divine promotion cheered me up. Surely divine promotion sounded better than conversion. It carried with it a solemn mission as a quantum leap of faith into a new and higher career calling in which God was my CEO. I quickly came to realize the radical changes I needed to make to align my life with God's purpose. How would my personal and professional obligations fit within God's will for my life? My Christian walk would require my ongoing commitment to steer my worldly demands, pressures, and personal desires to God's altar for complete submission to His leadership. The struggle to let go and let God lead is real. I took a deep breath and sighed, saying, "O Lord, help me." For comfort, I pulled my Bible from my briefcase and opened it to the bookmark, my eyes falling on a highlighted verse: "The Lord says, 'I will guide you along the best pathway for your life. I will advise you and watch over you'" (Psalm 32:8 NLT). What an encouraging and promising Word.

Ismet's flight arrived thirty minutes ahead of schedule. While waiting for his driver to pick him up, he called me, quizzing me again about my divine promotion. He tried all possible temptations to lure me into revealing the nature of such a promotion. Still, it was to no avail, I resisted and remained mysterious.

"I can't wait to hear all about it," he said. "It had better be a good one."

"Oh yes, it is," I said.

Throughout the evening, I thought about how to present my conversion as a divine promotion. What had made me tell Ismet about my conversion? Would he accept my new faith? After all, Ismet was Muslim—though he had radical views against the religion of Islam and didn't practice it.

Ismet once said, "All followers of a religion are narrow-minded and blind slaves to the person promoting that religion." Would his views about me change? Would he perceive me as narrow-minded and a slave? Slave to whom? Slave to Jesus? I did not mind the latter.

Would my conversion jeopardize our friendship and, more importantly, our business relationship? Suddenly, all these thoughts troubled me. I sank into my chair, regretting the entire conversation. For the first time, I was not looking forward to seeing Ismet.

Furthermore, would he accept that God's call on my life started in my childhood? My acceptance of God's calling and my belief in Jesus's deity was faith-based. I knew nothing about the Christian faith as portrayed in the world or as a religion. Reading the scriptures revealed to me God, not a religion. I realized that the little information I had learned to date about God and Jesus was not enough for an intellectual debate with Ismet, a walking genius. I felt so infinitely small for the task ahead of me of witnessing.

Mari walked in and saw me distracted. "What's wrong?" she asked. I shared with her my concerns about how to share my new faith with Ismet.

"Pray," she said. "Ask the Holy Spirit to speak to you and to open Ismet's heart to receive Him. That's all you can do."

Wow, what divine wisdom. Mari never ceased to amaze me. Her childlike faith helped to calm me in my intellectual pursuit to prove my faith.

19
DIVINE TESTING

Ismet arrived at 10:00 with two boxes. One had Turkish delight, *lokum*, from Ali Muhiddin Haci Bekir store in Istanbul, famous for Turkish lokum. The other box had frozen *lahmacun*, Turkish pizza.

I quickly arranged the lahmacun in the freezer. Mari prepared a tray in the kitchen: two small plates for lokum and two glasses of Campari mixed with orange juice—Ismet's favorite aperitif. "Mari," I said, "we are going to lunch. We don't have time for all this."

Mari gestured for me to slow down and take a deep breath. "Relax, madam. Did you pray?" she asked.

We held hands, and I quickly whispered, "Lord Jesus, please help me to explain my divine promotion."

Mari added, "For Your glory, Lord. Amen."

"I made a reservation for one o'clock," Ismet said loudly from the sitting room. When I joined him in the lounge, he said in an impatient voice, "Now, let me hear about your secret promotion. You sounded secretive; I can't wait to hear about it."

I sat on the other side of the sofa, facing him, and with great enthusiasm, I shared my divine promotion with him. I started with what had happened to me since February. I gave him the minute details of every step: the discovery of the lump on my thyroid, the supernatural presence in the Chapel, the divine calling from Jesus to follow Him, the rounds of doctors, the healing prayer, my miraculous healing through Jesus, and the doctors' denial of faith in spite of proof.

When I finished, Ismet looked like a deer caught in the headlights. Shock flashed over his face and stirred his inquisitive nature. He tilted his head down while his eyes bugged out over his eyeglasses, staring at me, almost penetrating through me. Silence reigned for a while; it seemed like an eternity. *Why isn't he saying anything? Did I say too much? I hate it when people are slow to respond. I hate the ticking of the clock; I must get rid of it.*

"Please say something," I softly pleaded.

Finally breaking the silence with a long sigh, he said, "That was a hefty surprise! I wouldn't have guessed it for a million dollars or even billions of dollars."

His comment made me smile because he was a man of wealth who weighed everything against money.

"Well?" I asked, prompting him for more comments.

"This is the most incredible story I've ever heard," he said.

"A story? A story?!" I protested. I shot up on my feet and objected in a serious tone, "This is *not* a story, Ismet! And more importantly, it is *not* incredible. You may call it supernatural, but incredible? Absolutely *not*, because nothing is impossible for God." Ismet's comment had annoyed me.

"Calm down," he said. "Sit down and let's discuss your experience intellectually and rationally."

I sat down. I reached for my glass and took one sip.

"Okay," he said. "We are many times more likely to be hit by lightning—or killed by a shark or hit by an asteroid—than to experience supernatural conversion or especially to be transported in the Spirit. It is hard to rationally and intellectually explain faith conversion, let alone a supernatural presence in the church and conversion."

"Where are you going with this, Ismet?" I interrupted.

"How are you going to explain your experience *intellectually*?" he asked.

Was his intellect standing in the way of believing in God's divine authority? The thought of intellectualism and faith in God flashed before my eyes.

"So, Ismet, the underlying issue is intellect versus faith. Are the two foes? Can they coexist?" I said, "You highlighted an interesting point. The presence or lack of faith in God shapes the direction of our thinking, our decisions, our emotions, and our lives, isn't it?"

I went on sharing with Ismet that while sitting at the church, I felt as if a spiritual heart surgery had taken place inside me that replaced my stone heart with a new one (Ezekiel 36:26 ESV). For the first time in my life, I felt real love embracing me. It was the love of Christ. It was that love that opened my eyes to see the unseen, granting me absolute faith in God.

"So, how do you explain it intellectually?" he asked.

"Although my new faith is in the infancy stage, I am sure it illuminated my intellect to know and understand the truth of God." The thought of examining faith from an intellectual perspective excited me. "Ismet," I said, "our discussion has made me realize how important it is to prepare myself to reach out to those who reject faith to gratify their intellectualism."

Quietly, we pondered our discussion. I had more of an appetite for debate than for lunch. I committed myself to proving to Ismet that my conversion was real and that Jesus is alive. I prompted Ismet to say something.

"Okay," he said. He walked to the window and stood there for a while as if to collect his thoughts.

"Yes?" I asked impatiently.

He turned to me and said, "How sure are you that it was Jesus who spoke to you? Who was Jesus to you at that point, the Prophet, God, or the Son of God?"

Ismet's questions suddenly highlighted controversial belief issues among Muslims, so I should have been prepared to answer.

"Ismet, are you testing my faith and conversion?"

"Yes," he said. "Consider it a divine test. As you may know, God takes us through trials to test our faith and where we stand with the Lord. So, do not be disappointed, depressed, or saddened when people question your experience at the Chapel. More importantly, do not be dismayed if people—including Christians—do not believe in supernatural conversions or healings.

I welcomed the challenge. Without any hesitation, I replied, "There is no doubt in my mind and heart that the voice I heard was the Holy Spirit of God. I am talking about Jesus as God! The thought of Jesus being a prophet did not even cross my mind. Whereas to Muslims, Jesus, like Moses, is regarded as a prophet. Period. I repeat, to me, Jesus is God, not a prophet."

I opened my journal and read what I had written on my conversion day: "Today, Jesus called me to follow Him. I said, 'Yes, Lord.' I finally can say, without any fear of punishment, that I believe that Jesus is 'God in the flesh.' He supernaturally came to earth as a humble man to bring humankind to God. Why? Because we human beings are sinners, and we are not holy enough to stand before the Almighty God. How I derived that conclusion in one encounter is a mystery."

"Someone might ask you, 'Who is God, and why is Jesus God?'"

A good question. I thought of the Christian nuns' prayers at my school. "Like the nuns and my Christian friends, I believe that God, Jesus, and the Holy Spirit are God. But I cannot explain more than this. I pray that God will reveal to me this mystery."

"This mystery is called the Trinity."

"Yes, I don't know why and how I believe in the Trinity. I cannot explain the surge of dormant beliefs in God. I have a lot to study and learn. But I repeat that my faith in Jesus is not based on comparison with prophets or other religions. I realize that to

Muslims, such a declaration is considered *the* unpardonable sin and lethal blasphemy against Allah. But I stand firm in my belief that Jesus is God. In my life, I never believed in anything by faith except my faith in Jesus; it was birthed, not inherited and not forced."

"Be careful, Miah," Ismet said with a warning tone. "Your renunciation of Islam and claiming Jesus as God are not only a bold declaration; they are also considered the greatest blasphemy in Islam, regardless of whether you practiced Islam or not. Have you thought that your conversion might get you in severe trouble?"

I understood Ismet's underlying warning. Some Muslim denominations and fanatic schools of thought regard apostasy as a crime deserving of the death penalty. In contrast, moderate Muslim scholars do not believe that apostasy requires punishment. In my mind, Muslim conversion highlights the difficulties of combining sharia law with modern legal frameworks and human rights, and questions the country's freedom of religion and multifaith identity.

After thanking Ismet for his genuine concern, I said, "Compulsion is forbidden in Islam. Surah al-Baqara 2:256[24] confirms, 'There shall be no compulsion in [acceptance of] the religion.' Therefore, God gave humankind the free will to choose the religion, so who is humankind to contradict Him or question Him? But some Muslim scholars through the centuries might have had different interpretations. Muslim children are assumed to be Muslim adults. However, nowhere in the Qur'an are Muslim adults mandated to adopt the parents' faith. Faith is in the heart. It cannot be forced; it is beyond compulsion."

Gazing at my family picture above the fireplace in which I was five years old, I said, "Looking back into my childhood, I called for Jesus at the age of five. Since that tender age, my heart

---

[24] *The Qur'an: Arabic Text with Corresponding English Meanings* (Singapore: Abul-Qasim, 1997), 56.

belonged to Jesus amid my Muslim upbringing. And now I am returning to my first love, Jesus. I am committed to renewing/restoring my relationship with God and having eternal fellowship with Him."

Silence reigned for a few minutes. Ismet looked pensive. "What are you thinking about now?" I asked.

"Miahciğm," Ismet said in his tender Turkish voice, "I am thrilled that Jesus has healed you."

Ismet's comment stunned me. *What? What?* my mind shouted. *Is* healing *the only bit he took from all that I have said?*

"But, Ismet," I protested in disappointment, "what happened to me was far more than healing. Did my healing overshadow Jesus's calling? Would healing be the only thing that people see in my conversion?"

"What else is there to see?" he casually said. "God has answered your prayer. Isn't it?" He took another sip of Campari.

"What else to see?" I shouted angrily. I jumped to my feet and shouted even louder, "What else to see?"

I was extremely disappointed and angry. At its ultimate crescendo, my voice choked with sadness. "Of course, there was far more than my healing," I moaned. "The whole experience of my conversion was *not*, and I stress *not*, about my healing. Jesus could have healed me without asking me to follow Him, or He could have called me to follow Him without healing me!"

I cried with fists hammering my knees. "Healing did not even cross my mind when I encountered the Lord, not for a second. My conversion is about accepting Jesus's call and recovering my relationship with God, not about my healing."

Ismet's comment shook me to the core. I felt jealous for the Lord, and my passion would not let me rest. I felt there was something I needed to say.

"You know, Ismet," I said, "I could have gone with Mari for prayer and left the church without being changed. But *no!*" I shouted, pounding my fists hard against my chest and knees.

"From your comment, I gather you've only focused on my visible physical healing, not my invisible spiritual healing. Now I understand the meaning of the scripture of 2 Corinthians 4:18: 'We fix our eyes not on what is seen, but on what is unseen, since what is seen is temporary, but what is unseen is eternal.'"

My vocal cords ached and my voice sounded hoarse, yet I could not keep quiet. In a cranky voice, I continued: "That Sunday was not an accident! On that day, the Holy Spirit of God manifested His glorious presence to me, breathed into my spirit, and kindled faith in me—an intense faith I'd never known before. The more I study the Word of God, the more the scriptures confirm to me what the Holy Spirit revealed to me. The revelation I received stands firm with the scriptures, attesting Jesus's deity as God. I realize that Jesus's incarnation is beyond human natural wisdom and comprehension. It is one of God's mysteries, of which the prophet Isaiah said 'His understanding no one can fathom' (Isaiah 40:28). The doctrine of the Trinity is another mystery of God. It is by faith that I believe and worship the *one* God who eternally manifests as three coexisting and distinct persons—God the Father, God the Son (Jesus Christ), and God the Holy Spirit—as 'one God in three divine persons.'"

Tears choked me. I covered my face with my hands. I felt jealous for the Lord because the world has turned their backs on the one and only true God who created the heavens and the earth but who also created humankind to have eternal fellowship with Him. I felt jealous for God, who took on Himself the world's sins and died in our place on the cross to erase our sins so we could stand holy before the holy God.

Between sniffles, I continued: "I marvel how the majestic God chose to touch and transform me, I, an unworthy, imperfect, minute, insignificant, and sinful person. I hope that you have something else to say other than my physical healing. The Lord has healed me in many ways, more than I can ever imagine or understand." I kept crying quietly with my eyes closed.

After a few moments of silence, Ismet's long arms embraced my shoulders. In a soft voice, he said, "Miahciğm, what else can I say? What do you want me to say when the Lord, the Almighty God of Abraham, Isaac, and Jacob, has spoken to you and touched you? Who am I to question God when He cried out from the cross, 'It is finished'? Who am I to question the Lord's action? The Lord chose you, called you, established you, and finished the path that He had set for you before the creation of the earth and which you are about to start. The Lord Jesus called you to the starting line of your race, and He will take you through it until the end."

Huh? What? my mind shouted. *What did Ismet say? Did I hear him correctly?* His comments sounded less aggressive and more agreeable.

Surprised, I frowned and looked at Ismet with curious eyes. I wanted an explanation of what he had just said. Ismet continued: "Miahciğm, I believe every word you said without any shadow of a doubt, and I stand in awe of your strong faith. I believe that you have truly received a divine promotion as you said on the phone! The Lord Jesus has personally touched you and called you, and more importantly, you responded. You chose the right path established by the one and only God, the God of Abraham, Isaac, and Jacob, and you now walking in the way, the truth, and the light. As a result, the Lord Jesus has transported you from darkness into the light, His light; therefore, your life will never be the same. Who am I to comment on what the Lord has done for you? Please forgive me for testing you and grilling you with questions as I did. I needed to know for sure that you are following Jesus, the Son of the living God."

Suddenly, his tears choked him. He pulled me to his chest and sobbed.

What?! What?! What is happening here? Did he say "Jesus, the Son of the living God"? Ismet's statement shocked me. I froze—even my tears froze on my cheeks! His words took my breath away! *Am I dreaming? Is this the same Ismet I knew, the powerful tycoon and billionaire businessman, a man both revered and feared in the corporate world, sobbing like a little child?*

Slowly, I pulled my head from under his chin and opened my eyes. A river of tears flooded Ismet's face, which was displaying a beautiful ensemble of emotions I'd never seen before. Wow! When I looked into his eyes, I saw a different twinkling. I saw sparks lighting a great faith hidden in the depths of his big heart. "Oh Lord, please free Ismet from his fear. May his wealth and business shepherd people to your kingdom and glorify You." We cried silently for a while; it seemed an eternity.

When the clock cuckooed at two o'clock in the afternoon, Ismet released me from his arms, jumped to his feet, and raced down the hall to the guest bathroom. A few minutes later, he returned to find me still sitting where he had left me, frozen in shock and bewilderment over his words. He fixed two fresh Campari drinks and sat at the table by the bay window overlooking the London skyline. I quietly moved and joined him, sitting at the other end of the table. I held my drink in both my hands and gazed into his eyes.

We sat quietly, listening to the ticking of the clock. Ismet cleared his throat a couple of times before breaking his silence: "Miahciḡm," he said, "I am sure that by now you have discovered that I have hidden my faith in Jesus for many years. I wanted to tell you, but you were an exceptionally stubborn atheist. But today, listening to your testimony broke something inside me—a dam of guilt," he said.

Bam! Further torrents of tears raced down my cheeks as he shared how the Lord Jesus had appeared to him in a vision while he was meditating and called him to follow Him. Unfortunately, he had kept his Christian faith secret out of fear of losing his family, his business, his wealth, and his social privileges. As a result of that, he was now living in guilt for cheating on the Lord.

I understood his fears. Following Jesus can come with a high price, but that price is nothing compared to the cost He paid on the cross. I gazed at Ismet with tears until I heard him saying, "I am extremely happy for you that you chose the true God."

What? What did he say? I shouted in my heart. My tears suddenly slammed on the brakes and stopped at midcheek. His words had fallen on me like a whetstone. Suddenly I heard my voice roaring, "*No, no,* a thousand times no! I strongly refute the opinion that my conversion was my own doing. *No!* It was *God* who chose me, found me, and called me. All I did was respond."

"My profound apologies," Ismet said. "You are right: the Lord chose you. It was not your doing; it can't be. God the Father, by His grace and mercy, calls us, and we accept His calling by faith in Jesus, God the Son." He pulled from his inner pocket a small Bible and read John 15:16:

> This is what the Lord Jesus says: "You did not choose me, but I chose you and appointed you so that you might go and bear fruit—fruit that will last—and so that whatever you ask in my name the Father will give you."

Looking at me, he said, "I thank God that you have responded to Jesus's high calling." He quickly added, "Well done, my little sister in Christ."

20
DIVINE FAMILY

I went to the bathroom to freshen my makeup. When I returned to the lounge, Ismet was pacing the room. A sad smile was on his face. I knew he wanted to tell me something. "What are you thinking about?" I asked. There was a brief hesitation before he explained that although he was thrilled with our discussion and personal testimonies, he was worried about one particular subject.

"Which is?" I asked, sensing a lingering concern in his mind. When he did not respond, I repeated my question: "Which is?"

He cleared his throat and said, "Do you know that now, through Christ, we both belong to one divine family, the family of God, and that I am your brother in Christ and you are my sister in Christ? And …" He paused.

"And?" I prompted him.

"And," he continued, "being your brother in Christ and your friend, I am concerned about you."

"What do you mean?" I asked, filled with curiosity.

"Please don't misunderstand me," he said. "I am overjoyed for your conversion, your 'divine promotion,' as you call it. But, uh, uh, I cannot hide my concern. I am genuinely concerned, even fearful and troubled, about your safety."

"What do you mean, Ismet? Would you please spell it out?" I urged him.

"Okay," he said. "Have you thought about some extremists out there who may react violently to your conversion?"

Having never doubted Ismet's sincerity, I was even more convinced that he was being sincere today. I knew what he meant. "Oh, that!" I sighed. His concern for my life touched me profoundly. "Yes, I've thought about it, and no, I am not concerned. We already discussed this topic, didn't we?"

"You are not concerned about objection and harassment?" He gasped in surprise. "Have you thought about the risks of deserting Islam to follow the God of Abraham, Isaac, and Jacob?"

Without any hesitation, I said, "Yes. I have. What if my parents were atheists or Christians and I wanted to convert to Islam? Why would it be acceptable then? And more importantly, why would Allah object to God? Unless Allah is different from God. There are people who are ignorant about Christianity and who refuse to study and understand God's plan for redemption and salvation through Jesus. They refuse to learn about the doctrine of the Trinity and its divine essence for fear of opening their eyes and seeing the truth. Like my sister, who is afraid of the name of Jesus." I reminded Ismet of Ibn Rushd's (Averroes's) quote "Ignorance leads to fear, fear leads to hatred, hatred leads to violence. This is the equation." In my mind, ignorance was human's biggest folly.

Ismet did not comment about that. He went on asking about my parents. "Okay! What about your parents?" he asked. "Have you thought about them or what they might say or do? What if they object?"

I paused and took a deep breath. I ran a mental check to see if my parents had ever been in my thoughts on that Sunday. They had not been. It was as if I'd had no parents. In a calm voice, I replied, "To tell you the truth, Ismet, when I stood on the steps of the church, I felt bare of my past life, history, and traditions, including my family. It was as if I had shed my old skin. The Lord emptied me to fill me with His presence and His Holy Spirit. I did not think about what my family's reaction might be. With all due respect to my dad and siblings, I am not responsible for their reactions. They are accountable for their actions, not I. I believe the reason for their objection to my conversion would be based merely on fear of Allah's judgment. You see, in Islam, Allah entrusts parents with instructing their children on moral behavior and religion. Take my sister for an example; she was against my conversion because she believes that she will be held accountable for my desertion of Islam. She believes that she will be subject to dire consequences on Judgment Day.

"I will respect their answers and any position they may take against me, but they will not be able to change what God has done in me. Should my conversion to follow the true God offend my parents, then I will ask them to judge for themselves whether I should obey God or humankind. I choose to obey God, not humankind. Shouldn't they also? Otherwise, they should evaluate their own faith.

"When I die, I will stand *alone* before God, not with my parents or siblings. I will receive God's judgment *alone* for my own doing, based on my own choices. I cannot blame my parents or traditions for making me reject His calling. It is God who specifically instructed me to follow Him, and from that moment on, I chose to obey *Him*.

"Besides, the Qur'an makes it clear that 'there is no compulsion in religion' (Qur'an 2:256), stating, 'For you is your religion, and for me is my religion' (Surah al-Kafirun 109:6[25]). Also, the Qur'an makes it clear that the belief in a religion is a personal concern, such as in 18:29: 'God is the judge of our faith, not Man.'"

I paused and took a deep breath. Looking back at what had

---

[25] *Qur'an: Arabic Text with Corresponding English Meanings* (Singapore: Abul-Qasim, 1997).

happened on that miraculous Sunday, I repeated, "I did not choose the Lord; He chose me. I did not call him; He called me. His Holy Spirit led me to that specific church. He did all the work; all I did was to say yes to Him. While God, by His grace, chose to call me, I, by my love of God and reverence for Him, chose to obey."

"I am stunned," Ismet said. "I have never heard you speak with such conviction. Your conversion is truly an amazing divine promotion and is truly from the Lord. Well done, my dear sister in Christ. As you said, God, the Almighty, adopted you into His divine family." He opened the Bible and read Isaiah 41:10: "'So do not fear, for I am with you; Do not be dismayed, for I am your God. I will strengthen you and help you; I will uphold you with my righteous right hand.'"

A long silence reigned in the room; we were both digesting the conversation.

"I am famished," I exclaimed. We looked at the clock and burst into laughter. We had missed our reservation by four hours!

Ismet called the restaurant to apologize and rescheduled for an early dinner. We drove to Oxford and continued our conversation.

21
DIVINE INSTRUMENT—END OF THE SECOND STRIKE

I agreed with the bank manager to pay my debts in monthly installments. The repayment devoured my salary. At first, I was very hurt and angry at Victor, but the scriptures kept jumping before my eyes, demanding that I forgive him. Grr! It was hard to comply with God's commands: "Do not repay evil with evil or insult with insult. On the contrary, repay evil with blessing, because to this you were called so that you may inherit a blessing" (1 Peter 3:9). In Leviticus 19:18 was another command that, at first, frustrated me: "Do not seek revenge or bear a grudge against anyone among your people, but love your neighbor as yourself. I am the Lord." Victor offered to repay my debts and correct my bank accounts, but I refused. I couldn't blame Victor; it was my mistake. Around that time, I noticed Victor's behavior had changed drastically. I thought guilt was weighing on him, and that made me feel guilty. One day, he asked me to go with him to see his psychiatrist. I did so. The doctor informed Victor that his tests revealed that he had mild autism in addition to his ADHD. What? I couldn't believe my ears, let alone my luck! My heart plunged in sadness. Victor returned to France for treatment. I was heartbroken, beyond words. Victor told me that given his medical conditions, I should move on with my life. It was one of the darkest days of my life. Forgiveness and God's love in my heart helped me to remain friends with Victor.

The repayment plan affected my lifestyle and reminded me of the civil war in Syria that had changed my family's lifestyle forever. I was ten years old at that time. Socialists toppled my dad's government, and many of the country's elites and government ministers and officials were jailed and persecuted. My dad was under house arrest. The new socialist government had confiscated my family's wealth and left us with no money. As a result, my parents had to dismiss the workers in the house. Since then, I have had a great fear of poverty. The repayment plan led me to relive the experience one more time. Letting Mari go devastated me the most.

One day, upon my return from a business trip, I found a message from the bank manager asking me to call him urgently. My heart sank. *What is it now?!* I cried in my head. With a trembling heart, I called the manager. Behold, the manager greeted me with a gracious tone and thanked me for paying off my debts.

What? What does he mean that I paid off my debt? Did I hear correctly?

"Sir," I interrupted him. "this is Mrs. Termanini speaking." For a second, I thought that he might have confused me with another customer.

"Yes, Mrs. Termanini." He continued, "As I was saying, I am pleased to learn this morning that you paid off the entire debt. For this reason, I called you to thank you for your full payment."

I could not believe my ears. Taken by complete surprise, I asked, "Would you please repeat what you just said?" I quickly added, "I hope this a crank joke. If it is, I am grossly displeased."

The manager assured me that he was not joking. He confirmed the receipt of the full payment.

"But how?" How could it be?" I asked in disbelief and a challenging voice.

"Well, we received a wire transfer from Switzerland, madam." The manager was surprised that I was not aware of the transfer. "Mrs. Termanini, I don't mean to pry, but you *do* have family in Switzerland. don't you?" The manager sounded wondrously curious.

Could it have been my dad? I quickly ran the matter through my mind. But I had not told my dad about my debt!

With a frustrated voice, I said, "Sir, it must be a mistake. I do not know anybody in Switzerland. As you know, I had no means to pay off my debt. For this reason, we agreed on a monthly payment schedule. So, I do not understand how, in a few weeks, my debts are now paid in full. I just do not understand it. Would you please recheck the wire? There must be a mistake. I am troubled by this call."

My strong reaction caught the manager by surprise. He put me on hold to recheck the transferred funds. While on hold, my mind raced to resolve this puzzle. It could not be my dad since he did not know my bank details or about my debt problem. *It must be a mistake—and a bad one,* I concluded.

Minutes later, the manager came back with the information. He confirmed that at ten o'clock in the morning, the bank had received a wire transfer to my account from their correspondent bank in Geneva.

"Wow," I said. "I still can't believe it." After a short pause, I asked the manager for the originator's name and the amount. At first, the manager hesitated to release the name over the phone, but I pressed hard enough that he told me that the wire was for the amount of $10,000, transferred by Mr. Ismet X.

"I presume you know Mr. Ismet X, right?" he asked.

I almost fell off my chair. Oh Lord! How could Ismet have known my situation? I had mentioned nothing to him about my financial predicament.

"Mrs. Termanini, are you there?" the manager shouted.

"Yes, I am still here," I murmured. "Yes, I know Mr. Ismet. But I had no idea of his generous gesture."

The manager explained that the ten thousand US dollars, when converted to pounds sterling, was the exact amount of my debt to the bank! Wow, this was undeniably a miracle from God.

We agreed that the transferred fund would pay off my entire debt to vacate the judgment against me and release my accounts. I also gave the manager my personal fax number to send me a copy of the wire transfer. That was the last time I spoke with the branch manager or had an issue with the bank.

Ismet's gesture blew me away. No one had ever done something like this for me. I spent the rest of the day thanking God for the miracle. In the afternoon, I received the fax from the bank. My eyes fell on the notes section: "Dear Miahciğm, thank you for sharing—a gift from the Lord Jesus."

A torrent of tears welled in my eyes, fell on my cheeks, and blurred my vision. I turned my seat toward the wall so no one could see me and sobbed for a long time, thanking Jesus for His miracle of blessing Ismet. Surely, God had used Ismet as an instrument to help me.

When my secretary Peggy came into my office to review the letters that she had typed for me, my tears scared her. "Are you okay?" she screamed. I jumped to my feet and hugged her.

"Oh yes, I am very much okay. I am much more than okay." Without giving any details, I told her that I had received good news. On the way home, I thought of the remaining puzzle: How could Ismet have known about my debt and account information?

When I got home, I called Mari and told her of Ismet's gesture. We praised God for a long while. Mari said that it was God's providence and favor that had led Ismet to help me—a testimony of how God uses people who obey Him as a vessel to help others. She referred me to Acts 9:15, 2 Timothy 2:21, and many other verses about how God uses ordinary people in unexpected ways for extraordinary missions. I spent the entire evening meditating on the verses Mari had mentioned, thanking God and praying God's blessings over Ismet.

Early in the morning, I called Ismet's office in Istanbul and found out that he was on a business trip. I asked his secretary to have him call me when it was convenient. The following day, Ismet called me from Switzerland. I thanked him with sincere gratitude for his incredible generosity. I asked him to explain how he had found out about my financial predicament and my bank details.

He reminded me of the last time he had visited me at home, when I received a phone call that seemed private. I was uncomfortable to speak and wanted to end the conversation, but the caller was persistent. So, he left the lounge to give me some privacy and joined Mari in the kitchen, who was preparing the dinner. At the kitchen table, he found an open letter from the bank; he apologized for reading it. From the letter, he learned of the debt issue and the bank's judgment against my accounts. He said he had written down the bank's name and address, as well as my account number. Weeks later, when he arrived in Switzerland for business, he felt the urge to help me out. Laughingly, he said, "It must be the Lord Jesus who prompted me to help you; I obeyed and followed His instruction." He quickly added, "Wholeheartedly, I must say. You can't imagine the joy I had after completing the fund transfer. It was as if the Holy Spirit had filled me with the joy of the Lord. I counted it a high privilege and honor to be an instrument in God's hand to reach you."

I was speechless and stunned. Normally I kept all bank correspondence in a folder in my briefcase. Also, Mari never left mail lying around in the house, let alone the kitchen. She meticulously kept it in a box. After the call, I immediately checked my briefcase. All the bank letters were in their folder under the pile of office documents! I was thunderstruck. To this date, I am unable to solve this mystery. Would Jesus remove the letter from the folder and place it on the kitchen table for Ismet to read? Had the Holy Spirit prompted the bank manager to call me when Ismet was visiting me, leading Ismet to the kitchen to read the letter and write down my bank details?

I ended the phone call with questions racing through my mind, mesmerized by how God moves in mysterious ways!

Glory to God for freeing me from the second strike.

PART VI
HE CONFIRMED ME

They saw what seemed to be tongues of fire that separated and came to rest on each of them. All of them were filled with the Holy Spirit and began to speak in other tongues as the Spirit enabled them.

—Acts 2:3–4

22
DR. R. T. KENDALL, WHAT'S NEXT?

After a month of business travel, I was eager to return to London, go to the Chapel, and share my healing news with Dr. Kendall.

After the service, Mari talked with the couple sitting next to her. She introduced them to me—Akiki and her husband, Natukunda (Natu for short). A few minutes later, I noticed from the corner of my eye that a handful of people had gathered behind me. I recognized Bill Reynolds and Benjamin Chan, whom I had met on my first visit to the Chapel. Bill introduced me to the others. "This is the woman whom R. T. told us about who converted from Islam." All were staring at me as if I were in a showcase or had just dropped from Mars. I blushed, feeling my cheeks heating up.

Before I could say a word, one of the people interjected, "Did R. T. tell you that you are the first convert from Islam in the history of this church?"

"Yes, he did," I replied.

They took turns welcoming me to the Chapel and asking questions about my conversion. Then, suddenly, the conversation stopped and all eyes turned behind me. I turned back and saw

Dr. Kendall walking toward us with a big smile on his face. His gracious smile was contagious; it triggered a smile on my face. "You came back," he said. We shook hands.

"Of course I came back," I quickly replied.

"We prayed for you. I was hoping that you would be back," Dr. Kendall said.

"Did you have any doubt?" I teasingly asked.

"I rested your case before the Lord," he said. "I see that you met the deacons. I am glad that you are here." (*Deacons? What does this mean?* I dared not ask.)

"Dr. Kendall, may I have a few minutes of your time?" I asked.

"Of course," he said. "Let us go to my office."

Mari left the church with Natu and Akiki. I followed Dr. Kendall to his office.

Dr. Kendall sat behind his desk, and I sat in the chair opposite. His gentle smile relaxed me. "I am so pleased to see you back," he said.

I explained that my absence was due to business trips, during which I was anxious to get back to London and return to the Chapel. I also mentioned that I had attended Sunday services at various churches in the different countries my business had taken me to.

"I trust you remember our last conversation?" I asked.

"Of course, I remember," Dr. Kendall replied. "How can I forget?" Quickly, he added, "I don't know if I told you that I have been the pastor of this chapel for many years, and you are the first convert from Islam."

"I pray to be the first of many more to come," I replied.

"Amen. And now, you wanted to see me. How may I help you?"

"Dr. Kendall, I have a few questions," I said. I pulled my list of questions from my purse and fired off my first question: "Now that I am attending church and reading the Bible, *what's next?*"

Suddenly, Dr. Kendall's facial expression changed; an inquisitive frown replaced the smile. "What's *next*?" he asked. "What do you mean?"

"What I mean is that I want to find out what next I need to do besides reading the Bible and attending the church to become a follower of Jesus and a child of God. Does the Chapel provide a course, a process of set steps for new believers? In John 1:12, Jesus says that to all who receive Him, to those who believe in His name, He gives the right to become children of God. Well, since I gave my life to Jesus, I want to know how to become a child of God.

"My next question is, is the Lord's Prayer, which Jesus taught to His disciples, the only prayer to recite during prayer time? In Islam, Muslims pray specific verses during salat.[26] Are there particular verses for effective praying and to know God the Father, Jesus, and the Holy Spirit?

"Third, are there any obligatory acts in Christianity similar to the five mandated pillars of Islam to gain eternal life in paradise? In Islam, Muslims must demonstrate that they put their faith first by performing the Five Pillars: recite the Shahada, pray the salat, give zakat, fast Siyam, and go to hajj. I am committed to working hard so I don't disappoint Jesus for choosing me and so I will be continually acceptable to God and earn His grace and mercy. What do I need to do to earn God's grace and mercy?

"Fourth, I do not wish—if I may say—any denominations to influence my faith and my worship of God. I want to stick to the scriptures, the Word of God. As you know, the scriptures do not teach about dividing the Christian faith into groups, sects, or denominations. Isn't it? For this reason, I want to be baptized only into the body of Christ, not into the body of a particular church.

"Last, and most important, what do I need to do so I don't

---

[26] In Islam, praying is observed five times each day at precise times.

lose my salvation, which God has gifted me? I need guidance for a perfect start to earn a perfect score with Jesus."

When I turned to the next page of questions, Dr. Kendall took a deep breath and said, "Well, well, well. I can see a fire in you, a passion for the Lord. You have fascinating questions. But"—he glanced at his watch (I realized that I'd already taken too much of his time) and rested his elbows on the desk—"we need more time to discuss your questions."

I felt so embarrassed that my face turned into a volcano, spitting fire and tongues of sweat. I quickly folded my list and pushed it into my purse. I wanted to leave the room, when suddenly a big gentle smile relaxed Dr. Kendall's frowning. "I like your questions," Dr. Kendall said. "But because I am pressed for time now, here are a few points I want you to know."

I quickly pulled out my notepad and took notes as fast as he spoke, telling me the following:

- God's Word is *the* only source for teaching. God, not human beings, is the author of the scriptures. If you have questions or need clarifications about a verse or a passage, ask the Holy Spirit. Make the Holy Spirit your teacher to reveal the meaning of the scriptures.
- There is *nothing* you can do to earn God's grace. *Nothing!* Grace is undeserved favor. You cannot earn God's grace through works. God's grace is His doing; it is God's *gift*.
- We all are sinners before God, and we all fall short before His glory. But what makes us acceptable to God is this: faith, repentance of sin, and confession in Jesus alone that He is our Savior and Lord. He died on the cross on our behalf, for our sins.
- God's salvation is God's *gift* by His grace through your faith in His Son Jesus as your Lord and Savior, and *not* by works.

- Work does *not* save a person. Once saved, you are always saved.
- Christianity is a *journey and a way of life*. To know God intimately, you need to build a *relationship* and *fellowship* with Him and know Him by reading His Word, not following religious rituals.
- As for how to identify the right from wrong teaching or something you hear or read: Test the spirit through studying the scriptures when they speak of questions and prayers. Be sure that what you're reading, hearing, or thinking is consistent with the scriptures.
- Prayers are about having a conversation with God, which involves both speaking and listening to God, not religious rituals.

Dr. Kendall suggested Robert Murray M'Cheyne's Bible Reading Plan as a good Bible reading and studying plan. He also said that he would ask his assistant Brian to meet with me.

Then, we walked toward the door. Right before he turned the doorknob to open the door, I remembered my healing news.

"Uh … oh yes. I forgot to tell you about my good news," I said.

"Oh?"

I knew that I was way over my time limit with Dr. Kendall, so I spilled the whole news, racing with my words to say that the Lord Jesus had answered the prayer Dr. Kendall had prayed over me with the deacons, and healed me. As a result, I wouldn't need surgery. When I finished, Dr. Kendall retracted his hand from the doorknob and stood utterly silent. My news had caught him by surprise. A few seconds later, which seemed like an eternity, he said, "Well, I don't know what to say other than to praise God."

Had I seen some doubt in his eyes? I quickly said, "I can ask for a letter from my doctors, so you'll believe me." I bet that he realized that I had heard the doubt in his voice.

"I don't doubt you," he quickly said. "We have seen a few miraculous healings here in the Chapel. Of course, the Lord heals. It is just …" After a short pause, he continued, saying, "I haven't seen a quick case similar to yours."

"A case? Which is?" I asked, anxious to hear what made my healing a "case."

"Well," he replied, "I praise God for healing you. I am truly happy for you. I am thrilled that you were healed within one week of your conversion."

Dr. Kendall's shock and probable doubt did not surprise me as he did not know me; he had met me just once, on the day of my conversion. But his last statement, "healed within one week from your conversion," hit me. What did Dr. Kendall mean by this comment? How many prayers does God require to heal a person? Is there a specific time needed between praying and healing? Would my miraculous "quick" healing lead people to seek God for healing over salvation? The thought that concerned me most was that people might base the motive of my conversion solely on healing. I felt I needed to defend my new faith.

"Dr. Kendall," I said with a firm tone of conviction, "the Lord brought me to this church in ways I cannot describe or understand. One minute I was at home, and the next minute I found myself at the church steps. I do not recall driving or parking. Some Christian friends said it was as if the Lord supernaturally transported me (God alone knows). The Lord called me to follow Him, and I chose to obey His calling. God be my witness that at that time, my illness was *not* on my mind. My obedience to Jesus's calling was *not* conditional on His healing me. I would have followed the Lord even if He did not cure me. The Lord Jesus healed people who had no faith. I pray that physical healing will not overshadow people's need for salvation, the healing of the soul."

I thanked Dr. Kendall for his time, and I left the Chapel with a heavy heart.

Once in the car, I rested my head on the steering wheel and sobbed, crying out, "Lord Jesus, You know the truth of my heart. I followed You for Your glory alone, unconditional on my healing. If You know of any hidden personal motives other than serving You and fulfilling the mission You have for me, please strike me down and end my life right now and right here." I cried all the way home. Mari was right; she had warned me that people might doubt the motive of my conversion.

I spent the rest of the day thinking of my conversation with Dr. Kendall. Like the widow who persistently pleaded to the judge for justice in Luke 18:1–8, I begged God to give me a sign confirming my conversion. I wanted a sign that *He* had called me to serve Him on a mission that He had purposed for my life and that my conversion was irrespective of healing. By the evening, I was exhausted, and yet I was not willing to give up pleading to God for a sign.

23
DIVINE CONFIRMATION—THE BAPTISM IN THE HOLY SPIRIT

It was late in the evening when the phone rang. I ignored it. Busy researching Dr. Kendall's points in the Bible, I refused any interruption. But the persistence of the caller annoyed me so much that I finally picked up the phone. In a soft voice, the caller asked me if she could pray for me. *Argh, not now, please,* my mind screamed. The caller shouted, "Please don't hang up. I am Akiki; we met this morning at the Chapel. Please listen to me for a second."

Is this a joke or what? Her interruption and intrusion irritated me. How could she pray for me when we had met only briefly today at the Chapel; she knew nothing about me. However, her persistence compelled me to listen. She explained that while she was praying at her home after the church service, her spirit stirred up and she heard a prompting in her ear to pray for me. When she started praying for me, she felt a heavy burden on her heart. While she was praying, her husband, Natu, a pastor, was also praying in another room. He had the same experience. Both of them—independently—had received the same message in their spirits to call me and pray for me and my burden.

For a few seconds, I was speechless and stunned. Why would God speak to Natu and Akiki instead of me, especially when I spent hours praying and pleading to Him to talk to me? A streak of disappointment found its way into my heart. But still, the fact that she and her husband independently had had the same praying experience and received the same message from God sparked my curiosity.

The more we talked about my conversion and her praying experience, the more I felt peaceful and comfortable with her. I was interested to know about her and her husband's faith and how they cultivated sensitivity to the Holy Spirit, the voice of God. Had Natu and Akiki experienced what the Lord Jesus said in John 16:13: "But when he, the Spirit of truth, comes, he will guide you into all the truth. He will not speak on his own; he will speak only what he hears, and he will tell you what is yet to come"?

The conversation infused me with a sudden burst of energy. I wondered if Akiki and Natu—since he was a pastor—would coach me to grow in the knowledge of God and the scriptures. I wanted to continually tune my spiritual ears to the whisper I had heard when I first encountered Jesus at Westminster Chapel.

Akiki and I spoke for a long while. I shared that I was wrestling with a troubling challenge (without giving details of the meeting with Dr. Kendall). I even admitted my disappointment that God had spoken to them about me instead of speaking to me. Akiki suggested that instead of praying on the phone, I should go to their home so that Natu could pray for me. Without a second thought, I accepted the invitation. I jumped in the car and raced to their home.

When I arrived, Natu and Akiki did not ask me any questions about my burden, nor did I volunteer any information. We went to their lounge and placed three chairs in the center of the room. I sat in the middle chair. Natu and Akiki sat on my sides. In my mind, I wondered how they would know what to pray for me. As if Natu had read my mind, he turned to me and said, "How do we pray? We follow the guidance of the Holy Spirit. The Spirit guides us on what to pray. We do not pray of our own." He flipped the pages of his Bible and read Romans 8:26: "In the same way, the Spirit helps us in our weakness. We do not know what we ought to pray for, but the Spirit himself intercedes for us through wordless groans."

Wow, Akiki and Natu never ceased to amaze me. Natu led in prayer, followed by Akiki. I joined them in prayer and prayed for God to release my burden, without disclosing the details. In my heart, I wrestled with my anxious thoughts of being misjudged by people who might believe that my healing was the only reason for my conversion. As for me, I am convinced without any shadow of a doubt that God's purpose for calling me on April 28 was *to heal my soul*. Physical healing was not on my mind. Not at all! It is God's will for all people throughout the ages to save them and have eternal life with Him through their redemption from sin. In John 3:16, the scripture says, "For God so loved the world that he gave his one and only Son, that whoever believes in him shall not perish but have eternal life." Following my conversion, prayers captivated my heart for people to seek redemption and salvation.

Minutes later, I found myself asking God to silence the negative voices in my ears, bullying me with catastrophic thoughts for deserting Islam. Images of my childhood shame flashed before my eyes and intensified my anxiety. I called for God's help and refocused my mind on praying with Akiki and Natu. Minutes turned into hours of praying and silent meditation. Suddenly, Akiki said, "Listen, Maha, this is what the Holy Spirit prompted in my spirit: 'Forget the former things; do not dwell on the past. See, I am doing a new thing! Now it springs up; do you not perceive it? I am making a way in the wilderness and streams in the wasteland'" (Isaiah 43:18–19).

As I listened to the scriptures, a tingling raced through my body and shook me violently, almost throwing me onto the floor. But nothing in this world could have prepared me for what happened a few moments later, when Natu laid his hand on my head and prayed. Suddenly my eyes saw things in a different realm. I learned later that I had had a spiritual vision.

In my vision, I saw myself standing at the foot of a giant golden throne that stretched beyond the sky. I had my face covered with my crossed arms as I leaned against the throne. I was sobbing intensely. Suddenly, something prompted me to turn my head. When I did so, I found a river running next to me in which three different streams were flowing next to one another. The first stream was of regular water running next to a golden water stream, next to a stream of long tongues of fire. The golden stream filled the air with bright light. The beauty of the throne and the streams took my breath away. Stunned by the majestic beauty of the landscape surrounding me, my sobbing turned into shouts of joy. My belly swelled and bubbled as if the three streams were running inside me. To this day, the sight of the throne and the river flashes vividly before my eyes and gives me goose bumps.

I do not know how long I stayed in that realm. When I opened my eyes, I found myself on the floor, flat on my back; a supernatural peace cocooned me. For a while, I could not move; my body had gone limp. Akiki and Natu were on their knees next to me, praying with their hands stretched over me. A few minutes later, I was able to move to the chair. I told Akiki and Natu what I had seen. When I finished, Akiki said with a big smile beaming on her face, "You just had a baptism of the Holy Spirit."

Natu explained, "Usually, the baptism of the Holy Spirit happens after the water baptism. But in your case, I believe the order changed because God wanted to confirm your request; He showed you that He had chosen you for a mission, unconditionally." Wow. How did he know that I had prayed for confirmation from God?

We praised God while having a celebratory tea with homemade sweets. As I prepared to leave, Natu handed me a paper on which he had written verses about baptism—baptism by water and baptism by the Holy Spirit. I thanked them and left, overjoyed and filled with the Holy Spirit.

24
DIVINE PROPHECIES—OUT OF THE MOUTHS OF BABES

My friend Ismet told me once that the Lord had set me apart from my childhood before He created the world. Ismet's statement reminded me of childhood events and dreams that, I now realized, were not fantasy or accidental. Remembering each of these events sparked loud and joyful aha moments as they prophesied life-changing phenomena decades later. To review those events, one weekend I brought home from the storage room the trunk where I stored my journals.[27] Every year, on the day following my birthday, I started a new diary and put the previous one in the trunk. I never had read any of the past journals until now. I sat on the floor, spread the notebooks around me, and started reading. The following are excerpts from my journals demonstrating the concept of "out of the mouths of babes"[28]—such as prophecies that God fulfilled many years later.

---

[27] I started journaling (scribbling and drawing) at the age of five.
[28] Matthew 21:16.

> *Important Note:* I want to make it clear that none of my Christian friends, my school classmates, the nuns, or the housekeepers at home had ever talked to me about Jesus.

I pulled out my first journal, dated 1958–59, written when I was five years old. The pages had faded and turned a yellow-orange. Some pages were hard to read, and some were stuck together. I oohed and aahed with tears mixed with laughter while looking at the drawings of me crying in front of a cross giving flowers to Jesus, whom I called Seigneur Dieu—God. For unknown reasons, which to this day I cannot explain intellectually, I believed that Seigneur Dieu was God and a loving one. The picture that touched me the most was of me flying hand in hand with Seigneur Dieu. The entire notebook had scribblings and drawings of the two of us. With lots of tears and cries of "ouch," illustrating my pain and anger at the horror I had gone through at that time, I turned the pages. I was amazed by my delight in the Lord at such a young age. My tender heart mysteriously loved this God. Every time I spoke to Him, I stopped crying and felt comforted. It felt like petting and giving a loving home to an abandoned and abused pet.

The scribblings and drawings triggered several aha moments. These showed how Seigneur Dieu had planted the seeds of faith in my young heart. It took several decades before they spiritually germinated to cause me to become the person God had created me to be! I marveled at how my child-believed hope in Seigneur Dieu to save me from abuse paved the road to my eternal salvation!

My second journal was thin and painful to read. I was six years old and suffering from horrific abuse. I was scared to tell anyone in my family out of fear; I thought they would not believe me. I was too young to know how to say what was happening to me. The only way I knew to display my anger and fear was by stabbing the pages several times with black and red pencils. Several pictures were of a child crying and praying before a cross. Others showed the child with arms extended to Seigneur Dieu, portrayed as an adult man in a white robe and a dark beard.

Another memory that came alive was from a drawing of a pendant necklace. The picture reminded me of when my mother had given me a gold Qur'an locket pendant to protect me from harm and the evil eye. I was in the 11ème class.[29] My mother repeatedly stressed that I should tuck the Qur'an necklace under my shirt every time I entered the toilet. One day my mother noticed that I was not wearing the pendant. She asked me if I had removed it. My response was that I was not aware of its absence from my neck. Of course, Mom grounded me for losing it. A few weeks later, Mom surprised me with another Qur'an pendant. Again, the necklace disappeared, and again I was punished. The third necklace my mother gave me had a shorter chain that felt like a tight choker with a childproof clasp.

When that pendant also disappeared, my mother accused my classmates, the teachers' helpers, and the cleaners at school. The following day, my mother took me to the school and met with Mother Superior. As I sat between them, they took turns questioning me. All attempts to make me recall what had happened to the three necklaces failed. Because of the sensitivity of the matter, Mother Superior treated the loss of the Qur'an necklace very seriously. She questioned the teachers, their assistants, the cleaners, the janitors, and everyone working at the school; she even asked my classmates if they had seen a Qur'an necklace. No one had seen it. Both my mother and the Reverend Mother were seriously puzzled by its mysterious disappearance. What puzzled me even more was that every piece of jewelry my mother had given me, whether a pendant or a charm bracelet, also surprisingly

---

[29] Equivalent to first grade.

vanished into thin air. To this day, I do not know how the childproof clasps could have come unfastened with the jewelry falling off me without my noticing.

Another drawing reminded me of the day I sang to my dolls a song I had made up with lyrics indicating that Seigneur Dieu was my friend and my God. My mother was not pleased when she heard me. She reprimanded Mary,[30] thinking that she was the one who had taught me the song. When several warnings did not stop me from singing the song, my mother finally punished me. She filled my mouth with cayenne pepper so I would never repeat it.

In the journal I kept when I was ten years old, I started asking Seigneur Dieu questions such as "Who are You?" and "Are You real?" and with statements such as "I want to know You." I seemed curious to know how and why Seigneur Dieu was able to soothe my pain and become a source of comfort when everything else had failed.

The journal also included drawings about the school recess periods, during which I used to go around telling the girls that I was Christian. My two older sisters were in the same school.

How had I gotten that strange idea? And why? Of course no one believed me! One girl challenged me, saying, "How could you be a Christian while your family is Muslim?" Some of my classmates called me a liar. Two of my older sister's friends took me to the side, scolded me for telling such a terrible blasphemy, and threatened to report me to Mother Superior and call my parents. I shrugged my shoulders and walked away. The girls' threats did not bother me. Nothing stopped me, including the thought of my mother's potential punishment (which usually shred my heart in fear). Claiming to be a Christian at such a young age puzzled me. Following my conversion, the Spirit of God reminded me of these recess sessions while I was reading Luke 6:45: "A good man brings good things out of the good stored up in his heart, … for

---

[30] A Christian housekeeper working at my parents' house at that time.

the mouth speaks what the heart is full of." To this day, I recall vividly the scenes and every word I said.

My journals also included letters to Seigneur Dieu, asking daring questions such as "Are You different from Allah? If You are different, why? And how are You different?" "How do You know me?" "Why do you Help me, a non-Christian?" and "Can You be my God? Please tell me how You can be my God." I repeated these questions in almost every letter and concluded the letters with a plea: "Please don't let my parents know that I talk to You and that we are friends. Please keep these letters our secret."

I marveled at how my tender child's mind made the distinction between Jesus and Allah and believed that they were different. In my heart, I believed that I was Christian, even from birth! I'd never questioned it.

I was eleven years old when, one day, I asked my mother to change my first name to Marie-Christine. At first, my mother sent me away with a scolding glare mixed with a funny smile. I repeated my request for several weeks, until one day she grabbed me by my arm and aimed her piercing eyes at my face. The pain in my arm paralyzed me, and yet I did not move; I pretended that I was not bothered. With her stern voice that shook the ground, she said, stressing every word, "No. You cannot change your name."

"Why not?" I softly asked.

"Because Marie-Christine is a Christian name and you are Muslim," she said.

I lifted my eyes to meet hers and boldly replied, "Well then, I will become Christian."

My reply shocked my mother. Her face flushed red with anger. My response brought severe punishment upon me. My mother threatened me to sell me like Sakina.[31] She ordered my governess to remove all my toys and to search my room for my

---

[31] Sakina was a maid, sold by her parents at the age of seven to work at my parents' house.

journals. Later on, she threw the toys and pages from the journals in the garbage. I was forbidden to leave my room for weeks (other than to go to school). Amid the physical pain, I found great consolation by feeling the presence of Seigneur Dieu. "Couldn't You stop her?" was always my first question to the Lord.

Decades later, during my baptismal ceremony, I changed my name on my baptismal document to Marie Christine.[32] My childhood desire was finally fulfilled! And yet I wanted God to give me a name. I waited and waited for my new name.

One year, my friend June and I decided to follow Robert Murray M'Cheyne's Bible Reading Plan. When we reached the book of Jeremiah, I started crying uncontrollably. From the first chapter to the end of the book (52 chapters, 1364 verses), I cried involuntarily. To this day, every time I read Jeremiah, I get emotional and cry. June told me that I was like Jeremiah, constantly weeping. So, I adopted the name Miah from the prophet's name, Jeremiah.

Several of my journals reminded me of praying in my heart the Lord's Prayer along with my Christian classmates. While the nuns and Christians prayed before starting each class, Muslims were forbidden to pray the Christian prayers or attend the catechism. Muslims' declaration of the Lord's Prayer was considered a confession, which in turn meant *the* unforgivable blasphemy. Although I did not understand the words of the prayer, I kept praying in my heart at home and at school.

One of my journals noted the day I had asked my older brother if he knew a man called Billy Graham. He said that he was an American priest. When he asked me about my question, I told him that I had had a dream about the man. Nana overheard the conversation and prayed over me, asking Allah to wash my mind and heart of Christian people's influence. Billy Graham's name

---

[32] It is worth mentioning that upon my baptism, I adopted a new Christian name: Marie Christine.

resonated in my ears for many years, until one day I found out that he was an evangelist. I shared my dream with his daughter Mrs. Anne Graham Lotz when she and I met in London in 2003. Mrs. Lotz signed my Bible and invited me to meet the legend.

I praised God for saving me. The memories of past events soaked my heart in a pool of sadness, heaviness, regret, and shame tinted with anger. I pulled my legs up to my chest, rested my head on my knees, and cried quietly; the drawings reignited my pleas to God, asking why He had taken so many years to save me. I lifted to the Lord a long list of whys, asking for answers. I wholeheartedly believed that if only the Lord had rescued me when I was a child, I would be a happier and confident adult. In the midst of my prayers, suddenly the Holy Spirit silenced me and reminded me of 2 Peter 3:8: "But do not forget this one thing, dear friends: With the Lord, a day is like a thousand years, and a thousand years are like a day."

Ecclesiastes 3:1 showed me that God works on a different timetable than mine; our schedules are not in sync. The thought of reconnecting with my childhood Seigneur Dieu filled me with immense joy. I wrote the following on the inside of the back cover of my journal:

> La grande retrouvaille du Seigneur Dieu de mon enfance. Le grand mystère de mon enfance est enfin résolu. J'ai finalement réalisé mes rêves et je suis sur le bon chemin qui m'a conduit au Seigneur Dieu, mon Jésus et mon Dieu![33]

I gathered all my journals and put them back in the trunk. I realized that all my childhood dreams and desires were

---

[33] The French translates as, "The great reunion of the Lord God of my childhood. The great mystery of my childhood is finally solved. God finally fulfilled my dreams. I am on the right path to the Lord God, my God!"

foretastes of God's will and plans for my life. I can say that when I was a child, Jesus manifested in my life on many occasions, but being a child, I did not understand. Besides, who would have believed me? Being severely punished, I kept those events to myself and in my private diaries. And now I genuinely understood the meaning of "out of the mouth of babes" (Psalm 8:2 KJV).

PART VII
HE DISCIPLED ME

I have much more to say to you, more than you can now bear. But when he, the Spirit of truth, comes, he will guide you into all the truth. He will not speak on his own; he will speak only what he hears, and he will tell you what is yet to come. He will glorify me because it is from me that he will receive what he will make known to you. All that belongs to the Father is mine. That is why I said the Spirit will receive from me what he will make known to you.
—John 16:12–17

INTRODUCTION TO PART VII

Examining the Source of My Faith—the Fuel for My Journey

Several years after my conversion, I visited Saint Catalina Church. Unlike on my previous visits, this time I entered the church as a Christian, a follower of Jesus. I held my head high, happy about my new identity. I sat at my usual place in the last pew. This time, I took the time to look around the sanctuary. Unlike Westminster Chapel, here the walls and the stained glass were not bare but were decorated with scenes from various Bible stories and images of Bible personalities. I noticed that they had installed a new lighting system; the lights that illuminated the crucifix were striking. I moved closer and stood at the foot of the cross. The lights dramatized the cross in such a way that made Jesus's wounds on His face and body look very real; you could hear His agonizing breathing and see His blood dripping over His cheeks and chest. Wow, I was looking at the event that had turned world history upside down. Jesus, who is God and the Creator of the universe and of humankind, with whom I fell in love, was crucified.

I bowed my head, too embarrassed to look at the horrific death He endured in my place. I lamented and cried my eyes out, recognizing that it was my sins that put nails in His hands and feet. A sorrowful pain hit my stomach, and a mournful cry flew through my lips: "I love You, Seigneur Dieu, Jesus, my God, my Lord and Savior." In slow motion, I took a few steps back to the closest pew and sat down. I was grieved by seeing His suffering on the cross and also smitten by His victory over sin and death.

An array of feelings lined up in my heart, ranging from sadness for Jesus's brutal death in my place, to thankfulness for His sacrifice, to humility that I was on His mind while He was dying on the cross.

While gazing on the crucifix, my mind took me to my childhood Christian kindergarten, which I attended at the age of five. My conversion reminded me of how, as a child, I related to Jesus and the Lord's Prayer. I adopted the Lord's Prayer as my daily prayer in spite of not understanding the meanings of the words, notably "God the Father." Nevertheless, I was fascinated with the idea that Jesus was not only God but also everybody's Father, including mine. So, I believed Jesus was my Father. Since I could not call Him "Father"—not to confuse Him with my earthly father—I called Him Seigneur Dieu.[34] I loved the idea of having two loving and caring fathers. (I loved my dad with all my heart; he was the best dad I've ever known.)

How did I, a five-year-old child, recognize that the baby in the manger and the man hanging on the cross were the same Seigneur Dieu? How did I believe that Jesus was both man and God even before reading the scriptures? I have no clue. In my child's heart, I believed He was the God who could rescue children and who could save and heal people when everything else had failed to help. I marvel at the choice of the words I used as a child, *save* and *heal*.

How did my child's mind get that knowledge and reach that understanding? Why did I, as a child, believe in the Christian God, who was radically different and whose deity was considered blasphemous to the teaching of Islam I had received at home? Had anyone taught me to believe in Jesus? I categorically say no. Why did Jesus reveal Himself to me when I did not seek Him? Why did Jesus wait many years before calling me to follow Him? What made me accept His calling when I had turned my back

---

[34] French for "Lord God."

on religion? What made me immediately and without hesitation declare Him as the true God? Where did the certainty come from that the voice whispering in my ear at the Chapel, calling me, was indeed the voice of the true God, not my imagination or a false god?

Was that faith? Yes! Yes! A thousand times, yes! It was my faith that suddenly leaped out from its dormancy and spurred my decision to respond to God's calling. I not only accepted the calling but also gave my life to Him. By faith, I accepted Jesus in my heart as the true God in the flesh, even before reading the Bible, as I did not need evidence. By faith, I raced to follow Jesus even before knowing the responsibilities and consequences associated with accepting His calling. I did not want to miss my second chance to receive Him in my life. I had lost Him once before, but no more.

How did my brain create my faith neurons and house them in my mind? I don't know, and I can't explain it intellectually. I candidly can say that I had never discussed the Christian faith with anyone.

So, what was the source of my faith? While I cannot explain my childhood belief, I do understand as an adult believer, from the apostle Paul's message to the Ephesians, that God gives everyone faith. By His grace, mercy, and love, God uses faith as an instrument to offer us the gift of salvation (Ephesians 2:8–9). It is up to us to either accept the gift or reject it. The scripture concurs with my belief that when I worshipped Jesus as a child, He planted seeds of faith that went dormant in my soul, only to revive decades later at a preset time.

God did not force me to believe; He gave me the free will to choose and to live out the consequences of my decision. Revelation 3:20 indicates that we select the path of our lives. The scripture reads that Jesus calls, "Here I am! I stand at the door and knock. *If anyone hears my voice and opens the door,* I will come in and eat with that person, and they with me" (emphasis added).

I accepted the calling and yielded to His will to begin a journey of discovery of His identity.

I don't recall how long I stayed at church, processing the drastic change in my life. On my way out, I saw a painting of Jesus preaching to a crowd of people. I stopped and said, "O Lord Jesus, if only I were alive at the time when you were on earth and had been at this place with these people, I would have said that I saw God in the flesh." With this uplifting thought, I left the church.

When people asked me what it was that had attracted me to the Christian faith that I could not find in any other religion, my answer was always "Jesus." My one-word answer inspired numerous debates with friends and heated criticism from my family. My siblings accused me of insanity and warned of the steep price I would pay. One of my brothers criticized my lack of knowledge of Islam and asked me to give the religion a second chance. My response was, "I am seeking God, not a religion. If I were to give anything a second chance, it would be Seigneur Dieu, Jesus."

I recognized that Jesus and the Trinity were always sensitive topics to debate with Muslim family and friends. How could God be a Father? How could God have a Son? How could Jesus, a man, be God? Is Allah the same God of the Bible? Is Christianity a monotheistic religion? How to prove the divinity of Christ, the Messiah? Why did God allow Jesus to be crucified? Why is the resurrection important? For Muslims, these questions represent the irreconcilable differences between Christianity and Islam, while they depict the tenets of Christianity.

Listening to my Muslim friends' and my family's questions and criticisms, I quickly realized how much Jesus's deity was grossly distorted and misinterpreted. It grieved me to see how much Jesus's enemies opposed His mission without understanding it. They proof-tested His words and works to establish a false ground for heresy to discredit Him and disfigure His divine identity so as to prevent people from believing in Him.

At first, my friends' and my family's hostile attitude saddened me; they rebuked me for converting. Friends and relatives deserted me. I wondered what Jesus would do in a similar situation. Two verses showed me Jesus's reaction to people's criticism:

- Mark 6:6—"He was amazed at their lack of faith."
- 1 Peter 2:23—"When they hurled their insults at him, he did not retaliate; when he suffered, he made no threats. Instead, he entrusted himself to him who judges justly."

Although Jesus was not powerless to retaliate, He did not criticize in return, nor did He get angry, wage war against his enemies, or get discouraged. Instead, Jesus focused on God and on the divine mission that God had given Him. So, I did not focus on people's criticism. Instead, like Jesus, I entrusted myself to God. The more I trusted God, the more He amazed me and the more I wanted to know Him. I longed for God and for His presence in my life. People's criticism motivated me to grow in the knowledge of Him and the scriptures, which enabled me to share my faith with biblical facts. I engrossed myself in studying both the Old Testament and the New Testament with the mindset of discovering God's nature and character.

The quest to satisfy these longings weaved a divine road map for my spiritual journey of discovery of the Godhead within the Trinity manifested as God the Father, God the Son, and God the Holy Spirit.

25
DISCOVERY JOURNEY TO THE TRINITY

Someone told me that the purpose of God is a mystery and unknown to humankind except when revealed by His divine revelation to those who seek Him. On many occasions, the apostle Paul used the word *mystery* to convey unique spiritual truths revealed to him by God through the Holy Spirit. Throughout the New Testament, the apostle Paul wanted to differentiate between God's mysteries and the mysteries of secret cults, which were then rampant. For example, in Ephesians 3:5, he wrote about the mystery of God's grace in the gift of redemption and salvation, "which was not made known to people in other generations as it has now been revealed by the Spirit to God's holy apostles and prophets." Surely, there is mystery in the Word of God.

One of the first mysteries in the Bible that captivated me was the use of the words *us* and *our* in Genesis 1:26 and *us* in verse 3:22. My mind thundered with questions: To whom was God speaking about making humankind? Did God need assistance to make humankind? Was He speaking to angels? Which angels? Can angels create human beings? No! God is the sole and ultimate Creator; besides Him, no one is a creator. Angels cannot create human beings; God created all angels. So, who was in God's presence, and to whom He was speaking?

> *Note:* Because God created angels, He instructed that humankind must not worship them (Matthew 4:9–10; Romans 1:25; Colossians 2:18; Revelation 22:8–9).

My curiosity fired me up, and I dove into the scriptures to identify the persons involved in the conversation.

Concordance

My friend June suggested I get a Bible concordance as a study tool. Oh boy. Did I get a small, compact concordance? Oh no! I got the largest one at the bookstore. Not only did its two-thousand-plus pages feel like a ton, but also I found it grueling to use and backbreaking to move it around. Following all the references to the verses and where they occur overwhelmed me and challenged me; quite often, I kept going off on rabbit trails. It took me awhile to get used to the concordance, until I finally managed to see its benefits for deepening my Bible study and my knowledge of the scriptures. It helped me to cross-reference the scriptures in different chapters of the Bible and to understand God's Word from different angles.

Plurality within the Trinity

The concordance led me to examine in parallel Genesis 1:1–2; 26–27; 3:22 and John 1:1–13. Hints of a plurality within the Godhead started to emerge before my eyes. I gasped out loud, surprised when I noticed the presence of three persons who performed distinct responsibilities in such a synchronized manner that it seemed as if they were one person. Oh my word, I cried with joy.

Could these verses be about the three persons of the Trinity? Oh, man! The mystery in these verses fired up my interest to trace the members of the Godhead in the Trinity.

I bought several books about the Trinity, thereby starting my quest to learn about it. I recall seeing my fingers moving so fast between the concordance and the Bible pages that they bled on numerous occasions. Studying the Trinity challenged me a lot. At times, it was hard to combat my brain's automatic reactions compelling me to stop, claiming that I would never understand the Trinity. Thank God for Dr. R. T. Kendall (1996[35]), who mentioned in one of his Friday Understanding Theology classes that the Trinity is "one of the most difficult subjects in Christian theology."

Contrary to what my Islamic high school education had taught me, that the Trinity was a false man-made concept, I believed the Trinity was real. Why? Since I was in kindergarten, I had loved the loving character of "Notre Père," God the Father. I found Him personable and close to me. I also loved His voice whispering in my ears words of comfort and peace in times of need. I loved seeing God as a caring and loving dad, especially for those who didn't have a loving dad and longed for one. I never shared my views with anyone. So, the moment I converted, I desperately wanted to explore the Godhead within the Trinity. I was thrilled to find my childhood belief reignited at my conversion. I wanted to learn about the oneness of God and to be able to explain the Trinity to others.

Someone described the Trinity this way: "If you try to explain the Trinity, you will lose your mind. But if you deny it, you will lose your soul." I love that!

I prayed for God's guidance as I tiptoed into my journey of discovery about the Trinity and writing my understanding.

---

[35] R. T. Kendall, *Understanding Theology*, vol. I (Ross-shire: Christian Focus Publications, 1998), 28.

Please note that I am not a Bible scholar. I am only sharing my humble and modest discovery journey of the Holy Trinity while the learning is in progress and ongoing.

★ ★ ★

Over a meal at a restaurant with my five Core friends and Mrs. Summons (i.e., my group), Gretchen asked about my Bible studies. I shared with the group my discovery of the plurality of the Godhead within the Trinity as discussed in Genesis 1:1–2, 26, and John 1:1–14. With these verses, I started my exploratory journey of the Trinity. I also shared with the group the meaning of the Godhead, the three persons—Father, Son, and Holy Spirit—as one God. I explained that each person is fully God; they interoperate distinctively and in unity at the same time, as one.

Boy! My brief explanation dropped a bombshell on the team.

Anwar, shouting from the end of the table, asked, "Miah, how can three Gods—Father, Son, and the Holy Spirit—exist in one God? And when Jesus died on the cross, did He die alone, or did all three Gods die? If God died, then He is no longer 'alive,' as Christians claim, is He? And who was running the universe while God was on the earth and died on the cross?"

Anwar seemed to have misheard me saying "*one* God." Being a convert from Islam, I understood Anwar's views. Hence, I had expected his questions. Muslims find the concept of the Trinity incomprehensible, even blasphemous. Anwar's questions attracted the group's attention. All eyes fell on me as everyone waited for my response.

Being a new believer, I knew in my heart that I did not have enough biblical knowledge or spiritual wisdom to respond intelligently and logically. I took a deep breath and said, "Well, Anwar, from a Muslim's point of view, your questions are valid. I am as curious and as interested to know about the Trinity as you might be. But this is what I can say for now. As you believe in the presence of Allah because the Qur'an says so, I also believe in the existence of three persons in one God because the Holy Bible says so (1 John 5:7–8). By sheer and deep faith, we both believe in the mysteries of God. How can our finite mind fathom God's infinite mysteries? There is no way! Besides, who am I to question God?"

I must say that I was trembling while responding to Anwar. Mervet, who was sitting next to me, put her arm around me and whispered, "Take it easy, Miah. Calm down."

I took a deep breath and continued: "I am currently studying the Trinity. We will get together again so I can share with you all my findings."

Mervet turned to Anwar and asked, "Anwar, how do you, as a Muslim, see the Trinity?"

Anwar was sufficiently informed to explain the Islamic point of view on the subject; he was pleased to share about Islam. He adjusted his position in his seat, pulled his sleeves up to his elbows, and said, "All Muslims, including me, deny any possibility of Allah being triune. In Islam, it is impossible for Allah to have a son; such a concept attacks Allah's *absolute* oneness, which is the fundamental doctrine of Islam and the Qur'an. We Muslims believe that associating a relationship with Allah, called *shirk* (i.e., association), is the greatest of all sins. *Shirk* is *the only thing* Allah does not forgive unless the person repents, rejects the *shirk* belief, and returns to Islam." Then he quoted the verse from Surah Ali-Imran 3:64:[36]

> Say: O People of the Scripture! Come to an agreement between us and you: that we shall worship none but Allah, and that we shall ascribe no partner unto Him, and that none of us shall take others for lords beside Allah.

---

[36] *The Qur'an: Arabic Text with Corresponding English Meanings* (Singapore: Abul-Qasim, 1997), 72.

He added, "Also, in Islam, Allah is too holy to have personal relationships with humans. The Qur'an reveals to us only Allah's will, not Himself."

Jacob followed: "And Jews, including me, believe that there is a one God, the God of Abraham, Jacob, and Isaac. Jews are blessed to have a personal relationship with God."

Nabil, sitting on my right, picked up the book *Understanding Theology* by Dr. R. T. Kendall[37] (1996), which I had brought with me, and put it in front of me. After searching the index and flipping through some pages, he said, "Listen to this." Quoting from the book, he said, "'The word *Trinity* is not mentioned in the Bible.'" Turning to me, he asked, "What do you say to that, Miah?"

I took the book from him and read the following lines from the same page: "'Some people feel that because it [the word *Trinity*] is not mentioned explicitly in the Bible—in and of itself—[this] is sufficient reason to reject both the term and what it means. But should we reject the book of Esther because the name of God is not found in that God-centered book?'

"By the same token, you may ask why Jesus is mentioned more than twenty times in the Qur'an, whereas the name of the Prophet Muhammed is mentioned only four times. What do you say about that?" But I reminded the group that we ought not to compare religions.

Everyone went silent. Mrs. Summons concurred with Nabil that the Bible does not explicitly mention the Trinity. Still, the Trinity is declared and confirmed throughout the scriptures in the Bible. The Trinity doctrine is *the* foundation of the Christian faith. She also added that the Trinity is undoubtedly the most mysterious doctrine of the Christian faith. She challenged us, asking, "If we only think of how complex and mysterious the

---

[37] Kendall, *Understanding Theology*, vol. I, 28.

makeup and nature of our bodies, minds, souls, and spirits is, then how much more complex and mysterious is God?"

Again, silence reigned, except my mind; it stormed on, on a questioning spree. Is God genuinely mysterious, and why? Why is the Trinity shrouded with such a mystery? Why do some people believe the Trinity while others don't? Why do other religions refute the Trinity? How to solve the mystery of the Trinity? Can humankind solve the mystery of the Trinity? I strongly doubt it, because the Trinity is one of God's mysteries, and "the Lord our God has secrets known to no one" (Deuteronomy 29:29 NLT). At one point, I asked God why He was not teaching me more about the Trinity so as to share my knowledge with others. Then, John 16:12 (KJV) gave me the answer in what Jesus told His disciples: "I have yet many things to say unto you, but ye cannot bear them now."

Admittedly, my mind would not be able to bear all the knowledge God might share with me.

Mervet's voice pulled my mind back to the group. She asked Mrs. Summons, "Do you believe that the Trinity practically applies to our everyday life?"

What in the world does Mervet mean by that? What an odd question! I thought. But Mrs. Summons praised Mervet for her perception and explained that God told us nothing that wouldn't apply to our everyday lives. She referred, as an example, to 2 Corinthians 13:14: "May the grace of the Lord Jesus Christ, the love of God and the fellowship of the Holy Spirit be with us all." Then, she said that the Godhead in the Holy Trinity aimed for the salvation of the world. Second Corinthians 13:14 tells us how salvation was originated: from the love of the Father, executed by the grace of the Son, and applied in our hearts by the power of the Holy Spirit. It is important, as believers, to exercise these virtues in our daily lives. Mrs. Summons mentioned a lot of things that I needed to research, understand, and apply.

The group raised more challenging comments and queries,

some of which put me in the hot seat. The group criticized my unfounded belief in the Trinity. Gretchen asked me on what basis I was establishing my knowledge.

I admitted to the group that I may not have had enough knowledge as of yet to satisfy their questions. "But one thing I know for sure," I said, "since the day I accepted His calling, God did not (and will not) leave me in the dark. The more I read the Bible, the more I ask Him questions. Gradually, God is revealing Himself and teaching me through His Word and His Holy Spirit. I learned that God reveals Himself according to my faith and my heart. My learning is in progress. And I will share with you what I learn."

In the end, Mrs. Summons reminded us that the words *Father* and *Son* are solely relational, not biological. Then she cautioned us by explaining that the Trinity has the divine essence, whereas we humans do not. As a result, humankind cannot comprehend the infinite mind, plan, and purpose of God. In the end, she encouraged me to complete my studies/research. She suggested to the group that they also read about the Trinity and bring their questions next time we met. On this note, we finished dinner and left the restaurant.

I spent the weeks following the dinner studying the main events mentioned in the Old Testament, considering the Trinity, and putting them in parallel with the New Testament. Not only did I find the scriptures interwoven throughout the Bible, but also I started seeing the presence of the three persons of the Trinity and their interactions with people throughout the entire Bible. From Genesis to Revelation, the evidence for the diversity-in-unity within the three persons of the Godhead was unquestionably noticeable.

The First Person of the Trinity—God the Father
When I researched the word *Father* in the Bible, I found it mentioned 660 times in the Old Testament, in some of which God

introduced Himself as the Father, as an endearment to emphasize His care and love for His people, for example, Deuteronomy 32:6; 1 Chronicles 29:10; Psalm 103:13; Proverbs 3:12; Isaiah 63:16, 64:8; Jeremiah 31:9; and Malachi 1:6, 2:10. So, I identified the covenant God of Israel as God the Father, the first person of the Trinity.

In the Old Testament and the Tanakh, I found the names Jehovah and Yahweh, among other names, referring to God the Father. In the following verses (to name a few), I found God calling His people who love Him as His "children": Hosea 1:10, 11:1; Isaiah 1:2; Exodus 4:22–23; Deuteronomy 14:1; and Psalm 82:6.

Over and again, the scriptures showed me a loving Father who was—and still is—continually calling the people to Him to bless them.

The Second Person of the Trinity—God the Son
I noticed that the scriptures in the Old Testament talked about a particular angel referred to as "the angel of the Lord/Yahweh" who interacted with people. Who was this angel of the Lord/Yahweh? What was so peculiar about this angel that he was referred to as "*the*[38] Angel of the Lord"? The verses seemed to be making a distinction between the angel of the Lord and all other angels.

What surprised me most was that only the Old Testament mentioned the angel of the Lord. I found no references to the angel of the Lord in the New Testament, i.e., after the birth of Jesus. At the same time, the Tanakh called the angel the "Malakh[39] of Jehovah" and the "Malakh of Yahweh." No particular titles are given to the other angels.

I also noticed that, unlike all the other angels mentioned in

---

[38] Italics for emphasis.
[39] "Angel" in Hebrew and in Arabic.

the Bible, *the* angel of the Lord spoke as God, proclaimed Himself God, and commanded and performed by divine authority as God. This is seen, for example, in Genesis 16:7–12, 21:17–18, 22:11–18; Exodus 3:2–6; Judges 2:1–4, 5:23, 6:11–24; 2 Samuel 24:16; and Zechariah 1:12, 3:1, 12:8.

Studying these verses convinced me that the angel of the Lord was not an ordinary angel. I noticed the following:

- When the angel of the Lord appeared to Hagar, she said, "You are the God who sees me," for she recognized Him as God (Genesis 16:7–13).
- People obeyed Him and did what He commanded them to do.
- People of the Old Testament who saw the angel of the Lord and recognized Him as God feared for their lives because they believed that they would die when they saw God—and yet their lives were spared (Exodus 33:20; the story of Gideon in Judges 6:22–23).

God alone knows how many times I read these verses trying to decipher whether the angel of the Lord was an earthly manifestation of God the Father, God the Son, or the preincarnate Jesus.

I quickly dismissed the thought that God the Father appeared to people in a physical form, for three reasons:

1. Exodus 33:17–23, and verse 20 in particular, where God said to Moses at Mount Sinai, "You cannot see my face, for no one may see me and live." God gave a strong warning and a direct confirmation that it is impossible to see God. So, the people of the Old Testament believed that they would die if they saw God.
2. However, when Jacob in Genesis 32:30, Gideon in Judges 6:11–24, and Manoah in Judges 13:22 saw God

face-to-face, they feared for their lives and thought they would die, and yet they lived! How come they lived? How come God's warning in Exodus 33:20 did not apply to them, unless the angel of the Lord they saw was not God the Father? And if such were the case, then who was he?
3. The apostle John stressed on three occasions that no one had seen God the Father (John 1:18; 6:46). The apostle Paul also wrote in 1 Timothy 6:16 that God the Father "who alone is immortal and who lives in unapproachable light, whom *no one has seen or can see*" (emphasis added).
4. God is Spirit (John 4:24; 1 Thessalonians 5:19; 1 Timothy 1:17).

> *Note:* Actually, the scriptures do not tell us that Adam and Eve "saw" God face-to-face but only that they "heard" the sound of the Lord (Genesis 3:8).

Therefore, I concluded that the people of the Old Testament who said they saw God and did not die must have seen a divine personification of God, the preincarnate Jesus.

One day I was in a bookstore looking for books about the Malakh of Yahweh. I randomly started flipping pages from the pile of books left on the table by previous browsers. I picked up the book *Systematic Theology* by Charles Hodge (1872). The title attracted me, causing me to hope that systematically I would arrive at my goal. The book was heavy reading that went way above my comprehension level. However, as I was flipping the pages, my eyes fell on the following paragraph:[40]

---

[40] Charles Hodge, *Systematic Theology*, vol. 1 (Peabody, MA: Hendrickson, 2020), 485.

> We ... find throughout the Old Testament constant mention made by a person to whom, though distinct from Jehovah as a person, the titles, attributes, and works of Jehovah are nevertheless ascribed. This Person is called the Angel of God, the Angel of Jehovah, Adonai, Jehovah, and Elohim. He claims divine authority, exercises divine prerogatives, and receives divine homage. ... But when this is a pervading representation of the Bible; when we find that these terms are applied, not first to one and then to another angel indiscriminately, but to one particular Angel; That the Person so designated is also called the Son of God, the Mighty God.

Wow, what a breakthrough! I read the paragraph several times and concluded that the angel of the Lord was "the Son of God, the mighty God, the preincarnate Jesus."

I jumped in a taxi to go home to call Mrs. Summons and share my findings. Mrs. Summons agreed with my analysis and concurred with Mr. Charles Hodge that the angel of the Lord is the person Son of God. Mrs. Summons referred me to the books of Micah and John.

Now that I had established that the angel of the Lord was the second person of the Trinity, I was determined to know more about Him.

I followed Mrs. Summons's suggestion and found that Micah 5:2 communicated God's promise that the ruler whom He would send to the world would have both (1) a human origin, born in Bethlehem (i.e., a Jewish background and a description that fits Jesus's birth town), and (2) a divine origin, the deity who existed "from of old, from ancient times," that is, everlasting, a detail that fit with God the Son. These two verses fit the description of the Messiah because, according to the scriptures, only a Jewish

Messiah from everlasting and of the lineage of King David could be ruler of Israel.

Jesus Fulfilled Prophecies
In verse John 8:58, Jesus confirmed two critical realities:

a) His divinity
   Jesus identified Himself as the "I Am." Jesus used the same name, "I am who I am," God had told Moses in Exodus 3:14.
b) His origin
   Jesus was present before the world was created and witnessed Abraham's life.

One of the most significant aha moments that happened while I was studying the Trinity was when I read John 1:1–3, 14. I found that the verses in John 1:1–3 echoed the opening of the book of Genesis, 1:1–2. By linking these verses together, I understood that the Holy Spirit revealed to the apostle John Jesus's divine identity as the *Word*. He is God the Son, with whom God the Father was speaking to in Genesis 1:26–27 and through whom He created the world alongside God the Spirit. As a result, I concluded that in the Old Testament period, the preincarnated God the Son appeared to people as the angel of the Lord. In the New Testament, the angel of the Lord came to earth as the incarnated God in the flesh—Jesus (John 1:14).

From John 1:1–3, I understood that in the beginning, God the Son was with God the Father and that God the Son was God, through whom all things were made; without God the Son, nothing was made that has been made.

I held the belief that the second person of the Trinity made preincarnate appearances in Old Testament times and appeared as the incarnated God in the New Testament as Jesus. I could not contain my joy at finally confirming my childhood belief that Jesus—my Seigneur Dieu—*is* God!

The New Testament clearly defines the relationship between the Word—God the Son, Jesus—and God the Father (John 8:28, 12:49–50, 14:10; Matthew 11:27).

I grew up in a culture that believes that we human beings are God's creation and descendants of Adam (in Arabic, Beni Adam). The Bible explains that God *brought each of us into existence* and loves us and looks after us with a fatherly care and love (Genesis 1:26–27; 1 John 3:1; Matthew 18:12–14). The Bible goes one step further and sheds light on a whole different level of relationship with God by becoming children of God through Christ. He is *begotten* as in John 3:16.

I wondered why the scriptures say that God *created* Adam and humankind and has *begotten* Jesus. What is the difference? C. S. Lewis in *Mere Christianity* gave me the best answer:

> To beget is to become the father of. To create is to make. And the difference is this. When you beget, you beget something of the same kind as yourself. A man begets human babies, a beaver begets little beavers, and a bird begets eggs, which turn into little birds. But when you make, you make something of a different kind from yourself. A bird makes a nest, a beaver builds a dam, a man makes wireless set—or he may make something more like himself than a wireless set: say, a statue (that may be looking very much like himself). But, of course, [the statue] is not a real man, it only looks like one. It cannot breathe or think. It is not alive.
>
> What God begets is God [i.e., what God the Father begets is God, something of the same kind

as Himself] just as what man begets is a man. What God creates is not God; just as what man makes is not man. That is why men are not sons of God in the sense that Christ is.

The Third Person of the Trinity—the Holy Spirit
When I first converted, I occasionally heard people in the church say, "The Lord spoke to me." I wondered what they meant, but I was too embarrassed to ask. Also, I was suspicious of people claiming to have heard from God. In Islamic belief, Allah spoke directly only to prophets and gave revelations through dreams to people—and that was limited. The Qur'an does not mention that Allah spoke (or will speak) casually to people. Instead, Allah warned about the Jinn (Satan) filtering in people's minds, whispering into their hearts, and leading them to believe they had heard from Allah. I never heard anyone in my family saying that Allah had spoken to them. For that reason, I doubted the faith of everyone claiming that God had spoken to them. I even distanced myself from them until I learned from the scriptures that God does indeed speak to His followers through the Holy Spirit!

While God the Son appeared to people as the angel of the Lord, God the Spirit manifested as Yahweh's/God's Spirit, the Spirit of the Lord, or the Holy Spirit. Having the same characteristics, nature, and personality as God the Father and God the Son, the Holy Spirit is referred to in the Bible as "He," not as "It."

Genesis 1:2 is where we find the first mention of the Holy Spirit, and Genesis 1:26 provides strong evidence that the three persons of the Trinity were present and participated in the creation of the world.

> *Note:* The use of the plural pronoun *us* in Genesis 1:26 describes the presence of three persons in one God and wipes out the concept of the plurality of majesty, as some claim.

Also, Psalm 33:6 proves the active participation of God the Son and of the Holy Spirit in the world's creation process.

In my mind, Deuteronomy 6:4, better than anything else, attests to the doctrine of the Trinity in one God: "Hear, O Israel: The Lord our God, the Lord is one." This is a declaration that Jesus repeated in Mark 12:29 to confirm the Godhead as *one* God. I also noticed that the apostle Peter in Acts 5:3–4 referred to the Holy Spirit not only as a person of the Godhead but also as God. Psalm 139:7–10 is another proof of the omnipresent person of the Holy Spirit, while 1 Corinthians 2:10 declares Him omniscient, and Luke 1:35 says He is omnipotent. Last but not least, the prophets acknowledged that what they spoke to people and prophesied, it was inspired by the Holy Spirit (2 Timothy 3:16; 2 Peter 1:20–21).

The relationship between the three persons of the Trinity is visible and clear in many verses, such as the following (to name a few):

- **1 Corinthians 12:4–6**
  "There are different kinds of gifts, but the same Spirit distributes them. There are different kinds of service, but the same Lord. There are different kinds of working, but in all of them and in everyone it is the same God at work."
- **Ephesians 1:13–14**
  "And you also were included in Christ when you heard the message of truth, the gospel of your salvation. When you believed, you were marked in him with a seal, the promised Holy Spirit, who is a deposit guaranteeing our

inheritance until the redemption of those who are God's possession—to the praise of his glory."
- **Ephesians 4:4–6**
"There is one body and one Spirit, just as you were called to one hope when you were called; one Lord, one faith, one baptism; one God and Father of all, who is over all and through all and in all."
- **Jude 20–21**
"But you, dear friends, by building yourselves up in your most holy faith and praying in the Holy Spirit, keep yourselves in God's love as you wait for the mercy of our Lord Jesus Christ to bring you to eternal life."

I was thrilled with my learning and findings, and I was eager to share them with the group. I knew in my heart that they were a drop in the ocean. I cannot say that I understand the Trinity, but I candidly can say that I believe in the Trinity.

During my preparation for the meeting with the group, I came across John 14:28. The verse threw me into confusion, derailing my writing. What did Jesus mean by saying that God the Father is greater than He, when the scriptures say they are equal?

The confusion over this verse caused me to miss a couple of nights of sleep, wondering about its meaning, until I spoke with Mrs. Summons. She explained that while the three persons are equal in divine characteristics and nature (for they are one God), each has a unique and distinct function. "But, Mrs. Summons," I apprehensively interjected, "the verse indicates the presence of some ranking in the Trinity for Jesus to say that the Father is greater than He." Mrs. Summons explained that the answer to my question lay within the nature of the Incarnation. She explained that during the Incarnation, Jesus, God the Son, took on human flesh. She also warned me of a form of heresy called subordinationism. Huh? What? I could hardly pronounce the word. Mrs. Summons stressed that there are *no* ranks or subordination among the three persons of the Trinity. She reiterated that while they are equal in nature of the one God, each person takes on different roles, some of which *may* seem subordinate to others. She referred to Genesis 1:1–2, 26–27; John 1:1–3; and Colossians 1:15–17, among other verses. When I studied these scriptures, I saw God's manifestation in the planner and commander's role in the creation and salvation of the world. At the same time, God the Son was the Means and the achiever of the Father's plans, and God the Spirit was the communicator between the Godhead and humankind.

Reading the Bible became more exciting as I managed to identify other evidence for diversity-in-unity, the plurality in the Godhead. For example:

1. Matthew 3:16–18 and Luke 3:21–22 state the presence of the plurality of the Trinity. In these two scriptures, the Godhead manifests in different roles: (a) God the Father revealed as the Voice, (b) God the Son revealed as Jesus, Son of Man, and (c) God the Spirit manifested as the dove.
2. John 14:16–17 and John 15:26 declare the presence and the different roles of the persons of the Godhead.
3. John 14:7–9 offers a strong testimony of Jesus's deity when one of Jesus's disciples, Philip, asks Jesus to show him God the Father. Jesus replies as follows:

> Anyone who has seen me has seen the Father. How can you say, "Show us the Father"? Don't you believe that I am in the Father, and that the Father is in me? The words I say to you I do not speak on my own authority. Rather, it is the Father, living in me, who is doing his work. Believe me when I say that I am in the Father and the Father is in me; or at least believe on the evidence of the works themselves.

Appendix A illustrates the diversity-in-unity within the Godhead, where the scriptures affirm the equality of divine nature of each of the three persons of the Trinity while preserving their distinct personhood.

You may find the Trinity confusing. Yes! It is confusing and complicated. Listen to what the theologian John Wesley is quoted as having said: "Bring me a worm that can comprehend a man, and then I will show you a man that can comprehend the triune God!"

I thought a lot about John Wesley's statement. Can a worm understand humankind, who is created in the image of God? Impossible! I understood from the theologian John Wesley that the Trinity is one of God's mysteries that *no* human being can fully comprehend. I will also add that it is not easy to understand all things of God.

Having said that, I would like to caution that this does not mean that we cannot comprehend God and that He is shrouded in mystery. I think it is wrong to say that God is unknowable or incomprehensible. That is not the God I came to know from the scriptures. While studying the Bible, I learned that God wants me (and you) to know Him intimately and to have a relationship and to fellowship with Him. However, it is true that God—for reasons He alone knows—has hidden things from us, for it is written, "The secret things belong to the Lord our God" (Deuteronomy. 29:29). Perhaps the human mind cannot bear all knowledge about the Godhead (John 16:12 ESV).

Nevertheless, God loves to reveal Himself to us through the sweet whisper of His Holy Spirit in our hearts. By the grace of God, God gives us the ability to grow in our knowledge through faith and according to the measure of our faith. For me, faith is like muscles. The more we exercise, the more we develop and strengthen our muscles. The same logic is true for faith. The more I study the Word of God, the more I strengthen my faith and the more I develop knowledge. Faith enables me to believe in the Trinity, God in three persons, in one essence.

Above all, do I need proof of Jesus's deity? Do I need proof of the Trinity? God forbid! Absolutely not! I call it pure faith, and I stress that it is not blind faith. More importantly, I do not apologize for my belief in the doctrine of the Trinity.

Summary

The more I researched the Trinity, the more it captivated me. I found it as one of God's most beautiful, intriguing, fascinating mysteries and a mind-boggling paradox. I quickly realized that understanding the Trinity is beyond the boundaries of my finite mind, as it is impossible to grasp God's infinite mind. Learning about the Trinity changed how I studied the Word of God. I started to look at the scriptures in the new light of the Godhead. Also, studying the Trinity convinced me that *Christianity is monotheistic, contrary to all false claims.*

In response to the questions I addressed earlier about Genesis 1:26–27 and 3:22, "Who was God speaking to about making humankind?" and "Who was in God's presence?" I candidly admit that the dialogue occurred among God the Father, God the Son, and God the Spirit. God the Father used the first-person plural pronoun (*us*) and kept *image* and *likeness* in the singular form, thus emphasizing that the three persons of the Godhead share the same nature and character as one God. The scriptures in both the Old Testament and the New Testament speak of the one living and true God who is the Creator of heaven and earth.

The Old Testament foretold the incarnation of God the Son as a man. The Old Testament attests to the appearance of God among the people as the preincarnate God the Son. The New Testament testifies that God the Son manifested on earth as the Son of Man, Jesus. The scriptures provide compelling testimony of Jesus's divine identity as God and foretell of His Second Coming at the end of time.

Finally, I define the Godhead within the Trinity as one and only one God—one Creator—who eternally exists in three persons: the Father, the Son, and the Holy Spirit. The three persons are distinct yet are coequal and coeternal, having precisely the same nature and attributes and being worthy of the same worship and obedience.

> *Note:* I believe that God the Father is the Creator and the *Source* of heaven, all the earth, and all life. I believe in Jesus Christ, the *Word*, the *Means* through whom God the Father created all things. Without Him, nothing was made that is made. I believe in the Holy Spirit as the *Spirit* of God and Christ (Ephesians 4:6; 1 Corinthians 8:6; Galatians 4:6).

26
DISCOVERY JOURNEY TO GOD THE FATHER

> Note: Unless otherwise mentioned, when I refer to God, I am referring to the Godhead: God the Father, God the Son, and God the Holy Spirit. The three persons of the Godhead are one God.

To fall in love with God is the greatest romance; to seek him the greatest adventure; to find him, the greatest human achievement.

—Saint Augustine of Hippo

The Lord's Prayer

As a person born into a Muslim family, I must pray to one and only one Allah. "There is no God but Allah." Islam forbids ascribing human physical characteristics to Allah. Therefore, addressing Allah as Father is blasphemy. Islam does not consider human beings as children of the Almighty but as 'Abd' (ع ب د), or a slave of Allah, with whom humankind cannot attain any degree of intimacy. The attribute "father" is not one of the ninety-nine attributes of Allah, nor does the relationship of father–child exist in Islamic theology.

One day, I asked my sister if we were children of Allah. She scolded me and reminded me that calling Allah "Father" is committing blasphemy. She warned me never to compare Islam with Christianity. Therefore, I concluded, we Muslims could not have a personal relationship with the Creator. Being a slave to Allah is humankind's highest honor.

Unfortunately, my sister's response stemmed from her misunderstanding of the metaphor embedded in the name. God chose this term *metaphorically* to say that He loves us with the fatherly love one has for a child.

As I read the Bible, I found that on many occasions, God spoke in figures speech and parables to emphasize an essential point or to call our attention to complex messages. At first, I had a hard time deciphering the metaphors. On many occasions, my misinterpretation of the messages embedded in the metaphors or parables misled me from seeing the truth. Dr. Kendall's sermons and teaching made me conscious of the need to correctly understand God's figurative language to get the essence of the point that God wants to convey. Otherwise, misinterpreting the figures of speech could lead to my making false claims, to believing the figurative expression literally as a fact. Gradually, I became conscious of God's figurative language in the scriptures so I could discern the message correctly.

I know some people who rejected Christianity on the grounds of heresy because they misinterpreted the figures of speech in the message. I found it disrespectful to refute God's scriptures because one doesn't understand the figurative language or doesn't want to believe it. E. W. Bullinger (1968) wrote:

> Applied to words, a figure [of speech] denotes some form which a word or sentence takes,

> different from its ordinary and natural form. This is always for the purpose of giving additional force, more life, intensified feeling, and greater emphasis ... to add force to the truth conveyed, emphasis to the statement of it, and depth to the meaning of it.

The article "Examples of Figures of Speech Used in the Bible. What Are They, Their Purpose, Recognizing Them ..." (2013) on the Truth or Tradition website expounds on the use of the figures of speech, saying:

> It is not honest biblical interpretation to call something figurative simply because you do not understand it or do not want to believe it. The words in God's Word are perfect. God has a reason for everything He says—where He says it; when He says it; to whom He says it; and how He says it. Figures of speech in the Bible are precise and exact, not haphazard.

One of the metaphors that caused great contention within my family was the addressing of God as "our Father," as in the Lord's Prayer. If God wanted to be called "Father," who am I to question Him or disagree with Him?

As a child, I memorized the Lord's Prayer; I had learned it in kindergarten.[41] I prayed the prayer countless times in spite of not understanding its words. I loved this prayer because it addressed Notre Père,[42] meaning "a father to all people and children," which included me. I turned the prayer into a conversation, talking to

---

[41] With my older sisters, I attended Franciscaine de Marie, a French Catholic school managed and taught by French nuns.
[42] French for "Our Father."

Notre Père, Seigneur Dieu, Papa. I believed that Notre Père / Our Father had the power to comfort me in times of need. His answering of my prayers was enough for me to love the Christian God. Of course, I carried my prayers, my love, and my belief in God the Father in secret in my heart. Otherwise, if my family ever found out, I would be severely punished. And I was!

There I was, decades later as a Christ follower, and my conversion had reignited my passion for the Lord's Prayer. I could not contain my joy when I read Lord's Prayer in Matthew 6:9–13. I admit that I felt unworthy and shy that Jesus would confer upon me such a high and unique privilege as addressing God Almighty as Father. I wanted to know the reasons why God desired to be a Father to His creation.

I started with Genesis. My curiosity swelled while reading the first chapters. I began to discover God the Creator. I knew the basics of God's creation from the movies, but I did not know who God was.

The book of Genesis provided me a window onto the dramatic Creation stage, where God performed the creation of the universe and of the human race. I was eager to know why God created humankind. For what purpose? I wondered if the connection between Jesus and the creation of physical human beings was the underlying reason.

God's Purpose for Creating Humankind
When I asked June, my friend from the church, why God created humankind, she said, "God created humankind so He could have relationships with them." I paused for a second, thinking about what she had said.

"June," I replied, "I have heard and read this answer from many sources, but honestly, I am not convinced simply because, in my mind, the verb *to have* underlines a *need*. This may be true for humans as we *need* human interaction and relationships as part of our survival and sustainability. But God? No way."

Immediately two questions popped into my mind:

First, does God "need" or lack something that humankind alone fulfills? Definitely not! God is the Creator of humankind and of all visible and invisible things in the universe. The human mind and all of today's and the future's technology cannot fathom the perfection and completeness in everything God has created. King Solomon wrote in Ecclesiastes 8:17, "No one can comprehend what goes on under the sun. Despite all their efforts to search it out, no one can discover its meaning. Even if the wise claim they know, they cannot really comprehend it." Also, Acts 17:24–25 reads, "The God who made the world and everything in it is the Lord of heaven and earth. ... And he is not served by human hands, as if he needed anything." Therefore, God lacks nothing.

Second, did God make humankind because He was lonely or alone? Absolutely not. God was never alone. He exists eternally in three distinct persons—the Father, the Son, and the Holy Spirit. The persons within the Trinity have an eternal fellowship with one another.

I was confident that there must be something more to why God created humankind. What was God's purpose for creating me? I kept praying for God's revelation, until one day, when I was studying Isaiah 43:1–7, I sensed that verse 7 might lead me to the answer: "Everyone who is called by my [God's] name, whom I created *for my glory*, whom I formed and made" (emphasis added).

I gathered from verse 7 that God created humankind for *His glory*. What is the glory of God? How does God manifest His glory? How can I, as a believer, glorify God?

I went deeper into Isaiah 43:1–7 and Ephesians 1:3–6, along with studying the epistles of the apostle John. I identified two key points:

1) Love Is the Heart of God's Glory

My childhood trauma sucked the love from my heart. As a defense mechanism, throughout my adult life, I expelled love from my life. So, reading about God's love was not easy for me. God's Word about His love for me entered my head, not my heart. How could God love me? I felt dirty and guilty about what had happened to me as a child. I did not allow God to love me because I felt unworthy of His love. Over time, through the gradual work of the Holy Spirit within me, something changed in me. Part of me wanted to taste God's love. But at the slightest attempt, quickly my stony heart shut down, froze my mind, and aborted the effort. I was fearful of getting hurt and especially afraid of failing to love God back.

For a few years, I struggled with God's love. Then one day, I had a vision where I was the prodigal child returning home. A powerful tingling came over my entire body as I entered the house and was greeted with open arms. I did not see the face of the greeter, but I sensed He was mighty. The moment His arms wrapped around my shoulders, a geyser-like blast of intense warmth raced through my veins. The greeter's warmth and kindness surprised me. Still, I was uncomfortable because He was too close to me; I did not want Him to see my brokenness. "No, no, don't touch my heart," I moaned, trembling. He silenced my fear. Then, suddenly, I felt powerless, yielding, and amazingly safe. My arms fell to my sides while my head rested on His chest. I sobbed my pain and poured my heart out for a long time, until my cries slowed into sniffles. I went quiet and still. Lo and behold, the greeter's hand went through my chest, unplucked my heart from its chamber, and put in a new one. I gasped for air.

For the first time, the scriptures that spoke about God's love came alive and entered my heart! For the first time, I tasted God's love! Wow, God loves me; He truly loves me! God filled the new heart with His love and the ability to love others. The vision ended with a climax when the greeter whispered in my new heart that for His glory, God's love and grace had redeemed me! What did He mean? Every fiber in me radiated with God's love. A soft breeze rolled over me and triggered a domino effect, changing my skin from lizard scales to human skin. I closed my eyes and took a deep breath, inhaling God's love inside my being.

When I opened my eyes, I was sad that the vision had ended. I sat tranquil, soaking in the power of God's love and taking in every word the greeter had said about God's love, grace, and redemption. The experience of God's love reminded me of His promise: "I will give you a new heart and put a new spirit in you; I will remove from you your heart of stone and give you a heart of flesh" (Ezekiel 36:26).

Following the vision, which I called a spiritual heart transplant, I started to enjoy the new feeling of love that had been birthed inside me. Scales of indifference and blindness fell from my eyes. Gradually, God's Word of love began to penetrate my heart.

I marveled at the knowledge that not only does God love me, but also He loved me *first*. He knew me intimately before the foundation of the world and fashioned all the days of my life before He created me. God's love is personal—custom made—for my needs. Above all, He calls me the apple of His eye and precious in His sight and shows me His kindness. I reflected on 1 John 4:19; Job 10:10–12; Psalm 139:13–16; Zechariah 2:8; ad Isaiah 43:1–4. Wow! These scriptures blew me away, because in them I found "such knowledge ... too wonderful for me, too lofty for me to attain" (Psalm 139:6). It was a moment of victory; I finally had found the love I had searching for, for my entire life.

I tasted God's love and found it unmatched by any human love, especially given that He loved me so much that He sacrificed Himself for me and died in my place. I stand in awe before such love. Sometimes I find it to be beyond my human comprehension.

When people ask me how I can be sure of God's love, I refer them to Psalm 103 (GNT), Psalm 145, 1 John 4:16, 18–19, and Jeremiah 29:11 so they will see the undeniable truth. And when they ask why God loves, I tell them of the most significant fact, that "God is love" (1 John 4:16), citing, "God demonstrates His own love for us in this: while we were still sinners, Christ died for us" (Romans 5:8). I wonder if love is the heart of other religions as it is in Christianity.

Given my trust in my salvation through my faith in Jesus Christ and the fact that "I have been crucified with Christ and I no longer live, but Christ lives in me. The life I now live in the body, I live by faith in the Son of God, who loved me and gave himself for me" (Galatians 2:20), I know that God loves me as His own. He delights in me as a father rejoices over his child. I rest in God's promise that "neither death nor life, neither angels nor demons, neither the present nor the future, nor any powers, neither height nor depth, nor anything else in all creation, will be able to separate [me] from the love of God that is in Christ our Lord" (Romans 8:38–39). I am confident that God sealed me with His promise and that He loves me "with an everlasting love."[43] So, how does God manifest His glory? Through love. How I glorify God? Through loving others, including my enemies.

In short, I found out that love is the essence of God's character and nature and is central to His glory.

2) Grace Is the Heart of God's Glory

I was intrigued by Moses's request to God to see His glory (Exodus 33:18) and wondered if I could make a similar request to witness the manifestation of God's glory. At first, I got scared, unsure that I, an unworthy person and a new convert, would be allowed to make such a petition to God. But one weekend, I worked up my courage and made the bold request to God to show me His glory. Not knowing what to expect, I waited patiently.

Around that time, the environment at the building where I lived suddenly changed. I found myself wrongfully accused. As

---

[43] Jeremiah 31:3 (ESV).

a result, hurtful rumors were spread about me. It was the darkest time of my life, I ran to God, pleading for His forgiveness, as I believed that my bold request to show me His glory had flared up His anger against me. I blamed myself for the destructive manifestations of God's wrath against me. Fear of God had pinned me to my knees, praying with all my might. I can't ever remember praying so hard for anything. I will never be able to put in words my fear of God's rejection when I most needed Him. The fear of losing my job and my reputation was negligible when compared to my fear of damaging my relationship with God. As the apostle Paul commanded in 1 Thessalonians 5:17, I prayed continually for God to manifest His grace and to forgive me and vindicate me (Romans 12:19).[44]

Weeks rolled into months of hard times. God kept my mouth shut. The injustice I endured was excruciating. I was helpless to defend myself or clearing my name of the false accusations. Reading Dr. R. T. Kendall's *God Meant It for Good* (1998) directed me to let God deal with the matter. Dr. Kendall wrote:

> If you are a child of God and you have been hurt by being falsely accused, God feels more deeply about it than you do, but if you try to defend yourself, he will back off. I promise you, you will find yourself in the biggest mess and in the deepest trouble. If anything, it will be worse than ever. But if you will only be quiet, say nothing, and to not try to manipulate the situation, God will be moved, and he will act. God loves to do that. (p. 54)

After long months of my persistent praying, God gloriously

---

[44] "Do not take revenge, my dear friends, but leave room for God's wrath, for it is written: 'It is mine to avenge; I will repay,' says the Lord."

stepped in! Breakthroughs started to come my way. I candidly say here that I witnessed God's grace displaying miracles before my eyes. God not only protected me but also cleared my name. By His grace, God manifested His glory in His perfect timing and in His perfect way; he cleared my name, defeated my accusers, and put them to shame, thereby demonstrating His justice.

Dr. R. T. Kendall (2000) explains: "Any manifestation of God's glory will be a manifestation of Himself. ... The most noble and God-honouring request we can make is to ask God to manifest His glory." What a relief! By His grace and for His glory, God answered my prayer to show me His glory. Hallelujah! From that experience, I learned to ask God to manifest His glory in everything I do as I wait eagerly to see His power. Equally, in everything I do, I learned to give glory to God.

Dr. Martyn Lloyds-Jones (1939) wrote: "Man's chief business in life is to serve and to glorify God. That is why the gift of life has been given to him. That is why we are here on earth."

My friend once cautioned me that by glorifying God, we do not make Him more glorious.

John MacArthur (1983) wrote in *Worship: The Ultimate Priority*:

> God is the only being in all existence who can be said to possess inherent glory. We do not give it to Him; it is His by virtue of who He is. If no one ever gave God any praise [or glorified Him], He would still be the glorious God that He is because He was glorious before any beings were created to worship Him. ... God's glory is essential to His nature; it cannot be taken away; it cannot be added to it. It is total glory that cannot be diminished. His glory is His being—simply the sum of what He is, regardless of what we do or do not do it in recognition of it. (166)

By His grace, God bestowed on me the privilege to be saved as His child to see His glory and to glorify Him. Psalm 29:1–2 reads, "Ascribe to the Lord, you heavenly beings, ascribe to the Lord glory and strength. Ascribe to the Lord the glory due his name."

Out of His love, God created humankind, with whom He wanted to have a father-child relationship. Understanding God's figurative language enlightened my spiritual perception of God as the Father. Full of adoration and humility, I cry out to God, "What is mankind that you are mindful of them, human beings that you care for them?" (Psalm 8:4).

Throughout the Bible, I found love to be the supreme and dominant attribute of God. God demonstrated His love by creating humankind. He said in Genesis 1:26–27, "Let us make mankind in our image, in our likeness …. So, God created mankind in his own image, in the image of God, he created them; male and female he created them." And, "Then the Lord God formed a man from the dust of the ground and breathed into his nostrils the breath of life, and the man became a living being" (Genesis 2:7). These verses motivated me to learn about God's creation of humankind, His purpose. Does today's human world fulfill God's plan? My studies took me back to Adam.

Adam, the First Creation

The first man whom God created was Adam. God created Adam from the dust of the ground. He personally "breathed into his nostrils the breath of life, and the man [Adam took a bodily form] became a living being" (Genesis 2:7). You may find it funny that I poured loads of questions onto God, one of which—Why did He create human beings in a bodily form different from animals and vegetation?—I wanted to highlight the truth of God's creation theory vs. the evolution gobbledygook. So, I researched it and found Dr. H. Morris (1990) explaining as follows:

> There is something about the human body ... which is uniquely appropriate to God's manifestation of Himself, and (since God knows all His works from the beginning of the world [Acts 15:18]), He must have designed man's body with this in mind. Accordingly, He designed it, not like animals, but with an erect posture, with an upward gazing countenance, capable of facial expressions corresponding with emotional feelings, and with a brain and tongue capable of articulate, symbolic speech. He knew, of course, that in the fulness of time, He would become a man. (74)

R. Grigg (1990) added, "God made Man in that bodily form which He Himself would one day assume—the form in which He wished to reveal Himself [to the world]."

Also, the fact that God instilled within Adam and Eve characteristics to display His nature and reflect His glory showed me that God honored humanity. God created humankind as superior to animals. The more I read about God's creation of humankind, the more I concluded that human beings could not be descendants of animals. I liked the description of R. Grigg (1994) of God's creation of humankind, where he emphasized the following:

> Man is not a close cousin of the animals, nor a distant relative of primitive plant life, nor a product of slime. Rather, he is someone great, wonderful and different, the most excellent of all God's works, and a special expression of the divine nature, created by God's own personal activity. God introduces him with solemnity, dignity, and the honour of an intimate deliberation on the part

of the Godhead. Although man was formed from the dust of the ground, God personally "breathed into his nostrils the breath of life; and man became a living soul" (Genesis 2:7 KJV). Man's life is thus, not the result of the spontaneous reorganization of molecules within his body, nor is it derived by evolution from any animal or "lower hominid" (as theistic evolutionists teach) but is a direct gift from God. This is further emphasized in the Bible by Luke's genealogy of Adam, where he designates Adam as being not the son of an anthropoid ape, but "the son of God" (Luke 3:38).

My research led me to remove the theory of evolution from my mind once and for all. When God created Adam, He made him after His image and likeness. He gave him a unique privilege of "sonship" (again, as a metaphor). The apostle Luke lists Adam as "son of God" for being the first offspring of God *by creation* (Luke 3:38). I want to stress that the meaning of "son of God" is utterly contrary to what some people's wild imaginations may assume and believe. For example, for some people, the term "son of God" is blasphemous merely because they find it unthinkable for God to bear a child. I totally agree! Yes, it is inconceivable for God to have a child because God is Spirit. I also believe that taking the term word for word is indeed blasphemous, even to Christian believers. The truth of the matter is that God chose this term to say *metaphorically* that He loved Adam with a fatherly love toward a child. And this is true for all of us.

Adam and Eve's story captivated me more so for their being my very first parents! In my mind, I visualized what it must be like to live in the presence of God, communing and fellowshipping with Him as Adam and Eve did. From the scriptures, I gathered that Adam knew that God was the Almighty, the Creator of the universe, who had created him from dust. Both Adam and Eve stood fear-free and guilt-free before God. There was no struggle for equality; there was divine order. Genesis 1:28–30 sheds light on their lives:

> God blessed them and said to them, "Be fruitful and increase in number; fill the earth and subdue it. Rule over the fish in the sea and the birds in the sky and over every living creature that moves on the ground."
>
> Then God said, "I give you every seed-bearing plant on the face of the whole earth and every tree that has fruit with seed in it. They will be yours for food. And to all the beasts of the earth and all the birds in the sky and all the creatures that move along the ground—everything that has the breath of life in it—I give every green plant for food." And it was so.

Wow, God created everything for humankind! I echo David's admiration of God: "What is mankind that you are mindful of them, human beings that you care for them?" (Psalm 8:4). Also, the scriptures showed me that God gave Adam and Eve some of His character and attributes. Therefore, they were in complete alignment with God. They were made "*in*" God's image and "*after*" His likeness (Genesis 1:26 KJV).

From the first two chapters of Genesis, I had many questions: How could God have an image since He is a spirit? Why would God give humankind His image and likeness knowing that humans would sin? How could a sinful and mortal person have a divine and eternal image and likeness? Where would the image and likeness of God reside, in the soul of the person, in his or her spirit, or in his or her body?

The first thing that caught my eye while reading Genesis

1:26 was that God used two different prepositions to describe His creation plan for humankind. Genesis 1:26 reads, "Let us make man *in* our image, *after* our likeness" (KJV). I concluded the following:

a) *Image* and *likeness* are not alike.
b) The preposition *after* means something we cultivate in our walk with God while living on earth for our afterlife.
c) What did God want me to know? Are God's image and likeness available to all?

M. Erickson (1998) wrote, "The image of God in humanity is critical to our understanding of what makes us human."

When I explored the meaning of "in the image of God" and "after the likeness of God," I found that God instilled in Adam and Eve godly characteristics and qualities that reflected His attributes. I learned from the scriptures that God's attributes are those characteristics that help us to understand who God is. God's attributes (to name a few) are eternity, goodness, holiness, immanence, immutability, justice, love, mercy, omnipotence, omnipresence, omniscience, righteousness, self-existence, sovereignty, and transcendence.

God's attributes gave Adam and Eve the spiritual and physical ability to walk with God and to perform their daily activities. As per the scriptures, their duties were to work, to exercise authority, to demonstrate obedience to God, and to build future generations (Genesis 1:27). This is also applicable to us.

Some of the critical characteristics of God's image and likeness that God wants us to display in our daily lives are holiness, faithfulness, graciousness, mercy, compassion, and love.

While living on earth, Jesus modeled these characteristics, demonstrating a total surrendering to the Father's will and glorifying God the Father. Although Jesus conducted miracles and people recognized Him as the "Messiah, the Son of the living

God,"[45] He still chose to give God the Father the glory instead of seeking His own glory.

The fact that God planned to extend to humankind, including me, His attributes and nature humbled me. Since the time I realized this, I have gained new attitudes beaming with hope and new abilities for my walk with God. The key lesson I learned was that only by reflecting these characteristics in everything I do, do I glorify God.

Unfortunately, to adopt God's nature and attributes and reflect them in everything I do is easier said than done. For example, before my conversion, loving others was outside my instinct and capabilities. Until I believed by faith in the life and death of Jesus and of the cleansing of my sins by the shed blood of Jesus and His resurrection, living by God's standards and loving others was impossible.

Walking with God meant that I had to allow God to reshape my nature and character. I felt as if God placed me in a washing machine running a repeat cleansing cycle. The more God cleansed me, the more I changed and the more I glorified God. I clung onto the hope of gaining God's likeness when I die and am resurrected with all believers, becoming a partaker of eternal life in God's presence. The verses John 3:16 and 1 Corinthians 15:35–58 are my assurance for resurrecting with a timeless Christlike image and likeness. Hallelujah!

In one of the corners in Oxford Circus, there was a man who distributed flash cards and shouted. "God is a spirit, infinite, eternal, and unchangeable in His being, wisdom, power, holiness, justice, goodness, and truth." How true!

---

[45] Matthew 16:16.

> *Note:* It is important to note that there are several other characteristics that are unique to God and that He did not share with humanity, such as omnipresence, omnipotence, omniscience, and self-existence.

Adam's Fall

I often wonder what the world would be like if Adam and Eve had not sinned. I also wonder what Adam and Eve's life looked like in the Garden of Eden when God created them. I imagine them as radiant for being sin-free, shame-free, guilt-free, and worry-free, living on holy ground in God's presence, reflecting God's image and likeness in nature and character, enjoying direct access and an intimate fellowship with God. What bliss! They lacked nothing; God gave them everything they could ever possibly want or desire for what I call a blissful life. The environment in which they lived was perfect as God pronounced it "very good" (Genesis 1:31).

Then, one fateful incident happened, and everything changed. The serpent, Satan,[46] fooled Eve by twisting God's Word with a lie that she would become like God if she ate the fruit from the tree of knowledge, the only tree from which God clearly forbade Adam and Eve to eat. Motivated by the false promise and a blind ambition to be like God, Eve chose to believe Satan's lie and disregard God's warning. She ate the fruit and led Adam to eat it too. Consequently, Satan's spirit of sin against God—the "sinful nature"—entered Adam's and Eve's souls and spirits. The sinful nature had dire consequences for Adam and Eve:

---

[46] As described in the next sections, Satan had previously rebelled against God and was expelled from heaven. Since then, he aims to take revenge on God's children, enticing them to rebel against God by sinning, because he knows that God hates sin. In other words, he kills people spiritually.

- They lost the likeness of God.
- Their God-given image was defiled and tarnished.
- Sin became a separating barrier between them and God.
- Their free access to, and fellowship with, God broke down.
- Their godly spirits died; they no longer heard the voice of God.
- They lost the privilege of eternal life with God, decreed physical death. God executed His warning, which they ignored: "You are free to eat from any tree in the garden, but *you must not eat* from the tree of the knowledge of good and evil, for when you eat from it *you will certainly die*" (Genesis 2:16–17; emphasis added).

Unfortunately, these bullet points describe my spiritual condition before conversion.

God expelled both Adam and Eve from His presence and cast them out of the Garden of Eden. God is holy and does not allow iniquities in His presence. Eve's ambition to be like God drove her to believe Satan's lie and disobey God.

Wow. "Wasn't that a harsh statement, O God?" I cried one day to the Lord. "What is it in sin that You hate so much that You decreed physical and eternal death?"

Adam and Eve's obedience to the serpent (evil) infected them with sin in the very core of their being. Because God is holy, He could not look upon sin; He could no longer commune with imperfect and blemished souls. Consequently, He expelled them from the garden and from His presence because of their conscious disobedience against Him. God's original plan to have a relationship with humans could have ended. The knowledge that Adam and Eve had transferred the tendency to sin to their descendants, the entire human race, throughout the ages threw me into an abyss of fear.

Why God Hates Sin

God hates sin because it is against His holy and righteous nature. There is nothing like God's holiness; it is God's most sublime attribute. Throughout the Bible, God describes His holiness and demands His followers to be holy. For example, God's instructions to Moses were as follows:

> I am the Lord your God; consecrate yourselves and be holy, because I am holy. Do not make yourselves unclean by any creature that moves along the ground. I am the Lord, who brought you up out of Egypt to be your God; therefore be holy, because I am holy. (Leviticus 11:44–45)

There is no way my finite mind can fully grasp the grandeur of God's majestic holiness.

God's original plan for Creation was (and still is) to give us, the human race, the privilege to have intimate and eternal fellowship with Him, to be bonded with Him in love, to reflect His glory, holiness, righteousness, love, and power, and to live in His presence eternally. In contrast, Satan's original plan was (and still is) to take revenge against God by enticing humankind to follow him and worship him instead of worshipping God. How? By using the same strategy he used with Eve: subtly twisting our minds and leading us to live by the world's standards instead of God's, thus luring us to sin against God. Boy, did I fall into this trap! I witnessed how in the world the wrong became right and vice versa.

The prophet Samuel addressed God: "There is no one holy like the Lord" (1 Samuel 2:2). The scriptures throughout the Bible emphasize God's holiness. God's holiness reflects His moral perfection. God made clear that an imperfect, defiled, and sinful nature cannot be in His presence. For this reason, God hates sin because it separates us from Him (Isaiah 59:2) and disconnects our fellowship with Him. The absence of fellowship with God leads our spirits to die. As a result, we lose sight of God's will for our lives; we derail from the lives for which we were created and originally intended to have. So, why does God hate sin? I went back to the Bible and found sin described as immoral, evil, and offensive conduct, practices, or actions that twist or break the law of God.

The psalmist explained why God hates sin by saying, "For you are not a God who is pleased with wickedness; with you, evil people are not welcome" (Psalm 5:4). King Solomon summed up the sins that God hates: "There are six things that the Lord hates, seven that are an abomination to him: haughty eyes, a lying tongue, and hands that shed innocent blood, a heart that devises wicked plans, feet that make haste to run to evil, a false witness who breathes out lies, and one who sows discord among brothers" (Proverbs 6:16–19 ESV).

I grieved at the knowledge that Adam's and Eve's "sinful nature" had impacted all of humanity. The consequences of their fall, their sinful traits, became hereditary and were passed through their DNA to their descendants. From one generation to another, through the centuries, sin has corrupted the whole population of our world to our present time (Romans 5:12). Because of the sinful nature, humankind holds the attitude of a predisposition to do wrong, an inclination toward evil.

In 2009, I went back to college to earn a degree in early childhood education and psychological development. We studied children's characteristics inherited from parents and past generations. My interest in DNA expanded to explore the sinful nature carried in the DNA. I found that scientists confirm that DNA holds the traits and temperaments from generation to generation. Interestingly, DNA carries the characteristics that entice us to sin against God's laws.

One day as I was meditating on God's creation process, notably, Genesis 1:26–27, my mind traveled to a similar process when God regenerated me. Father God declared me a new creation upon my confession of Jesus Christ as my Lord and Savior (2 Corinthians 5:17). During the regeneration process,[47] I envisaged that God breathed out through His Holy Spirit and into my nostrils with the breath of the new life. As a result, the DNA of my human spirit was fused with the Holy Spirit's DNA, the two coiling together into one strand. Like a newborn baby becoming a child of the Father of similar DNA, my regenerated spiritual DNA granted me the privilege and honor to have a God-child relationship with my heavenly Father.

With this in mind, I saw a parallel between God's regeneration of believers and the divine creation process where the Holy Spirit fuses and coils together with a regenerated human spirit, thus becoming one and forming a new creation (2 Corinthians 5:17).

Upon God's promise in 2 Corinthians 6:18, "And, I will be a father to you, and you will be my sons and daughters," I built the foundation of my faith. The fatherhood of God filled me with eager anticipation and excitement for the hope of abiding by what was required of me to be His child and experiencing the privileges of being His child.

The more I learn about the essence of sin in my soul and spirit, the more I feel ashamed and regretful. The thought that one day I will stand before the judgment throne of God, looking at all my sins like watching a movie, distresses and scares me most. What excuses will I have when I give an account of my sins? As the apostle Paul said in 2 Corinthians 5:10, "For we must all appear before the judgment seat of Christ, so that each of us may receive what is due us for the things done while in the body, whether good or bad."

O where would I go to hide from God's judgment? Where would I hide? The scriptures warn me that "nothing in all creation

---

[47] Regeneration is a spiritual rebirth, also known as being born again. More on this in chapter 30.

is hidden from God's sight. Everything is uncovered and laid bare before the eyes of him to whom we must give account" (Hebrews 4:13).

When the subject of sin came up in one of the meetings with my group, some of us downplayed the seriousness of sin, calling our sins innocent mistakes and making excuses such as "It wasn't my fault." It was a delicate subject to discuss because each one us claimed to be a decent person, not a sinner. My friend Nabil said that calling someone a sinner is a terrible insult. Mervet added that she was not a sinner because she has not committed any crimes. Jacob criticized us, saying that sin is a pet topic of Christians to preach on although Christians are not perfect. Gretchen pointed out that white lies are not sins if told to save the day. Mrs. Summons listened carefully to our interpretations of sin. When we finished, she asked us if any of us had taken a pencil or a notepad from the office without permission or called in sick to work when we were not sick. "Yes" was the answer. "Then," she said, pointing to all of us, "you sinned." Ouch!

Gretchen asked why we lie even when we do not want to lie. I shared my regrets about things I should not have done. Mervet expressed her regrets for the times she had found herself unintentionally entangled with the wrong crowd and involved in wrongdoing. Mrs. Summons explained that humankind is far from perfect. We all, intentionally or unintentionally, sin, and no one likes to be wrong. Sadly, instead of owning our sin, we come up with all sorts of excuses to downplay the sin. God knows our human weakness. Mrs. Summons read what the apostle Paul wrote:

> I do not understand what I do. For what I want to do I do not do, but what I hate I do. And if I do what I do not want to do, I agree that the law is good. As it is, it is no longer I myself who do it, but it is sin living in me. For I know that

good itself does not dwell in me, that is, in my sinful nature. For I have the desire to do what is good, but I cannot carry it out. For I do not do the good I want to do, but the evil I do not want to do—this I keep on doing. Now if I do what I do not want to do, it is no longer I who do it, but it is sin living in me that does it.

So I find this law at work: Although I want to do good, evil is right there with me. For in my inner being I delight in God's law; but I see another law at work in me, waging war against the law of my mind and making me a prisoner of the law of sin at work within me. What a wretched man I am! Who will rescue me from this body that is subject to death? Thanks be to God, who delivers me through Jesus Christ our Lord! So then, I myself in my mind am a slave to God's law, but in my sinful nature a slave to the law of sin. (Romans 7:15–25)

Then she explained that the wrongdoing that we do is due to the sinful nature DNA that we inherited from Adam. Some people have a tendency, more than others, to do wrong. All we have to do is to watch today's news to be inundated with headlines of crimes and violence and to see how wickedness has powerfully invaded the human heart all across the world.

Nabil asked if there were different degrees of sin, that is, if some were more pardonable than others. Mrs. Summons explained that there is no distinction between sins. She referred to James 2:10: "For whoever keeps the whole law and yet stumbles at just one point is guilty of breaking all of it"—meaning that God sees all sins alike and weighs them equally. Ouch!

Also, Mrs. Summons, pointing out that the scriptures use the terms *sin, iniquity, transgression,* and *trespass,* referred to Psalm 32:5 as an example: "Then I acknowledged my sin to you and did not cover up my iniquity. I said, 'I will confess my transgressions to the Lord.' And you forgave the guilt of my sin."

Sin: the transgressions of God's law. Sin means "to miss the mark" and is a general term for falling short of God's standards. Romans 3:23 reads, "For all have sinned and fall short of the glory of God." Sins can be intentional or unintentional (Numbers 15:27). Sin is not just doing something wrong but is also failing to do what is right (James 4:17).

Transgression: intentionally disobeying God's command, coupled with a willful trespass or violating of a boundary; going beyond one's right.

Iniquity: twisting and distorting God's law; an intentional plan to sin. The scriptures in Galatians 5:19–21 present examples of tendencies or instincts from within us that drive us to defile our character and body and repeatedly sin over and over. Iniquities are characteristics that are passed down from one generation to another.

In the end, Mrs. Summons stressed that God takes sin very seriously. Still, His gracious forgiveness is unlimited. She read Exodus 34:6–7:

> The Lord, the Lord, the compassionate and gracious God, slow to anger, abounding in love and faithfulness, maintaining love to thousands, and forgiving wickedness, rebellion and sin. Yet he does not leave the guilty unpunished.

Note: For ease of reference, I will use the term *sin* for all types of disobedience listed in this chapter.

I learned the following:

a) For God, a sin is a sin no matter what it is. Even looking at something the wrong way is a sin (Matthew 5:28).
b) God looks not only at the sin but also at the root cause of the sin that leads us astray. For example, in my case, it was the fear of punishment from my mother that caused me to lie to cover up my wrongdoing.
c) Sin punishes itself. There is an Arabic proverb that says, "The rope of lies is short."

The question that occupied my mind was: Are newborn babies born with a sinful nature? I always believed that babies were innocent at birth. But Psalm 51:5 shed light on the truth: "Surely I was sinful at birth, sinful from the time my mother conceived me." Psalm 58:3 helped too: "Even from birth the wicked go astray; from the womb they are wayward, spreading lies." In light of the scriptures, I am convinced that *no* human being is born without a sinful nature, including newborn babies. It is worth noting that newborn infants are *not* born sinners, but they carry in their DNA the sinful nature; they become sinners only when they sin. I also learned that there is no innocent sin. I observed my one-year-old niece manipulating her parents to get her way. In other words, to become a sinner, we have to commit a sinful action.

> *Note:* Science confirms that traumatic experiences and consequences are also carried in the DNA!

I like Bjorn Nilsen's explanation:

> The god of this world, the devil, is active as well. He also wants to get a hold of our human spirit, to

influence us to do his will. He has come to destroy us, and he speaks to our flesh. "The flesh" refers to mankind's earthly desires and lusts which we have inherited from our forefathers (1 Peter 1:18) and which originate from the fall. Here there is a battle between two forces, and in this battle, God is a jealous God. He is zealous (jealous) for our spirits. He wants us to be zealous, with "God's zeal" in this battle.

One of the greatest lessons I learned is this: While God hates the sin, He loves the sinners.

Relationship and Fellowship with God the Father
My friend June was right when she said, "God created human beings to have relationships with them." I stand in awe before God who He loves me so much that He wants to have a personal relationship with me. The privilege of having a relationship with God (through my faith in and my confession of Jesus as my Savior and Lord, and having the Holy Spirit dwelling in me) permitted me to be called a child of God and to belong to the family of God, thus giving me an eternal identity.

I came to understand from the book of Genesis that God had two purposes for creating humankind in His plan: to have a relationship with human beings and to fellowship with them. It is my understanding that my relationship with Christ started when I received Him in my heart. Once I established the relationship with Christ, my fellowship with Him began when I started walking with Him and living by His Word. Both relationship and fellowship are critical. I noticed that I could not have fellowship with Christ if I had not established a relationship first. The verses John 1:10–13 and Ephesians 6:10 illustrate the scope of the relationship and fellowship; we have to be in the Lord first to be strong in the Lord. In other words, having a relationship with God is a personal reason for God. Through fellowship, God equips us to achieve the lifework He designed us to do for Him on the earth.

I also learned that relationship has two dimensions: one is vertical with the Lord, and the other is horizontal with other believers. The apostle John explained that when I received the Lord Jesus Christ as my Savior, I gained fellowship with the Father and the Holy Spirit, as well as with all believers in the family of God (1 John 1:3).

On the one hand, I marveled at the knowledge that God desires to have a personal relationship with me. On the other hand, terror and doubt snaked their way into my mind, reminding me of the numerous broken relationships that marred my past. I lamented my broken life and the many bridges with people I loved I had burnt; the most recent one was my dad's disowning of me when he learned of my conversion.

Sharp nails of doubt and fear bit into me for days. I feared to repeat with God the same fate of my previous relationship experiences. *If Adam and Eve's divine relationship with God lasted for no more than two chapters, then ultimately my relationship with God wouldn't last either,* I thought. I grieved at the thought that my sinful nature had broken my relationship with God. Now I wanted to know how to fix it.

I became desperate for an immediate solution to earn God's forgiveness, to become His child, and to have a long-lasting relationship and long-lasting fellowship with Him. Was I asking for too much? Was there a solution? What was it? What were God's requirements to become His child? For a few hours, which felt like an eternity, doubts injected my mind with beliefs that my sins and the sexual abuse I experienced would prevent me from following Jesus and cause me to lose my calling. Fear stole my sleep at night and my peace every waking hour. I meditated on the psalms. When I reached Psalm 27, the tenth verse startled me: "Though my father and mother forsake me, the Lord will receive me." The verse confused me a bit. Was the verse confirming my dad's decision to disown me for my conversion, or was it telling me that God would not expel me as he did with Adam?

For a while, I doubted my calling. I meditated on the verse until one night I heard myself speaking in my sleep, saying Isaiah 54 and Jeremiah 31:3. In the morning, I looked up the two chapters. Both chapters describe God's unshakable, unfailing, and everlasting love:

> "Though the mountains be shaken and the hills be removed, yet my unfailing love for you will not be shaken nor my covenant of peace be removed," says the Lord, who has compassion on you. (Isaiah 54:10)
>
> I have loved you with an everlasting love; I have drawn you with unfailing kindness. (Jeremiah 31:3)

I cannot describe the bliss and the joy of the moment. These two verses affirmed God's love for me. From that moment on, I prayed to God to guide me on *how* to approach Him and *what* I needed to do to become His child and enter into fellowship with Him. It is worth noting that the concept of having a relationship and fellowship with God was utterly foreign to me, let alone the idea of calling Him God the Father.

Fatherhood of God the Father

Once I had established that God the Father was my heavenly Father, I wanted to know how to become His child. Mathew 18:3–4 gave me the answer. Jesus said, "Truly I tell you, unless you change and become like little children, you will never enter the kingdom of heaven. Therefore, whoever takes the lowly position of this child is the greatest in the kingdom of heaven."

I understood from this verse that God wanted me to go to Him with a childlike faith. But what does it mean to have childlike faith? Around that time, my niece and her family arrived in London for vacation and stayed with me. I observed the interaction between my niece's one-year-old baby and her dad and mom. And it dawned on me: there was an unshakable trust between the child and her parents. God wanted me to trust Him and depend on Him 100 percent in every aspect of my life. I turned to the book of Proverbs, where King Solomon imparted wisdom to his son, saying in Proverbs 3:5–6, "If you want favor with both God and man, and a reputation for good judgment and common sense, then trust the Lord completely; don't ever trust yourself. In everything you do, put God first, and he will direct you and crown your efforts with success" (TLB).

At first, it was a bit scary; for my whole life, I had held the reins of my life and ran it my way, the best I knew how. So, letting go of my self-trust and self-serving life plans and letting God take the reins of my life was challenging. "I'm afraid, Lord," I cried.

The Lord's Prayer gave me the blueprint to build the foundation of my faith. It mapped my spiritual transformation needed if I wished to adopt an attitude of submission and a childlike dependency on the Lord in my daily life. Through His grace, I grew aware of my partnership with God and with the feeling of His power and hope within me, telling me that I needed to face life's challenges. The Lord's Prayer became my daily spiritual and mental workout to let go of my self and let God. Like a clingy child, I gripped God's hand to sail the journey of life and receive His promises. The privilege of calling God as Father led me to discover and experience His infinite love for me.

The knowledge that struck me most was the fact God loved me *first*, way before I loved Him or answered His calling. From the time He created the world, He knew about me and loved me! Even when I rejected Him and worshipped idols,[48] God did not stop loving me. Even when I sinned against Him and broke many promises I had made in His name, God did not stop loving me. His unconditional love continued to pour upon me. (*Note:* Though He grieved seeing me doing wrong, God hates the sin but loves the sinner.) Even when I cursed or swore falsely in His name, God's love never ceased and never gave up on me. Tragically, it was I who had given up on Him when I thought I could do things without His help or was angry at Him when tragedy came my way, thinking He could have prevented it but did not. But, wow! How wrong I was when I learned not only that God not only loves me (and you) but also that He loves us unconditionally no matter how many times we fail, who we are, or what we have done.

One evening when I was listening to Reverend Billy Graham's radio station, one listener sent the question "Does God ever give up on us? I have failed Him so many times that I do not even ask Him to forgive me anymore. I've got to get my life together, but I don't know how." The person who sent this question was speaking my mind.

Reverend Graham replied, "God never gives up on us. Our sins may drive us farther and farther away from Him, but even then, He still loves us and yearns for us to repent and turn to Him for the forgiveness and help we need." One of the most significant treasures in the Bible is the truth that God is love! The apostle John wrote in 1 John 4:8, "Whoever does not love does not know God, because God is love." How true! Before my conversion, it was difficult for me to love and to receive love. Then, God broke down the walls of hatred. Love burst into my heart. I never had had such strong emotions and feelings before. Love was gushing

---

[48] Throughout the years, I created my own idols, idolizing my job, my salary, etc.

out of me as if from a broken fire hydrant shooting water high up in the air.

The more time I spent with God, the more I learned about His loving nature and the more I loved Him. God's love created in me an intense desire to talk to Him. I learned that we speak to God in prayer and that He speaks to us as we study His Word. My prayers became natural conversations with God, pouring my heart out to Him. In every prayer, I asked God to increase my faith and to help me to love myself and others. I meditated on God's love as expressed in Psalm 103:8–11:

> The Lord is compassionate and gracious, slow to anger, abounding in love. He will not always accuse, nor will he harbor his anger forever; he does not treat us as our sins deserve or repay us according to our iniquities. For as high as the heavens are above the earth, so great is his love for those who fear him.

The Manifestation of Sin in My Life
Before my conversion, I did not believe that I inherited Adam and Eve's sinful nature and would suffer their sin-consequences. I thought that the effects of their sin had disappeared with the passing of thousands of years. I was proud of my ethical values, crediting my professional success to my dad's wisdom, diplomacy, and good ethics—all things that he taught me. I established the boundaries of right and wrong based on my own experiences and the world's standards. I sailed through life, believing that I knew my needs better than Allah did. I hated making mistakes. I was hard on myself whenever I made them. However, my mistakes were my learning base. I used to laugh at the cook Fatma at my parents' house when she blamed the devil for every wrongdoing

in her life and in the world, saying, "Allah yel'an al-sheitan," meaning, "May Allah curse the devil."

Overall, I was pleased with the way I had turned out. I thought that I was doing well in life and thought I was a good person until I read Romans 5:12: "When Adam sinned, sin entered the entire human race. His sin spread death throughout all the world, so everything began to grow old and die, for all sinned" (TLB). This scripture rocked my world. It took awhile for the reality of Adam's sin to sink into my head. I started examining my character, personality, behavior, and lifestyle. Gradually, I came to realize that I was not as okay as I had thought; instead, I was a sinner! How could Adam and Eve's sinful nature get passed down to me? Is it possible? Well, according to scientists, yes.

Scientific research indicates that I inherited my parents' physical characteristics through DNA, their genes, passed down to them from their parents and their ancestors before them. Similarly, the scripture indicates that I inherited a sinful nature from my parents and ancestors. I join David's cry: "Behold, I was brought forth in iniquity, and in sin did my mother conceive me" (Psalm 51:5 ESV).

I cried in pain for realizing that I had been born physically alive but spiritually dead. I realized that throughout my life, either consciously or unconsciously, knowingly or unknowingly, I had acted on the sinful traits that were passed down to me—acts against God. My own actions had robbed me of the privileges that God originally meant for me. When I look back into my past, I notice that the following things were true of me without my knowing:

1. I defiled my heart and body. I grew angry and lost confidence in people; I did not trust anyone. In my anger, I rebelled against my family and my religion. I adopted man-made philosophies that derailed my mind from the truth, replacing

it with lies and false hope diffused by Satan. I followed false gods to glorify myself according to my pride.
2. Irenaeus (AD 200) wrote that humankind, "having been created a rational being [at the Fall], ... lost 'true rationality,' and he began to live 'irrationally,' opposed to the righteousness of God, giving himself over to every earthly spirit and serving all lust." How true! Yes, I was irrational and lived irrationally. While God loved me (and you) before the creation of the world, He did not show Himself to me before my conversion. Why? Because my mind, heart, and soul were in an ungodly and irrational condition.
3. Living irrationally had led me to choose to ignore God and not fear Him. The absence of the fear of God in my heart led me to lack humility and care for others. Unconsciously, arrogance grew in my heart. The absence of the fear of God led me to spiritual idolatry (e.g., putting my security in my income instead of in God, thereby placing something ahead of God). The lack of the fear of God led me to rebel. I believe that the saddest phenomenon in today's world is the loss of the fear of God and the hemorrhaging of the conscience, soul, and spirit. The lack of the fear of God in today's world is leading people to rebellion, violence, and destruction.
4. Spiritually, I was deaf, blind, and dead. The apostle Paul calls this condition in Ephesians 2:1 "dead in [my] transgressions and sins." Sin separates me from God and strips me of righteousness, holiness, and the love of the truth.

The scriptures opened my eyes to face the reality that I am a sinner. I realized that once I allowed sin into my life, I came under its grip and it controlled my heart and mind. While repenting my sins, out of fear of God's judgment, I gave excuses for why I had done what I had. But God does not accept any excuses. It is of no avail to offer him any. Don't even try. To God, a sin is a sin no matter how small, trivial, or foolish and regardless if fails to affect or hurt others. It is a sin. Period!

Until God showed me how my choice to sin had led me to catastrophic consequences that almost destroyed my life, I did not know the depth and height of His grace, mercy, love, protection, and forgiveness.

Until I learned how much my sins grieved God, I did not know the real feeling of mourning. To escape the pain and sorrow of the many disappointments in my life, I echoed David's cry: "Oh, that I had the wings of a dove! I would fly away and be at rest. I would flee far away and stay in the desert; I would hurry to my place of shelter, far from the tempest and storm" (Psalm 55:6).

Until I understood the biblical meaning of idolatry, I did not realize that idolatry is not limited to the lifestyle of the ancient Israelites and their inherited traditions. According to the scriptures, I practiced modern idolatry.

Until my conversion, I thought idolatry was merely worshipping, bowing down, and praying to false gods, carved images, statues, or natural phenomena. God has prohibited idolatry, warning us, "You shall not make for yourself an image in the form of anything in heaven above or on the earth beneath or in the waters below. You shall not bow down to them or worship them; for I, the Lord your God, am a jealous God" (Deuteronomy 5:8–9). The scriptures taught me that idolatry is giving something or someone a priority above God or worshipping something or revering someone other than the one true God. In both the *New International Version* and the *English Standard Version*, Colossians 3:5 mentions that covetousness and greed are idolatry! J. Lallier wrote:

> [Worshipping] carved images may have declined in popularity [today], but believers must contend with an ever-growing pantheon of false gods. These gods are worshipped at the altars of employment, electronics, entertainment, money,

and many other distractions of modern life. An idol does not have to be made of wood or stone. An idol can be anything a person puts before God in his or her life.

Therefore, idolatry is not limited to revering a statue or idolizing a person. A pastor once mentioned that if the latest gadgets or our personal appearance continuously consumes our minds, then that's idolatry. If the highest priority in our lives is our family (above God), even that is idolatry. For example, I have a friend who adores his only son and calls him his god.

Evaluating my life, I realized that I had committed idolatry. As happened to Eve, the world's culture had persuaded me to worship man-made philosophical ideologies. I exalted my career and my income as my gods. When God said, "You shall have no other gods before me,"[49] He wasn't just talking about the imaginary deities. God was talking about *anything* that takes His place as number one in our hearts. The scriptures opened my eyes to the fact that Satan desires that I (we) become God's enemy by sinning against Him and worshipping false gods. His sole purpose is to keep me under his control, instead of within God's will. He kidnaps me and blinds me with defected lenses so I see that which is right as wrong and that which is wrong as right (Isaiah 5:20 TLB). He masquerades wrongs as fictitious, make-believe, innocent acts. I never knew that by sinning (whether consciously or unconsciously), I was obeying the devil and worshipping him. This thought blew every fuse in my being.

God also made it clear that I should not worship other gods, for He is a "*jealous* God." In Exodus 20:4–5, I registered God's warning: "You shall not make for yourself an image [idol] in the form of anything in heaven above or on the earth beneath or in the waters below. You shall not bow down to them or worship

---

[49] Exodus 20:3.

them; for I, the Lord you God, am a jealous God, punishing the children for the sin of the parents to the third and fourth generation of those who hate me." In Exodus 34:14, God says, "Do not worship any other god, for the Lord, whose name is Jealous, is a jealous God."

What? God is jealous? God is perfect and is love, so how could He be jealous? Doesn't the scripture say that "Love is patient, love is kind. It does not envy, it does not boast, it does not proud" (1 Corinthians 13:4)? The more I thought about God's jealousy, the more I learned that His jealousy stems from when we take from God what rightly belongs to Him and give it to someone else.

At the time of writing this section, I thought of the evil things I've done in my life, some of which found me acting like Adam and Eve. Like Adam, I witnessed wrong actions happening in front of me where, while I had the power to either stop them or refuse to get involved, I chose not to exercise that power. Similarly, I recall circumstances where, like Eve, I was fooled and allowed temptation to swell my pride, leading me to participate in malicious activities and bad relationships. I demonstrated the nature of rebellion in many ways. My parents gave me ample opportunities to follow the laws and rules of Islam. Still, I rebelled and chose to do my own will, to do things my way. I created gods, depending on my circumstances. I admit that the consequences of my wrongdoing were destructive and costly. The sinful nature and temperament darkened my soul. They put blinkers on my eyes to focus my attention on running down dangerous avenues with sharp and blind turns. Once the enemy[50] had secured me away from God, he left me to battle life alone, bound to fear, frustration, and despair. I lost sight and derailed from the path God had established for me.

On my own, I could not get out of the hole I had put myself in. Instead, I kept slipping and sinking, until one day, God said

---

[50] The devil is known as the enemy.

"Enough is enough" and pulled me from the pit of destruction. Only when I immersed myself in the Word were my sins paraded in front of my eyes, showing me how spiritually dead I was. I grieved, and guilt filled me with shame when I learned that God was watching me sinning against Him. One day while praying, my sins flashed before my eyes, some of which made me so embarrassed that I got angry at God; I shouted, "Lord, why did You not stop me?" No, God did not stop me, because He gave me the free will to make my own decision, the ones I made having looked good at the time. Nothing is hidden from God. God sees everything and knows the hidden secrets of our hearts (Hebrews 4:13; Luke 8:17). O how much I wished I did not have free will.

In short, I learned that I could choose my actions but I could not choose their consequences.

Atonement

At the end of a discussion on sin, Nabil said, "Oh man! I wish we had never opened this subject. It is a downer."

"I wonder how the world would be if all of humanity were to stop sinning. Can we stop sinning? Even for a day?" I asked.

"Impossible," Mervet nervously said. "We sin every day."

"So, in other words, we are doomed to hell," Gretchen said.

June shared that if we break one of the Ten Commandments, we are guilty of breaking all of them.

"How could a loving God allow all humanity to perish in hell?" Jacob criticized.

On this somber note, with melancholy, we quietly closed the meeting.

A few months later, my friends and I met with Mrs. Summons for another round of debate and brainstorming. We all acknowledged that the sin subject had occupied our minds and made us worry about our final destination after death.

Gretchen admitted that the sin subject stressed her so much that she could not concentrate at work. She shared, "Since I am born a sinner, and since I will carry the DNA of the sinful spirit until my last breath, I feel like I am doomed no matter what I do. The thought that scares me most is that I don't know what my fate will be after I die."

Nabil said, "Perhaps we have to accept that this is the way God created us."

June turned to Nabil and said, "So, Nabil, are you saying that we shall go on sinning because we don't know what else to do?"

Mary asked, "What else to do, June? How has God dealt with humankind's sins over the ages?"

Mervet asked, "How to stop sinning? Can we stop sinning?"

Anwar responded, "Yes, we can stop sinning if we focus on Allah. And if we sin and repent, Allah forgives us." Then he cited Surah al-Tahreem 66:8:[51]

> O you who have believed, repent to Allah with sincere repentance. Perhaps your Lord will remove from you your misdeeds and admit you into gardens beneath which rivers flow [on] the Day when Allah will not disgrace the Prophet and those who believed with him. Their light will proceed before them and on their right; they will say, "Our Lord, perfect for us our light and forgive us. Indeed, You are over all things competent."

Anwar had a valid point. Repentance and forgiveness are paramount.

Mervet said, "But in this case, we would be trapped in an infinite loop of sin, repent, repeat. What happens if we die before repenting? There must be a permanent solution. Right?"

Jacob asked, "How many times will God forgive us for sinning?"

---

[51] *The Qur'an: Arabic Text with Corresponding English Meanings* (Singapore: Abul-Qasim, 1997), 810.

Mary asked, "What happens on Judgment Day? Will God judge us on all the sins we have committed and all the mistakes we have made throughout our lives?"

Gretchen said, "Will we be judged on mistakes as well?" With tears filling her eyes, she said, "I am doomed."

Jacob said, "June, how does *your* Jesus judge your sin? Don't you guys believe that His blood erases sin!?" Behind his faint smile, Jacob's tone was peculiar.

Suddenly, the reality of the consequences of sin unexpectedly hit us hard, all of us feeling as if a wrecking ball had hit us right in the face. A terrifying silence descended upon the room and stayed for a long while, each one of us in deep thought stemming from our having taken a trip down memory lane and observing our past lifestyles.

With a broken and fearful voice, Mervet broke the silence: "Now that I know the truth, that I am a sinner in God's eyes *and* that I sin every day, and now that I know the fate of sin, what hope do I have? What is the way out? Is there a way out? Surely, God knew about humankind's sinful condition, so what is His solution? Are we doomed to eternal punishment in hell, as Gretchen said?"

"I don't think so," June said. "Listen to what God said in Psalm 103:14: 'For he [God] knows how we are formed, he remembers that we are dust.'" Then, she explained that God knows that we are weak and easily tempted, adding that it is not easy to live a righteous life in today's world. "So, what is God's solution?" June, her big eyes wide open, scanned the table. I looked at her in anticipation of hearing God's solution. I hoped for a miracle to eradicate my sins.

June reminded us of the fact that we can't redeem ourselves or others. For this, God devised a perfect solution that would restore our souls and our lives, bind up our wounds and brokenness, and lead us to freedom from the bondage of sin.

"How?" she asked us all. No one gave an answer. "Jesus is the answer!" she exclaimed. "The power of His blood, which He shed on the cross on our behalf, offers salvation, the only permanent solution." June's voice echoed her assurance and confidence in Jesus.

"What is so special about Jesus's blood?" Nabil asked.

June answered, "Unlike animal sacrificial blood, the power of Jesus's blood covers our sins and purges them so God will remember them no more. Why? Because the blood that Jesus shed on the cross satisfied God's judgment and wrath on sin. In short, without Jesus's work, we cannot be *saved*. Think about this: God the Almighty, the second person of the Trinity, dies for us to forgive and purge our sins."

"What's the catch?" Nabil asked.

"Return to God and believe in Jesus as your Lord and Savior," June replied. She flipped the pages of her Bible and said, "Listen to these verses," then read the following:

> If my people, who are called by my name, will humble themselves and pray and seek my face and turn from their wicked ways, then I will hear from heaven, and I will forgive their sin and will heal their land. (2 Chronicles 7:14)

> I [God] will forgive their wickedness and will remember their sins no more. (Jeremiah 31:34)

While God's forgiveness and the purging of our sins captivated all of us, the fact that Jesus is the only way to God[52] offended some of my friends. On that note, we closed the meeting.

I could not sleep that night. I stared at the ceiling, thinking that while I did confess Jesus as my Lord and Savior, did I put 100 percent of my faith in His blood? What did I have to do for God to remember my sins no more so I could be saved? I wanted

---

[52] "Jesus answered, 'I am the way and the truth and the life. No one comes to the Father except through me'" (John 4:16).

to understand the components of the Atonement and the process that leads to salvation. In other words, I wanted to know the link between Jesus's atonement and my salvation.

I started my research with the first atonement in the history of humankind, which happened in Genesis 3:21. God made a garment from animal skin to cover up Adam and Eve's nakedness (with nakedness representing their sin of disobedience).

Studying the atonement process in the Old Testament, I found it is based on three elements: the "offeror" (an animal in the Old Testament era), the "offering" (blood and body), and the "recipient of the offering"—humankind. In other words, atonement requires the shedding of the blood, which represents life. Leviticus 17:11 explains: "For the life of a creature is in the blood, and I have given it to you to make atonement for yourselves on the altar; it is the blood that makes atonement for one's life." Also, the book of Hebrews stresses the importance of the blood offering even more by saying, "In fact, the law requires that nearly everything be cleansed with blood, and *without the shedding of blood there is no forgiveness*" (Hebrews 9:22; emphasis added). Wow, undoubtedly, the blood is mysterious and a sacred means for forgiveness.

In the Bible, I found many scriptures informing of the importance of the blood in purifying sins. But the verse about the atonement process that attracted my attention was Hebrews 10:4: "It is impossible for the blood of bulls and goats to take away sins." As if God was saying that to purge humankind's sins and satisfy[53] His judgment, the offering blood had to be from a human (like for like), not the blood of an animal. More importantly, the scripture stressed that the atoning human must be sinless. So, who is that human? And what was God's plan to redeem us and save us through the forgiveness of our sins?

---

[53] Theologically, the word *satisfaction* does not mean gratification or enjoyment as in common usage, but rather "to make restitution": mending what has been broken or paying back what was taken.

27
DISCOVERY JOURNEY TO GOD THE SON

Redeeming the God-Creation Relationship (Redemption and Salvation)
What Did God Do to Redeem and Save Humankind?

Throughout the Old Testament, I found God, moved by compassion and mercy for His people, sending his prophets to nations to call them to repent of their sins. To repent means that we choose to turn away from our transgressions and return to God. It is a 180° move. By doing so, we restore our broken relationship with God, and He blesses us and delivers us from Satan's destruction. Unfortunately, humanity at large has disregarded God's warnings that He will not excuse sin. God will by no means leave the guilty unpunished (Exodus 34:7). For a while, Exodus 34:7 scared me, keeping me awake for several nights. God's judgment for creating and believing in idols will be to punish "the children and their children for the sin of the parents to the third and fourth generation." I pleaded for God's mercy and forgiveness for seeking tarot cards and fortune-tellers to tell me about my future. My mother (RIP) was superstitious and used the divination technique of lead-pouring on the water to protect us from the evil eye (Nazar in Turkish). Believing in such superstitious practices is idolatry. By faith, I stood in the gap for my siblings. I washed myself and my siblings with the blood of Jesus, canceling the spirit of idolatry over me and my siblings.

The Bible warns us that wickedness will increasingly become rampant in the human heart. Genesis 6:5 reads, "The Lord saw how great the wickedness of the human race had become on the earth, and that every inclination of the thoughts of the human heart was only evil all the time." God affirms in that "the intention of man's heart is evil from his youth" (Genesis 8:21 ESV).

Mrs. Summons commented once that while God could have destroyed humankind through a natural disaster such as the flood in Noah's time, when the world became corrupt and pervert (Genesis 6:9–13), He, by His grace and mercy and for His glory, devised a plan to rid the world of evil without eliminating humankind; the plan was *redemption* and *salvation* (Ephesians 1:7). The theologian M. Henry (1662–1714/1997), in *Concise Commentary on the Whole Bible*, explains the verse Exodus 34:7:

> The Lord God is merciful, ready to forgive the sinner and to relieve the needy. Gracious; kind, and ready to bestow undeserved benefits. Long-suffering: slow to anger, giving time for repentance, only punishing when it is needful. He is abundant in goodness and truth; even sinners receive the riches of his bounty abundantly, though they abuse them. All he reveals is infallible truth; all he promises is in faithfulness. Keeping mercy for thousands, he continually shows mercy to sinners. He has treasures, which cannot be exhausted, to the end of time. Forgiving iniquity, and transgression, and sin; his mercy and goodness reach to the full and free forgiveness of sin. And will by no means clear the guilty; the holiness and

justice of God are part of his goodness and love towards all his creatures. (p. 116)

With every waking breath, I sought God's divine guidance to aid me in understanding the connection between atonement, redemption, and salvation.

Definition of Redemption and Salvation
Redemption and *salvation* were two new terms to me. Not long after my conversion, I started attending Dr. R. T. Kendall's theology classes on Friday evening. In one of the sessions, Dr. Kendall (1998) addressed the sovereignty of God with regard to redemption and salvation and defined them as follows:[54]

Redemption means "setting free for a ransom." God bought us back by the blood of His Son (1 Peter 1:18–19).

Dr. Kendall gave me a great picture of redemption. He wrote the following:

> The picture is this: we have been redeemed (bought back) by God, the price paid for our release being the blood of Christ.
>
> (1) We fell to Satan in the Garden of Eden and have been held captive ever since.
> (2) But Jesus Christ by His blood bought us back; we are now owned by God—bought with a price (1 Corinthians 6:20).

---

[54] R. T. Kendall, *Understanding Theology*, vol. 1 (Ross-shire: Christian Focus Publications, 1998), 41, 52, 116, 117, 137.

(3) The life of Christ was apparently an agreed price paid to secure our freedom from bondage to Satan.

In other words, redemption refers to Christ's blood buying us back from the lost condition into which we were born.

Thanks be to God, redemption means undoing the effects of sin for me, you, and the entire human race.

Salvation means the following:
1. God has spared us (saved us) from the wrath to come by the blood of His Son (Romans 5:9). This will necessarily include being saved from the penalty and power of sin.
2. We are delivered from our sins (Matthew 1:21). This salvation comes by God's initiative and provision:
    a) by Christ's blood (Romans 5:9)
    b) by Christ's life (Romans 5:10)
    c) by God's purpose (2 Timothy 1:9)
    d) by God's grace (Ephesians 2:8–9).

To better understand God's redemption and salvation, I needed to study God's grace and His mercy as these are *the* basis or foundation for our redemption and salvation.

Grace: Dr. D. Prince, in *The Spirit-Filled Believer's Handbook* (1994), expounded on Paul's explanation of God's grace (Romans 11:6) by contrasting it with works. He wrote:

> By grace, Paul means the free, unmerited favor and blessing of God bestowed upon the undeserving, and even upon the ill-deserving. By works, Paul means anything that a man may do of his own

ability to earn for himself the blessing and favor of God. Paul states that these two ways of receiving from God are mutually exclusive; they can never be combined. Whatever a man receives from God by grace is not of works; whatever a man received from God by works is not of grace. Wherever grace operates, works are of no avail; wherever works operate, grace is of no avail. ... Through Jesus Christ, the free, unmerited blessing and favor of God are now offered to all men on the basis of what Christ has done on man's behalf. This is grace.

Through faith in Christ, God's grace covers my sins and my failures; I do not get the punishment that I genuinely deserve for my sins. Grace is God blessing me even though I do not deserve it (Romans 3:23–24). Grace is extending kindness to unworthy and sinful humankind.

Mercy: Dr. Kendall explained that mercy is "when God [by His grace] chooses not to punish us (Exodus 33:19; 2 Peter 3:9)."[55] "When we ask for mercy, we are ask for what we don't deserve,"[56] instead of the punishment that we deserve for our sins. Mercy is deliverance and freedom from judgment.

Who Is the Redeemer and the Savior?

For weeks, I studied all the verses referenced in the concordance relating to these three topics, atonement, redemption, and salvation. I gathered a lot of information that I wanted to share with the team. I invited the group to my flat. We revisited the importance and the role of the blood atonement and how the Bible stresses that no good deeds can atone for our sins or save us

---

[55] Ibid., 41.
[56] Ibid., 119.

from eternal life in hell (Titus 3:5). Therefore, our redemption and salvation is entirely dependent on God's grace and mercy.

Mervet asked about God's plan to forgive and purge our sins and the requirements to get to heaven and have eternal life.

June explained that the solution is God's redemption plan through a Redeemer to redeem us and save us (i.e., salvation).

Nabil asked, "A redemption plan?"

Anwar quickly added, "And who is this Redeemer?"

Gretchen asked, "What makes you think that a Redeemer was needed? To do what?"

Mary asked, "What's the difference between redemption and salvation?"

I shared my learning with the team that there is a difference between redemption and salvation. Redemption is the *method* the Godhead devised so we human beings can receive the gift of salvation. In other words, redemption is the payment that Jesus paid on the cross on our behalf to set us free from the grip of Satan and to save us from eternal death—which is the price we pay for our sins.

For a few minutes, we questioned why God needed a Redeemer and the underlying causes that necessitated a redemption plan to receive salvation.

June answered, "Redemption was necessary to restore the Creator-Creation relationship, which Adam's Fall broke, causing Satan to take hold of the entire human race."

In one accord, the team shouted, "Satan?!"

June's comment about Satan gave us the shivers.

Gretchen said, "June, what do you mean by 'causing Satan to take hold of the entire human race'?"

Then, Mary asked, "Satan? What did he have to do with God's plan for redeeming humankind?"

Mrs. Summons asked us what we thought of Mary's question. Some said that Satan had nothing to do with God's plan for redemption, while others thought redemption had something to do with Satan's adverse actions toward humankind, but they did not know how and why. When my turn came, I said that the purpose of redemption is to invalidate Satan's revenge. I shared with the group my understanding that Satan had a high position in heaven as the chief of angels. Satan was a beautiful angel, and for this, he was called the Morning Star. Satan became proud of his beauty and his high position.

Satan's God-defying arrogance and self-exaltation not only made him refuse to serve God but also led him to want to be served. He rebelled against God. Motivated by his pride, Satan wanted to become God and seize for himself God's authority over Creation, the universe, and the angels. God expelled him from His presence out of heaven, along with the angels he had persuaded to follow him. Since that day, Satan has devoted himself and his followers to revenge.

I saw a parallel between Satan's fall and the fall of the King of Tyre in Ezekiel 28:11–19. These verses depict how God hates pride and casts down the proud into the pit. God's judgment on Satan is described in Isaiah 14:12–15; Revelation 20:7–10; Luke 10:18; 2 Peter 2:4–10; and Jude 6. In the end, I explained that Satan's reaction was to take revenge.

The word *revenge* took everyone aback.

"What? Satan wants revenge on God?! Why and how?" Mary asked.

I said, "How? Satan strategized to break and destroy the Creator-Creation relationship through sin and death because he knew that God hates sin and that the penalty of sin is death (spiritually and eternally)." I added that because God had expelled Satan from His presence, the latter aimed to take revenge by destroying all the good plans that God had for humankind. Satan does not want anyone to enjoy God's blessings while living on earth and then, upon death, to join God in heaven. How does he do this? By luring people to do things that on the surface may appear logical and beneficial but that, in reality, are against God's Word and have dire destructive consequences in the long run.

Starting with Adam (Genesis 3:1), and throughout the ages, Satan has plotted the destruction of nations and people and has subjected humankind to rebel against God, that is, to sin. Of course, this is done unconsciously. In other words, since every person carries the sinful nature DNA, Satan lures us to sin; the human mind is his field of play. By being lured to sin, we are unconsciously trapped and fall as prey into Satan's den. We, humankind, will stay bound to Satan's control until we acknowledge our sins, confess, repent, turn to God, and ask His forgiveness and deliverance from Satan's bondage to freedom.

So, if we don't repent and turn to God before we die, we will be eternally punished in hell, not enjoy afterlife in God's heaven. And this is Satan's ultimate goal for the entire human race.

Genesis 6:5 explains that the Godhead saw how Satan's evilness overtook humanity and lead them to an intolerable level of iniquity with no one to help them (2 Kings 14:26; Acts 7:34). Satan's purpose remains[57] to entice people to turn their backs on the Godhead and die spiritually and physically, thus preventing them from having eternal life in heaven. On many occasions, the apostle Paul confirmed that humanity is enslaved to sin. Without the help of God, we cannot, on our own, free ourselves from living under the spell of the devil. The more I learned of Satan's destructive strategy, the more I thanked God for His redemptive plan.

Mervet said, "I think it would take someone who meets God's holiness and purity standards to be His creation's Redeemer, isn't it?"

"Exactly!" I exclaimed. "And who meets God's holiness and purity standards?"

---

[57] And still is and will remain until the end of the world, that is, until the Second Coming of Jesus Christ.

For a while, we discussed the potential person in 1 Corinthians 3:15. Some said that the prophets were the ones who met such standards; others said the seers. I referred to Psalm 49:7, Zephaniah 3:17, Isaiah 61:10, and John 8:36 and noted that the Redeemer had to be divine.

Jacob asked, "And whom do you suggest?" After a quick pause, staring at me, he flashed his index finger. "No, no, no," he said, as if he had read my mind, which was thinking of Jesus. "I don't agree with the Redeemer business *if* there were such a thing." Jacob accused me of misinterpreting the verse; Anwar and Nabil agreed with Jacob. I noticed that the meeting suddenly had turned into a heated debate, bearing in mind that the three topics—atonement, redemption, and salvation—represent the core differences between Judaism, Christianity, and Islam.

Why Do We Need a Redeemer?
Mrs. Summons quickly intervened to keep us from derailing the discussion. She said, "Let's summarize the key points. The scriptures tell us that we, humankind, deserve death for our sins, and yet God did not want humanity to die (2 Peter 3:9). Therefore, God devised the Covenant of Redemption. Although God revealed the covenant in Genesis 3:15 in the Old Testament, He only unfolded it when 'the fullness of time had come,' in other words, in the New Testament (Galatians 4:4–5 ESV)."

"What? What? A covenant?" Nabil asked. Putting his lawyer hat on, he continued: "Who were the parties of this covenant, because a covenant is a contract?"

Mrs. Summons explained, "Yes, Nabil, the Covenant of Redemption was a binding contract between two parties. But unlike all other covenants made between God and humankind, such as the Noahic covenant,[58] Abrahamic covenant,[59] Mosaic

---

[58] Genesis 9.
[59] Genesis 12.

covenant,[60] and Davidic covenant,[61] the Covenant of Redemption was, in reality, a last will and testament between the persons of the Godhead. The Godhead knew of humankind's Fall, and of the explosion of sin and corruption in the world, and planned the redemption covenant as a method to redeem humankind and allow them to receive salvation."

Following the meeting, I did more research into the redemption covenant. I found that God spoke through the Old Testament prophets such as Jeremiah (see Jeremiah 31:31–34).

> *Note:* Why did God create humankind when He foreknew of the Fall? This question deserves a separate book. At this present time, this topic is outside the scope of *I Thought I Was Doing Well Until* ....

A couple of weeks later, we resumed our discussion about the redemption covenant and the identity of the Redeemer. Anwar warned the team of blasphemy. While the group's questions rained down on Mrs. Summons, my mind traveled, visualizing the planning meeting for the Covenant of Redemption between the three persons of the Godhead in heaven. Putting my business hat on, I wondered how the persons of the Godhead would conduct divine meetings and agree on divine plans and assign responsibilities. Suddenly, I found myself focused on Anwar's question, "Why would God come to earth instead of sending prophets or even angels?" I lost count of how many times I had pleaded to God to give me an answer that would satisfy Anwar and silence the skeptics. Suddenly and unconsciously, I shouted, "Why not?" My shout startled the team, including me,

---

[60] Exodus 24:1–8.
[61] 2 Samuel 7.

interrupting Mrs. Summons in midsentence. All eyes shifted to fall on me, seeking an explanation for my action.

My face turned red, steaming intense heat. I apologized for my reaction. I turned to Anwar and said, "Why not, Anwar? Why wouldn't God come to earth to His people, whom He created? Does He need our permission? God is an all-powerful and all-capable God, isn't He? Are we questioning what He can and cannot do? Are we restricting God's power to fit our limited minds, our constrained and legalized reasoning, by controlling beliefs?"

The group looked confused and shocked by my answer. Before they started questioning, Mrs. Summons asked me to clarify my thoughts. I shared my point of view that questioning or rejecting the possibility of God's coming to earth is, in my mind, blasphemy. My statement shocked my friends. Nabil and Jacob roared, "Woe." I went on explaining my view, saying that by rejecting the possibility of God's coming to earth, we are (1) denying God's works and miracles, (2) constraining God's freedom to do what He wants to do in His timing and way to satisfy His purpose and will, and (3) disbelieving and rejecting the authority, power, and capability of the Godhead, the all-powerful, all-knowing, and all-capable Creator of the universe, the great I Am. To finish up, I said, "In my mind, rejecting the thought of God's coming to earth *is* blasphemy." I paused. My friends remained silent.

"That said," I continued, "I believe God welcomes us when we go to Him with sincere questions when we don't understand a verse or a passage. We can even ask God to help us process His works and miracles mentally, intellectually, or spiritually. In my experience, I have found that the more I ask God, the more I get to know Him. I believe God loves to reveal His nature and character to serious seekers. So, suppose you have doubts and questions about Jesus or the Trinity. In that case, I highly recommend that, instead of rejecting Him, you go to Jesus and ask *only Him* to reveal to you the truth. If you are seeking Him with sincerity, He will answer you."

Anwar interjected, "Why should I go to Jesus?"

I replied, "Because you willfully rejected Jesus without knowing Him or even seeking truth or any knowledge about Him directly from Him."

Then, I continued sharing with the team that the scriptures throughout the Bible had shown me over and over that nothing is impossible for God. "If we *genuinely* believe that God is omnipresent, omniscient, and omnipotent and that He is the Creator of the universe, then what is preventing us from believing that He came to earth? Why do we limit God's infinite power to fit our finite human reasoning and logic? Why do our mouths recite prayers and verses about God's majesty and power when our hearts and minds don't honestly believe? God did not create barriers between Him and humankind. On the contrary, it is humankind who created religions as barriers between God and humankind. Or could it be that we, humankind, have conditioned our minds to reject everything that contradicts our ancestral traditions and beliefs or that disapproves of our lifestyle?"

My comments caused the meeting to derail into side discussions. We took a short break. When we reconvened, Mary asked me to clarify what I was trying to say.

I responded, "Who is more qualified to restore God's reflection of His glory on humankind other than God Himself? Who has the power to pull humankind from the claws of Satan and his fatal dominion other than God? Who is more qualified to redeem us than the One who created us? Human beings cannot redeem themselves or others. No prophets or angels can redeem us. The scriptures have taught me that the basis of the redemption covenant is as follows:

1. The Creator is the Redeemer. The prophet Isaiah prophesied, "Our Redeemer—the Lord Almighty is his

name—is the Holy One of Israel" (Isaiah 47:4). At least fifty-plus other verses attest that God is the Redeemer.
2. Redemption requires a *divine* personality because humankind cannot redeem themselves or others (Psalm 49:7).
3. Redemption requires a pure and holy blood sacrifice from a pure and holy human to atone for the sins of humankind. Only divine blood can appease God's wrath against Satan and satisfy His justice (Isaiah 53).
4. Divine atonement is our only hope for an eternal relationship with God in heaven (Hebrews 10:1–18)."

All went quiet. Silently, some rose to leave. Had I said something offensive? Our session would have ended if it weren't for Gretchen. She signaled with her hands to the team to stay, and asked Mrs. Summons to resume her explanation of the Covenant of Redemption and salvation and provide feedback on my comments.

While Gretchen was speaking, Anwar quickly picked up the concordance and checked the index several times. A few seconds later, he said in a sharp tone, "There are no references in the Bible to the redemption covenant."

Mrs. Summons asked us to take our seats and agreed to continue. In my heart, I prayed to God to increase our faith to understand this complex topic. Mrs. Summons first concurred with Anwar, saying that as with the word *Trinity*, the Bible does not explicitly mention the Covenant of Redemption. Still, she stressed that the scriptures throughout the Bible confirm the concepts of the Trinity and the Covenant of Redemption. They are the foundation of the Christian faith.

Regarding the Covenant of Redemption, Mrs. Summons compared the covenant to a contract where the parties engaged in the contract are qualified and responsible for executing the contract and fulfilling the agreement. Then, she applied the scenario to the Covenant of Redemption, saying that since the involved parties are the persons of the Godhead, the only person "qualified" to fulfill the covenant is the Godhead.

Why Did God Send Jesus Instead of Sending a Prophet?

I admit that the redemption topic was challenging. I had to look deeper into the scriptures from Genesis 3:14–15 to Revelation to glean an understanding of the Covenant of Redemption and Salvation. Romans 3:23 says, "We all [humanity] have sinned and fall short of the glory of God." Psalm 49:7 confirms that because humankind is sinful, "None of them can by any means redeem [either himself or] his brother, nor give to God a ransom for him" (AMP) for the condemnation of death. Since the Redeemer has to be a human being with divine purity and holiness as the Godhead, then the Redeemer can only be the *Godhead Himself*. You may say that this is a naive statement!

Given the diversity of functions among the persons of the Godhead, each person may perform a different divine function that would contribute to the completion of the common purpose and will. Like the creation process, the Covenant of Redemption patterns the diversity of roles among the Godhead.

Being a visual learner, I visualized the Covenant of Redemption meeting as such: God the Father was the planner and executor in heaven; God the Son was the executer on earth; and the Holy Spirit was the revealer (John 16:8–13; Ephesians 3:1–4; 1 Corinthians 2:9–10).

After a careful examination of Genesis 3:15; Matthew 26:28; and Hebrews 9:9–17, I finally had an epiphany when I began to understand the Covenant of Redemption with new insight as a last will and testament (or "will" for short) to be executed at a predestined time and in a predestined way.

1. In Genesis 3:15, God announced that the Covenant of Redemption and Salvation would be executed by "he" (later found to be the second person of the Godhead).
2. In Matthew 26:28, Jesus (the incarnated second person of the Godhead) announced to His disciples that He was about to inaugurate/execute the will.
3. Hebrews 9:16–17 expounds on the necessity for the testator's death to make the will valid.
4. Hebrews 10:8–10 sheds more light on the Godhead's agreement for a "new testament/covenant" for redeeming, saving, and sanctifying humankind.
5. In Hebrews 10:9, the second person of the Godhead (God the Son, Jesus) said to the first person of the Godhead (God the Father), "'I have come to do Your will.' He sets aside the first to establish the second." God the Son came to earth to execute the New Testament (covenant). Hebrews 10:9 told me that the sacrifices of the old covenant were only meant to be symbolic of the real resolution for redeeming humankind and purging our sin, which came through the incarnation and death of Jesus Christ.
6. In Matthew 26:28, Jesus announced that He was about to execute God's will by offering His body on the cross, as if Jesus had inaugurated the new covenant.

God, by His grace, devised a redemption plan as a last will and testament to offer the gift of salvation to humankind. The terms of the will were to rescue us from enslavement to Satan, cancel his claim upon us, cleanse us from sin, and bring us back to God's presence and fellowship. In the eye of the law, a last will and testament can only be executed at the death of the testator. Biblically speaking, an atonement is needed (i.e., shedding *holy* blood as a price to repurchase us to God). The second person of the Godhead agreed to come to earth, become a man as Jesus, and atone Himself for humankind.

God the Son, driven by His infinite love for humankind, agreed to inaugurate the New Testament. He left His high position amid the majesty of heaven, the purity of heaven, and its peace, joy, and glory, and lowered Himself to come to earth. God the Son foreknew of the degraded condition of the world on earth and the immorality of humankind. He also foreknew that few would believe Him and receive Him as the Son of God, Christ the Messiah. Still, He willingly entered the earth as an infant born to a virgin. His name became Jesus. He lived among people to identify with our human sorrows and the pains of temptation we endure from Satan's advances. I am very grateful that Jesus understands my humanity, my struggles.

Jesus achieved God the Father's plan, dying on the cross in exchange for the life of the human race. From God's perspective, redemption satisfied His divine justice on sinners' wrath. From my human perspective, I "have redemption through His [Jesus's] blood, the forgiveness of [my] sins, in accordance with the riches of God's grace" (Ephesians 1:7). Through redemption and by God's grace (as well as through my faith in Jesus), God offered me His gift of justification and salvation. As a result, I am justified and saved by God's grace through Jesus Christ (Romans 3:24).

Thanks be to God for the Lord Jesus Christ, who is the only one who offered me salvation through His death on the cross. The blood that He shed on the cross washed me and restored me to the image and likeness of God. O the precious grace and mercy of God demonstrated in salvation!

I wonder what the Old Testament people would have done if they had known that the prophecies proclaimed in the Old Testament would be personified in the person of the Messiah, Jesus Christ, thousands of years later in the future.

I like the pictorial description of C. K. Cummings (1987):

> Throughout the entire Bible there is one underlying message; it is the message of salvation

by a Redeemer. And either you trust in this message or you do not for in the end it is all we really have. The Old Testament prophesies that the Savior will come. The New Testament tells us that he has come and what he has done. This underlying message of salvation serves as a unifying principle, connecting the various revelations of the Bible and uniting them into a harmonious whole. Like a winding stream it connects the many rivulets and streams of thought that run throughout the Bible and unites them into one river of holy history converging with the Spirit of God and the plan. The covenant of grace is that plan of redemption which runs through the Bible. An understanding of God's covenant will acquaint one with the central message of the Bible and at the same time provide an outline of its history and revelation that more sin means more suffering. Thankfully God's mercy rules overall.

Incarnation and Virgin Birth

The topic of Jesus's incarnation and His virgin birth prompted several questions among the team. Both the Qur'an and the Bible acknowledge that Jesus was conceived by the power of the Holy Spirit and born to the Virgin Mary.

Qur'an al-Anbiya 21:91 reads,[62] "And [mention] the one who guarded her chastity [i.e., Mary]. We blew into her [garment] through our angel [i.e., Gabriel], and we made her and her Son a sign for the world." The Arabic version of the Surat indicates that Allah breathed His Spirit into Mary.

---

[62] *The Qur'an: Arabic Text with Corresponding English Meanings* (Singapore: Abul-Qasim, 1997), 448.

Chapter (21) sūrat l-anbiyāa (The Prophets)

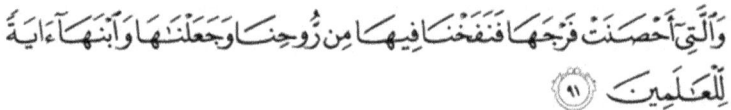

Also notable is Qur'an Surah Ali-Imran 3:45:[63] "[And mention] when the angels said, 'O Mary, indeed Allah gives you good tidings of a word from Him, whose name will be the Messiah, Jesus, the son of Mary—distinguished in this world and the Hereafter and among those brought near [to Allah].'"

It is written in the Bible in Luke 1:30–37:

> The angel said to her, "Do not be afraid, Mary; you have found favor with God. You will conceive and give birth to a son, and you are to call him Jesus. He will be great and will be called the Son of the Most High. The Lord God will give him the throne of his father David, and he will reign over Jacob's descendants forever; his kingdom will never end." "How will this be," Mary asked the angel, "since I am a virgin?" The angel answered, "The Holy Spirit will come on you, and the power of the Most High will overshadow you. So the holy one to be born will be called the Son of God. ... For no word from God will ever fail."

Before my conversion, I believed that Jesus was born of a virgin simply because the Qur'an says so. And it is written in the Bible, "nothing will be impossible with God" (Luke 1:37 ESV). So, if God wanted to come to earth in a bodily form born

---

[63] Ibid., 69.

to a virgin and live among people as a human being, who am I to question the omniscient and omnipotent God? Although the Incarnation of Jesus Christ is above my human comprehension, I read the scriptures in the Bible with a believing heart as the ultimate truth, not with a critical spirit. By faith, I believe that God came to earth as Jesus.

When Mervet asked me why God came to earth and why believing in the Incarnation was so important, I told her what my friend once told me: "God came to humankind to bring humankind to God." In other words, God demonstrated His sovereign and gracious initiative to atone for and redeem humankind[64] (like for like). Jesus came to earth to reveal God to people, to redeem us, and to mend our broken relationship with God. To this day, I shiver every time I think that if only had I lived in Israel during Jesus's time, I would have seen God! I get goose bumps at the mental image of "Anyone who has seen me [Jesus] has seen the Father" (John 14:9). John 1:18 reads, "No one has ever seen God, but the one and only Son, who is himself God and is in closest relationship with the Father, has made him known." O how I wish I had lived at Jesus's time!

God could have chosen to come to earth in any other form of His choice. Still, He decided to appear as a human being with a human nature to identify with our human race. We, as humans, identify with Jesus's humanity. Jesus was born as all of us are born (Luke 2:6), grew up as we all grow up, and lived a human life prone to all human suffering, even death (Philippians 2:6–8). Having said that, although Jesus lived a human life like us in every aspect, He did not sin. He resisted temptation (Hebrews 4:15; Matthew 4:1–11). By doing so, Jesus revealed His divine person and human nature.

After reading Philippians 2:5–11 in different Bible versions,

---

[64] Matthew 1:1–25; Luke 1:26–38.

I found the interpretation of J. B. Phillips (1972), in *The New Testament in Modern English*, the best exposition of the scripture:

> Let Christ himself be your example as to what your attitude should be. For he, who had always been God by nature, did not cling to his prerogatives as God's equal, but stripped himself of all privilege by consenting to be a slave by nature and being born as mortal man. And, having become man, he humbled himself by living a life of utter obedience, even to the extent of dying, and the death he died was the death of a common criminal. That is why God has now lifted him so high, and has given him the name beyond all names, so that at the name of Jesus "every knee shall bow," whether in Heaven or earth or under the earth. And that is why, in the end, "every tongue shall confess" that Jesus Christ" is the Lord, to the glory of God the Father.

Philippians 2:5–11 humbled me and brought me to my knees. Did I understand that the Almighty God, the Creator of the universe, left heaven to come to earth to save me and redeem me? Me, an insignificant person? Wow! What a striking contrast with the world's leaders who take every opportunity to glorify their pompous selves as gods while the almighty God humbled Himself to become human and serve humanity! Instead of the glory and privileges of remaining in heaven, Jesus "made himself nothing by taking the very nature of a servant, being made in human likeness. And being found in appearance as a man, he humbled himself by becoming obedient to death—even death on a cross!" (Philippians 2:7).

What I learned from Philippians 2:5–9 is this: during His

life on earth, the incarnated Son of God, Jesus, existed in two natures, fully God and fully human simultaneously. In other words, Jesus did not diminish His deity. Instead, He acquired a second nature, a human nature embodied in body and soul, to identify with our nature—this along with God's character and attributes. By entering our world as a human being, God exalted our human race.

The *Encyclopedia Britannica*[65] helped me to understand incarnation intellectually:

> The word *incarnation* (from the Latin *caro*, "flesh") may refer to the moment when this *union*[66] of the divine nature of the second person of the Trinity with the human nature became operative in the womb of the Virgin Mary—the permanent reality of that union in the person of Jesus.

I saw the divine union in John 1:14, when the Word (the second person of the Trinity, God the Son) became flesh as a human being without diminishing His heavenly deity. The scriptures showed me three crucial facts about Incarnation: the divine person of Jesus, the human nature of Jesus, and the divine union of the human nature with the divine nature in the divine person of Jesus. Undoubtedly, the conception of Jesus was purely supernatural by the Holy Spirit, not done through a biological process. For this reason, believing in the Incarnation is significantly essential.

By studying the scriptures and the prophecies in the Old Testament, I am convinced that the Incarnation of Jesus was not accidental; the Godhead meticulously planned the Incarnation

---

[65] *Encyclopedia Britannica*, s.v. "Incarnation," https://www.britannica.com/topic/Incarnation-Jesus-Christ.
[66] Italics added for emphasis.

before the genesis of time. It was one of the Godhead's many mysteries and miraculous plans similar to the Creation, where God spoke and it was done. The prophets Isaiah and Micah prophesied about the Incarnation (Isaiah 7:14, 9:6, and Micah 5:2, respectively.)

One of the critical lessons I learned is that while the Incarnation of Jesus does not save by itself, apart from Incarnation, where the Word became flesh, there is *no* salvation. In fact, our salvation entirely depends upon Jesus's coming to this world in human form to atone for the sins of humankind. Romans 5:8 clearly states, "But God demonstrates his own love for us in this: While we were still sinners, Christ died for us."

Studying the Incarnation was valuable and precious in many ways. The incarnation process affirmed that God is love and that He calls us to love others. The source of love in my heart is God! Love is my seal in God (1 John 4:7)! I discovered the God who endlessly loves us, the human race. Incarnation demonstrated God's unconditional love by His willingly giving up heaven and coming to earth to redeem us. Chapter 53 of the book of Isaiah is one of many examples displaying God's unconditional love for us by His suffering in our place for our sins. John 3:16 sums up God's love for us: "For God so loved the world that he gave his one and only Son, that whoever believes in him shall not perish but have eternal life." I always take a moment of silence when I read or think of this verse. God, the majestic God, the Creator, died for me! Do you get it? I don't know of anyone who would do that for me. Do you? I am utterly speechless. How can I thank God for His sacrifice? How can I thank God for His unconditional and everlasting love?

My friend June brought to my attention that the Incarnation edified humankind and glorified God. Apart from God's Incarnation as Jesus Christ to be our Redeemer, there is no hope for the world.

Additional Critical Points I Learned of Incarnation:
1. Mary, mother of Jesus, did not create the divine person of Jesus; He existed with God the Father and God the Holy Spirit from the genesis of time, and He exists throughout eternity.
2. The virgin conception and His birth in Bethlehem does not mark the beginning of the life of the Son of God. Instead, it marks His physical entrance into our world.
3. Jesus said that by knowing Him, we will be able to know God. Jesus modeled how to deal, speak, and fellowship with God. Jesus spent time alone with God.
4. God, by His grace, mercy, and love, did not abandon us, the human race, as it was falling into corruption and decay. Jesus came as a Redeemer to reestablish the fellowship of humankind with God.

So, Why Is Incarnation So Important?
(My Response to Mervet)
1. By offering His own body, Jesus wiped out, for believers, eternal death in hell through redemption and salvation. I naively wonder if God created humankind in a human form, planning for His incarnation (Hebrews 2:14 NLT[67]).
2. I and all believers in Christ have a hope that we will not die condemned (Romans 8:1). Instead, we die with the hope and certainty that we will be resurrected at the end of time.

Resurrection
Similar to His incarnation, Jesus's resurrection was a supernatural and divine phenomenon that never stopped amazing people

---

[67] Because God's children are human beings—made of flesh and blood—the Son also became flesh and blood. For only as a human being could He die, and only by dying could He break the power of the devil, who had the power of death.

worldwide throughout the centuries. Jesus's resurrection shook the world and turned it upside down then, as it still does to this day. What is unique and of utmost importance about Jesus's resurrection is that He rose by the power of the Holy Spirit.

Like the Incarnation, the death and resurrection of Jesus are the foundation of Christianity. The apostle Paul wrote, "If Christ has not been raised, your faith is futile; you are still in your sins" (1 Corinthians 15:17). Since my conversion, Christmas and Easter have a special meaning in my heart. I celebrate the Lord and what He has done in me and in the human race at each of these holidays.

The Cross and the Blood of Jesus
The uniqueness of Jesus's sacrificial blood on the cross is that He sacrificed His own blood for the entire human race once and for all (Hebrews 9:22–26). By contrast, the Old Testament blood sacrifice ceremony was repeated every year by the high priest using animal blood, not the priest's own.

The scriptures throughout the Bible demonstrate that God is love. Out of His everlasting love, God breathed life into Adam and created the human race. Out of love, God created the Garden of Eden for Adam. When God sent Jesus to redeem us by His death on the cross, He did it out of love for every single person on this earth (me and you). God loves us and will do everything to redeem us back to Himself so we don't perish in hell (John 3:16).

Ah, the power in the blood of Jesus! It is unique and unequal! It is the precious blood of Jesus that redeemed me and saved me—nothing else.

The Prophecies about Jesus
Jesus fulfilled more than three hundred Old Testament prophecies.[68] One of my favorite pastimes is to trace the time

---

[68] See appendix B.

line of the prophecies in the Old Testament that Jesus Christ fulfilled, for example, the Virgin Birth (Isaiah 7:14; Psalm 2:7; Luke 1:26–38; Matthew 1:18), the parables He spoke, the miracles He performed (Matthew 9:24–25), the sins He forgave (Matthew 9:6), His crucifixion in Psalm 22:16–18, His appearance to His disciples after being resurrected from the dead (Luke 24:36–39), His eternal existence (John 1:1–3; 8:58), His authority to forgive sin (Matthew 9:6), His acceptance of worship (Matthew 14:33), and His ability to predict the future (Matthew 24:1–2). The writer of Hebrews tells us that Jesus is superior to angels (Hebrews 1:4–5) and that angels are to worship Him (Hebrews 1:6), and He suffered death on our behalf to break the power of death—the devil (Hebrews 2:14–15). Also, Micah 5:2 confirms the identity of Jesus as the Messiah.

Wow, is not it something to find that these prophecies took place about a thousand years before Jesus's birth? Everything Jesus did or spoke during His life on earth proves that Jesus the man was indeed God in the flesh.

I found that God spoke throughout the Old Testament through prophets, saying that a Savior would come to save people and deliver them from spiritual bondage and eternal life in hell. The New Testament reveals the arrival of the Savior—Jesus Christ, the Messiah—who fulfilled the Old Testament prophecies. Also, the Old Testament foretold and provided a foretaste of salvation, for example (to name a few):

- The book of Exodus displays the concept of salvation rooted in the Israelites' deliverance when God commissioned Moses to perform His mighty acts to save His people from living in bondage in Egypt and take them to the Promised Land. In parallel, God offered the gift of salvation to the world through the miraculous Incarnation of God the Son, who entered the world and manifested as Jesus. The scriptures in Exodus, Deuteronomy, and Joshua reflect a parallel between my salvation and the salvation of the Israelites. At an appointed time, God led me as He led the Israelites out of Egypt, which represented bondage and slavery to sin, to the Promised Land, which signified resting in peace, resting in Christ.

- While reading Numbers 21:4–9, I was perplexed to see God instructing Moses in verse 8 to build a statue of a snake and to lift it up in front of all the people before putting it on a pole. Why would God want a statue when He was fiercely against idols? Then it dawned on me when I studied John 3:14, when Jesus said, "Just as Moses lifted up the snake in the wilderness, so the Son of Man must be lifted up." I loved Jesus's statement telling the Jews at His time over and over that He eternally existed even before Moses and that Moses's action foretold of Jesus's work of salvation.

Numbers 21:4–9 paints a picture of how salvation will be brought to humankind through Christ. Moses's reaction illustrated a parallel between the bronze snake on the pole (for whoever looked at the snake was rescued and lived) and Jesus's crucifixion (victory over death on the cross—and whosoever believes in Him will live eternally). In Numbers 21:4–9, the Israelites were suffering from the snakes' bites and dying as a result of their disobedience to God. Their hope for not dying, and their hope for healing, was derived simply by looking at the bronze snake on the pole, showing the people that healing from death comes from God's power, not their own. In the same way, we, humankind, suffer as a result of sin (Romans 5:12). Our only hope of being rescued from eternal death (Romans 6:23) is salvation, which is granted by God's grace, not based on our own works (Romans 5:6). Faith in Christ is not a "work" or something we do, any more than the

Israelites' choosing to look at the bronze snake was one of their works.
- God foretold the Jewish people that the Leviticus sacrifices (Leviticus 17) would be overshadowed by the saving grace of Jesus Christ, who alone has the power to save Creation once and for all (Hebrews 9:6–15).

I enjoyed reading John Wesley's sermons, notably, "On the Holy Spirit" (2008), where he stated: "When he [Jesus] was incarnate and became man, he recapitulated in himself all generations of mankind, making himself the center of our salvation, that what we lost in Adam, even the image and likeness of God, we might receive in Christ Jesus."

Athanasius's statement "He [Jesus] became what we are that we might become what he is" confirms that we are saved because of Christ God Himself, who became a human being and died a human death. "He [God the Son, Jesus] became what we [humankind] are that we might become what he is. ... God became a human to make humans divine; the immortal became mortal to raise mortals to immortality. No mere creature could achieve this, but only the very Word of God [God the Son, Jesus]."

God did not create barriers preventing me from getting close to Him; on the contrary, it was me, my doing, my choice to push God away. And now, I aim to be Christlike and follow Jesus's steps as He modeled the ultimate obedience to and fellowship with God the Father.

> *Note:* Jesus is the one who enables salvation for us through His death on the cross. Through His blood, Jesus restores us to the likeness of God.

The Meaning of Christ Jesus in the Old Testament

Several of my friends asked me if Jesus was present as the God of the Old Testament. My usual response: "Of course He was! God does not only show up in the New Testament."

I believe that the Old Testament bears witness to the New Testament. I wouldn't be able to understand the New Testament without the Old Testament, being the introduction. Jesus, the angel of the Lord in the Old Testament, became incarnated in the New Testament and united all scriptures together in one tapestry, weaving the first chapter of Creation with the final chapter of Revelation—the end of the world.

I mentioned at the beginning of the chapter that the Old Testament describes events of the angel of the Lord appearing to people. The New Testament confirms that Jesus Christ, the second person of the Trinity, came to earth for a short time in angelic form.

I found in the Old Testament eleven encounters of God, manifested in different elements with various people. Each occurrence reveals the nature of Jesus.

- In Genesis, He appeared to Hagar as the angel who offered her hope amid her despair (Genesis 16:7–14).
- In Genesis 18:1–15, He emerged as a person, one of three strangers who came to Abraham and Sarah. He prophesied/promised that Sarah would have a son in a year, which she did, a year later; God fulfills His promises.
- In Genesis 18:20–33, He appeared as a person with divine authority, speaking as God, who heard the outcry against Sodom and Gomorrah and who pronounced His judgment on the cities for their wickedness.
- In Genesis 22:1–10, He appeared as the angel who stopped Abraham from sacrificing his son Isaac. Verse 16, "I swear by myself, declares the Lord," testifies to the authority of the angel as God.

- In Genesis 32:22–30 and Hosea 12:4, He appeared as a helper and a source of blessing when Jacob cried out to God for help and wrestled with an unknown man. Jacob refused to let go until the man realized it was God who had blessed him.
- In Exodus 3:2, 14, the voice that spoke to Moses from within the burning bush and as an angel was later self-revealed as the Great I Am and the God of Abraham, Isaac, and Jacob.
- In Exodus 13:21, He appeared to the Hebrews as a cloud by day and a pillar of fire by night. He rescued them from slavery and guided them out of Egypt and toward freedom in the Promised Land. Wouldn't you say that this passage in Exodus is another redemptive plan? The apostle Paul connected Jesus with God's redemption plan in Exodus, saying, "They all ate the same spiritual food and drank the same spiritual drink; for they drank from the spiritual rock that accompanied them, and that rock was Christ" (1 Corinthians 10:3–4). Both the Old Testament and the New Testament illustrate God's redemptive plan in Jesus, the One who died to free us from the slavery of sin.
- In Judges 6, God appeared to Gideon as an angel and commissioned him to fight the Midians.
  At first, Gideon did not realize that God the Son was speaking with him, until the flames spontaneously erupted and devoured his offering. Only then did Gideon realize he had encountered God, and immediately fear gripped him because he thought that for sure he would die. But God put Gideon at peace by responding, "I will be with you" (Judges 6:16). Just as Jesus led Gideon to victory, Jesus does the same thing for you and me; He fights on our behalf and commands our victory.
- In Judges 13:22, the angel of the Lord appeared twice to a barren Israelite woman and her husband Manoah

and told the woman that she would give birth to a son (Samson). He also said to them that their son would rescue the Israelites from the Philistines. Manoah told his wife that they were doomed to die because they had seen God.

- In Isaiah 6:1–10, the prophet Isaiah narrated his encounter with Christ in His glory in a vision (John 12:41), saying, "Woe to me! For I am destroyed! For I am a man of unclean lips, and I am living among a people of unclean lips, for my eyes have seen the king, Yahweh of hosts!" The prophet feared for his life after seeing God, but God assured him with His acceptance and commissioned him to spread the truth and the message of hope, life, and salvation. I, like the prophet and all believers, say to the Lord, "I am here. Send me" to witness to Jesus (Isaiah 6:8). John 12:41 reiterates that the prophet Isaiah testified about seeing Christ in His glory. Jesus's message of hope, life, and salvation has not changed.

In Daniel 3, King Nebuchadnezzar claimed that he saw a fourth person with Shadrach, Meshach, and Abednego when they were in the blazing furnace for refusing to worship the king. Commentators believe that the fourth person was none other than Jesus. In my heart I believe this to be so because Jesus stands by His promise that He will never leave His faithful children or forsake them.

Just as Jesus stood with Shadrach, Meshach, and Abednego in their dire time, Jesus, I know, will stand beside me in times of need and amid my most heated difficulties. Is it difficult or impossible for God to appear to humankind? *No!* Nothing is impossible for God.

In all these incidents, the people who have seen and heard, have seen and heard God the Son, who is the Word.

Micah 5:2 attests that Jesus was preexistent with God the Father and God the Holy Spirit before Adam lived. John 1:1–3;

Colossians 1:15–20; and Hebrews 1:2 affirm the supremacy of the Son of God, Jesus, as *the* One through whom God created all things. Each of the Godhead has all of God's attributes and nature for each is fully God, fully eternal, infinitely holy, omnipresent, omnipotent, and omniscient.

Athanasius summarized that Jesus is the God of the Old Testament, the God who was known to His people not under philosophical categories, but in His dealings with them as a Father, the Deliverer, He who would accomplish all things for those who waited on Him, the God of the covenant. He is the God of the New Testament, God in Christ reconciling the world to Himself, manifesting His righteousness in the gospel of Christ to whomsoever believes. In Christ, the Christian learns that God is love.

Conclusion

One of Jesus's names is Emmanuel, which means "God with us" (Matthew 1:23). And one of God's great promises is that "He will never leave you nor forsake you" (Deuteronomy 31:6; Joshua 1:5). In Hebrews 13:5 too, God promises, "Never will I leave you; never will I forsake you." I hold onto these verses with my life; they affirm that Jesus is the best friend, helper, protector, and confidante I can have for *all* times. I candidly can say that when I look back over my life, which has been plagued with danger, I see that God did not leave me to be prey. He stood by my side even when I did not feel His presence. He quietly lifted me up and rescued me. The scriptures have taught me to say with confidence, "The Lord is my helper. I will not be afraid. What can mere mortals do to me?" (Hebrews 13:6). God's promises and Word evoke in my heart a great power, comfort, and hope.

I never forget the day when I was driving through Richmond Park and thought of my dad. The park was one of his favorite places where we spent hours together walking and talking, with me holding his arm. His death left a big hole in my heart. I stopped the car and cried; I missed him so much. Some minutes later, I felt the warmth of giant arms embracing me. Wow! God the Father gave me, through His Spirit, what I needed. He is with us and closer than our own breath. God the heavenly Father wanted me to know that He will never leave me feeling abandoned and that He can and will give me what I miss from my earthly father—and much more.

God is a God of life. The Bible is pro-life because humankind is created in the image of God. Every person is valuable in God's eyes, including those aborted and killed before their births.

28
DISCOVERY JOURNEY TO GOD THE HOLY SPIRIT

How I Met the Holy Spirit

Before my conversion, I hardly knew anything about the Holy Spirit. A few days after my conversion, I learned that it was the Holy Spirit who had effected my supernatural transportation to the Chapel. I also learned that it was His gentle whisper that I had heard for the first time at the Chapel, calling me to follow Jesus. The still whisper of the Holy Spirit led me to convert. I will never forget the first time I heard the Holy Spirit whispering in my spirit. Ah, the softest and sweetest whisper! As the Lord Jesus said, the Holy Spirit became my Helper, Comforter, Advocate, Intercessor, Counselor, Strengthener, and Teacher (John 14:26 AB). Without the Holy Spirit, I could never have understood the scriptures; as a mentor, He revealed (in His own timing and His own way) the meaning and the purpose of scriptures, especially the metaphors.

In the first years after my conversion, I had numerous visions and dreams that showed me events that had happened in the past and those that will occur in the future. The Holy Spirit taught me how to test the spirits (1 John 4:1–6) and helped me interpret the visions and dreams according to God's Word (Joel 2:28).

With teaching and counseling came convicting and disciplining. The Holy Spirit never missed an occasion to discipline me. At times, I admit that I was stubborn and reluctant to change or confess my sins, or too embarrassed to expose the skeletons in my closet. But nothing compares to the times when I feel the presence of the Holy Spirit near me. Irrespective of my circumstances at the moment, whether I am asleep or awake, goose bumps crawl my body and I start smiling. With no exception and without fail, the Holy Spirit prepares me emotionally and spiritually for events about to happen or for prayers I need to pray. Quietly, He instructs me what to do.

Looking back at the day before I had a nervous breakdown in 2006, I now believe that the Holy Spirit prepared me. I was in the office working as usual, when suddenly my eyes went blurry and I could not read the lines in front of me. For a few minutes, my heartbeat was extremely fast, and I became confused as if I had lost my memory. I feared a heart attack. I cannot describe the panic of the moment that went on inside me. I closed my eyes and prayed. When my heartbeat stabilized, I called Dr. Smith, my GP, for an immediate appointment. I switched off my PC, turned my chair around to face the window, and watched the fleeting clouds in the sky. Suddenly, a gentle breeze tickled my neck, throwing goose bumps over my arms. "O Holy Spirit, I welcome You," I whispered. A tsunami of tears flooded my face. I could not stop crying. I do not remember what I prayed, but what happened in the following hour changed the course of my career and my life.

Suddenly, I had the urge to clear my desk. *What is the Holy Spirit up to now?* I thought. Although I did not understand the reason for packing, I complied. I can only say that my mind was beginning to shut down. Without any hesitation, I opened my drawers and file cabinets, removed my personal items, and stacked them in a box and in my briefcase. My packing felt very mechanical, more like a robot, not human. All I wanted was to leave the office. The walls seemed to be closing on me; anxiety mounted in my heart.

Once I had finished packing, I called a taxi. I told my secretary about my doctor's appointment. I picked up my box and briefcase and walked down the hall to the elevator. I ignored the comments of my colleagues who passed me by. By the time I reached the lobby, the taxi had arrived. I went through the revolving door, and before getting into the cab, I raised my head to peer at my office on the twelfth floor and gave a big sigh. In the taxi, I cried all the way. I did not know why. By the time I arrived at the doctor's office, I was in total hysteria. I broke down at the doctor's office. Two hours later, the doctor and his nurse escorted me to a taxi to take me home. The doctor handed me a letter, which I read at home. It was a copy of the letter he said he would send to my employer informing the management that he had signed me off work. He requested "indefinite leave" due to a severe nervous breakdown. When I look back on that day, I stand in awe at how the Holy Spirit prepared me to remove my personal items from the office, because I never went back to work. That was my last day in the office. The nervous breakdown led me to a psychiatric hospital, where I stayed for several long and hard weeks.

With a heavy heart, I resigned. Leaving the job that I loved broke my heart. For a long time, I mourned the loss of my career. Was God punishing me? He took what was precious in my eye, my self-identity, my income, my independence, my self-reliance. To escape it all, I left the country and moved to the United States. In one hand, I carried my past. With the other hand, I held on to God.

I joined a new church and enrolled in biblical counseling. Sunny, my counselor, was a gift from God. Gradually, she helped me release my anger against those who had hurt me. Sunny helped me see how I had created idols of my job, my income, and my self-identity. Unconsciously, I had worshipped my good-size income, and now I could not handle the fact that I had lost it. One day, Sunny reminded me of Matthew 6:24, where Jesus said, "No one can serve two masters. Either you will hate the one and love the other, or you will be devoted to the one and despise the other. You cannot serve both God and money." And it dawned on me. I repented. I realized that what I had gone through was part of God's will for my life. I submitted to God's will. With the guidance of the Holy Spirit, I walked on new ground. Sunny gracefully helped me open my spiritual eyes and ears to the Holy Spirit. Thank you, Sunny!

In my new walk, the Holy Spirit taught me one of the greatest lessons in my life that improved my Christian walk. It happened when the Holy Spirit led me to Luke 4. I read the chapter several times, wondering what the Spirit wanted me to know. The difference in the two verses is the position of the presence of the Holy Spirit within us. In Luke 4:1, it is written that Jesus was "*full* of the Holy Spirit," while in Luke 4:14 the Word of God says that "Jesus returned to Galilee *in the power of the Spirit*" (emphasis added). Then it dawned on me. When God regenerated me, the Holy Spirit indwelled in me; in other words, I became "filled" with the Holy Spirit (Luke 4:1). And Luke 4:14 taught me that if I wanted to perform the mission God had assigned to me to do, I needed the power of the Holy Spirit to empower me to achieve the task. I understood from Luke 4:14 that Jesus performed His miracles in Galilee through the power of the Holy Spirit. Also, Luke 4:14 showed me Jesus's humanness. Wow, what a revelation! From that moment on, I learned that I must invite my Teacher and Counselor, the Holy Spirit, to empower me in everything I want to do.

I felt the power of the Holy Spirit on several occasions. But for the purposes of *I Thought I Was Doing Well Until ...*, I will mention three events where the power manifested in different ways:

1. Following my conversion, my feelings toward my family began to soften. My conduct changed drastically from indifference and hatred to love, kindness, and self-control. My gentleness not only surprised my family but also surprised me. I never thought I could forgive my family. I

even pleaded to God to keep me away from them. But the magnetism between us became so strong, it kept pulling me to them. I knew that it must have been the power of God's Holy Spirit, who has not only changed me but also enabled me to show my family the fruit of the Spirit. God the Father, in the name of Jesus and through the power of the Holy Spirit, keeps working on me. God's teaching and changing are never-ending. They are continually in progress.

2. I always preferred witnessing for Jesus by writing instead of speaking. While applying for graduate school to study leadership, I shared in my Statement of Purpose my interest in a master's degree in leadership. I wanted to apply Jesus's leadership style in my life. More importantly, I took the Statement of Purpose as an opportunity to witness for Jesus.

At first, I struggled to find the right words to impress the admissions committee. For a couple of days, I wrote only one paragraph. I thought perhaps I needed help with my English language. My English teacher friend gave me a few writing clues. Still, I was not pleased with the letter. Frustration mounted as the submission deadline was nearing. I almost gave up on my dream of earning a master's degree, when suddenly I felt a familiar nudge and the tingling of goose bumps. And it dawned on me. I lacked God's power, not language skills. I needed the power of the Holy Spirit, not an English-language expert (with all due respect to my friend). I prayed, "O Holy Spirit of God, come and empower me to witness for Jesus. Flow Your words into my mind and out into the letter."

What I could not do in three days, the Holy Spirit empowered me to complete in one afternoon. While writing, not only did I feel the outpouring of the Holy Spirit, but also I found myself under His powerful teaching. I recall my fingers were racing to type what the Holy Spirit was dictating to me. When I read the statement, I could not believe my eyes. The language of the letter was powerful. There was no way I could have written the letter on my own as I had not mastered the English language to write such a persuasive letter.

It was the power of the Holy Spirit that empowered me to witness for Jesus, not only through the Statement of Purpose but also throughout my college years to professors and students.

3. The Word of God spoken through the prophet Zechariah reads, "This is the word of the Lord to Zerubbabel: 'Not by might nor by power, but by my Spirit,' says the Lord Almighty" (Zechariah 4:6). This verse never fails to prove that God will deliver on His promises for me and will work miracles in my life whenever I depend on the power of the Holy Spirit. *I Thought I Was Doing Well Until ...* is my testimony of the power of the Spirit. When the Lord asked me to write it, I did not know how to start. If it were not for the power of the Holy Spirit to empower me and encourage me, I could not have written this book on my own. As the Holy Spirit was influential in teaching me the scriptures and revealing their meaning, He was equally instrumental in *I Thought I Was Doing Well Until ...* in that He equipped me with writing abilities to achieve this goal.

I learned from Zechariah 4:6 that whenever God wants me to do a task, He will equip me with the talents and abilities to successfully achieve His purpose for His glory.

The Holy Spirit is the third person of the Trinity; He is God, along with God the Father and God the Son. God the Spirit has the same nature and characteristics as the Father and the Son, and yet He has distinct functions and roles. I gather from the scriptures that the Holy Spirit is the communicator between the Godhead and humankind. According to His will and grace, God sends His Holy Spirit to speak to humankind, to convict us, and convert us, and help us in seeking the kingdom of God. And this is what happened to me. The Holy Spirit regenerated me, led me to accept God's gift of salvation, and revealed to me the path to Jesus by seeking the kingdom of God and becoming His child.

Regeneration

I believe that God planted the seeds of faith in my soul when I was a child. However, it was only on Sunday,[69] April 5, 1996, that God the Holy Spirit supernaturally germinated the seeds and imparted to me a new spiritual life.

I understood later that on Sunday, April 5, 1996, God gave me two gifts: the gift of a new heart and the gift of faith. These two gifts led the seeds of faith in Jesus to suddenly sprout and come alive. By faith, I responded to His calling at the Chapel and proclaimed Him as my Lord and Savior. In other words, God "regenerated" me with a new heart, which activated my childhood faith and enabled me to convert. Without God's regeneration, I would not have accepted Jesus and converted. The entire conversion process was the work of God alone through the Holy Spirit. I had nothing to do with it; it was entirely out of my control. Therefore, no one can predict or plan his or her conversion. I thank God that my conversion was supernatural, so that no one can take credit for it. The conversion revived my spirit from being spiritually dead to spiritually alive.

The prophet Ezekiel prophesied the process of regeneration within believers with words spoken by God:

> I will give them an undivided heart and put a new spirit in them; I will remove from them their

---

[69] Either on that day or anytime before.

heart of stone and give them a heart of flesh. Then they will follow my decrees and be careful to keep my laws. They will be my people, and I will be their God. (Ezekiel 11:19–20)

With my new heart and revived spirit and faith, I became what the scripture calls "born again."[70] I craved Jesus's teaching and had the desire to learn everything about Him, especially how to follow Him. I committed to walk in Jesus's statutes, to keep His rules and obey them. I began attending weekly Bible studies at Mrs. Summons's house and Dr. Kendall's weekly Understanding Theology evening classes at the Chapel. I was like a sponge gathering information, some of which, I admit, went over my head. But I pressed on with full excitement and unwavering commitment.

Not long after my conversion, Melvyn and his wife Jane, a lovely couple I met from the Chapel, invited me to lunch. We went to the restaurant across the street from the church. As soon as we sat down, Jane asked me if I was saved. Huh? Otherwise, she said that I *needed* to be born again and saved to receive God and enter the kingdom of God. Huh? Jane's question caught me by surprise. Before I could ask her what she meant, Melvyn seconded Jane's comment and added that attending church or Bible studies would not save me. Melvyn stressed that I *must* be *saved* to become a child of God and have eternal life.

Salvation

The words *need* and *must* challenged me. In my mind, I believed that I was born again and was saved from the moment I accepted Jesus's calling and confessed Him as my Lord and God. I passionately believed that my confession assured me that Lord Jesus had saved me from the penalty of eternal punishment in

---

[70] Also called regeneration.

hell for my sins and had granted me eternal life in heaven. Isn't that what salvation means? Wasn't I then saved? Also, I based my salvation on the scriptures, as follows:

1. Acts 16:30–31
   When the jailer asked Paul and Silas, "Sirs, what must I do to be saved?" they replied, "Believe in the Lord Jesus, and you will be saved—you and your household."
2. Romans 10:9–10, which reads, "If you declare with your mouth, 'Jesus is Lord,' and believe in your heart that God raised him from the dead, you will be saved. For it is with your heart that you believe and are justified, and it is with your mouth that you profess your faith and are saved."
3. 2 Timothy 1:9, where the past tense of the verb assures my salvation. "He *has saved* us and called us to a holy life—not because of anything we have done, but because of his own purpose and grace. This grace was given us in Christ Jesus before the beginning of time" (emphasis added).

Dr. R. T. Kendall (1998[71]) wrote:

> What could possibly be more important than the Atonement? ... Nothing assures us of being saved like a clear understanding of the atonement. This is because it is not great faith that saves, but only faith in a great Savior.

The magnitude of Jesus's sacrifice and atonement on my behalf is beyond my mental ability to grasp (although I accepted it by faith). I am confident that I am saved by believing and putting my faith in Jesus, the great Savior. For His love for me, He endured

---

[71] R. T. Kendall, *Understanding Theology*, vol. I (Ross-shire: Christian Focus Publications, 1998), pp. 113, 114.

suffering, even death on the cross, and the shedding of His blood as the ransom to free my soul held captive by sin.

I can't tell you how relieved I am to have the Holy Spirit indwelling in me as my Counselor and Helper. I look to His counsel and wisdom in decision-making and taking action. Experience has shown me that relying on the Holy Spirit has saved me time and heartache in completing tasks, reaching better decisions, and achieving goals. Waiting on the Holy Spirit is not as easy as it sounds. I learned the hard way that God's timing, will, and means are different from mine. I recall those times when I failed to ask for the guidance of the Holy Spirit or I was too impatient to wait for a response; oh boy, did I regret it! When I make mistakes, the Holy Spirit always gently makes me aware of my faults. He speaks to me, for example, "You did not pray about it, did you? Okay, let's work it out together." It is not only guilt that leads me to repentance; it is the fear and the reverence of God, compounded with the hearing of the cry of Jesus on the cross, echoing in my heart, "Abba, forgive ..." that makes me run to God for forgiveness. When the Holy Spirit exposes my sinful actions, instead of condemning or convicting me, He leads me to the truth in God's Word. He reminds me of who I am in Christ. The Holy Spirit tells me that God, by His grace and my faith in Jesus's atoning sacrifice, has justified me and regenerated me to be righteous in Christ (Romans 3:28, 4:5, 5:1; Titus 3:1–8). The knowledge of who I am in Christ warns me, with big flashing lights, from going down a wrong path. Daily, I ask the Holy Spirit to strengthen my self-control to turn away from sinning or making wrong and hasty decisions.

After my conversion, the Holy Spirit started bringing to my mind past actions or behaviors of which I needed to repent. Perhaps it was part of God's regeneration of my spirit. The more I meditated on Jesus's sacrifice, the more I regretted my past life attitude and disbelief, and the more I repented and asked His forgiveness. It was not that I repented of my past sins and then stopped sinning. It wasn't that I started doing good deeds for God to save me. This would have been considered salvation by way of works. And this is incorrect because the scriptures say that we are saved by faith in Jesus, not by works.

I quickly learned that repentance is the result of regeneration, not the cause of it. Repentance is essential to salvation and cannot be separated from it. The scripture says: "Godly sorrow brings repentance that leads to salvation and leaves no regret" (2 Corinthians 7:10). Based on my experience, I found that repentance and salvation are linked. I could not have been saved unless I was willing to repent and turn away from the sins I had been living in. For example, I changed my lifestyle and behavior to please God and live according to His commands (Romans 2:4). One of the first changes that I made was to ask Victor, my boyfriend at the time, to move out. When he protested, I broke up with him once and for all. I have not seen him since.

I studied the verses and the commentaries about salvation; I gradually started to realize that salvation is *not* a deed-related earning. And that was a tough one for me because I had to reprogram my brain since, for years, I believed that my good deeds were my passport to enter paradise. Whereas in Christianity, the scriptures stress that good deeds will not grant salvation, simply because *salvation is God's gift to me through His grace* and *my faith in Jesus*. The scripture affirms, "For by grace you have been saved through faith [in Jesus], and that not of yourselves; it is the gift of God, not of works, lest anyone should boast" (Ephesians 2:8–9).

God's grace, coupled with my faith in Jesus's work, as well as my repentance, was a catalyst for my salvation. I learned from the scriptures that two parts are involved in receiving salvation: God's part and humankind's part. God, by His grace, offers humankind the gift of salvation, and the Holy Spirit leads a person to repentance and stirs his or her heart to receive God's gift. It is our choice to either accept or decline God's gift of salvation, which He extends to us. That's what happened to me.

God, by His grace, freely offered me the gift, and I willingly chose to accept it and take it. My salvation formed a partnership/relationship between God and me. The question remained as to how to manifest this partnership in my life to glorify God. What is next to salvation? How to serve Jesus and fulfill His calling? For a long while, I prayed Colossians 1:9–14 for wisdom and guidance.

The Holy Spirit guided me to Matthew 6:33: "Seek first his kingdom and his righteousness, and all these things will be given to you as well."

But how to seek the kingdom of God? Again, Jesus's Word gave me the answer by saying, "Very truly I tell you, no one can see the Kingdom of God unless they are born again" (John 3:3).

"But, Lord, I am born again!" I cried to God. "And my conversion attests to my faith in Jesus."

I revisited Melvyn's and Jane's comments regarding the words *need* and *must* and wondered if they were bringing to my attention "receiving the kingdom of God."

Quickly, I found out that the kingdom of God is one of God's mysteries. I read many views, some of which pointed to the future time when God will create a kingdom reigned over by the Messiah as the King. Other descriptions pointed to Jesus and God's rules. In my mind, I believe the kingdom of God encompasses both interpretations.

It is my understanding that Jesus inaugurated the kingdom of God when He came to earth and unveiled the gifts of redemption and salvation to the world. Jesus told His people that the kingdom of God is "is in your midst," "near," and "upon you" (Luke 17:20–21; Matthew 3:2, 12:28). I believe that in these three verses and throughout the New Testament, Jesus was speaking about Himself. He was and still is present and alive. Jesus Christ *is* the King right now. When Christ returns to earth, He will establish His kingdom with believers. At that time, the invisible kingdom of God will become visible and all people around the world will see Jesus, the King, ruling the kingdom. Hallelujah!

I rejoice in the assurance that I have received Jesus, the kingdom of God, in my heart. His power and truth live inside me. In other words, I live under Jesus Christ's lordship, seeking His righteousness, peace, and joy through the Holy Spirit.

For months, I felt a gradual longing to become a child of God. The Holy Spirit led me to John 1:12–13, which reads, "Yet to all who did receive him, to those who believed in his name, he gave the right to become children of God—children born not of natural descent, nor of human decision or a husband's will, but born of God." Romans 8:13–14 states, "For all who are led by the Spirit of God are sons of God." I learned from this verse that unless the Holy Spirit is dwelling in me, then I am led by the Spirit to understand the Spirit's written Word (the scriptures), hear in my heart His whisper, change my life, and become a child of God.

I invited my group for another round of discussion. Mrs. Summons suggested going around the table so each one of us could share our understanding of the verses.

Nabil said, "I see mandates and conditions to receive the right to become a child of God."

Gretchen said, "I don't see them as mandates or conditions; I see choices. Some believed, and some did not. God gives us choices, yeah? It is up to us to choose the path of life we want, and when we do so, then we have to accept its consequences."

Anwar said, "Is becoming a child of God a right you earn or a gift you receive when you convert? If the latter, then it should be free. If the former, then I see God putting mandates and conditions on it, things you need to do to earn the right. What happens if you do not meet the conditions? Isn't enough to declare your belief in Jesus to become a Christian? In Islam, converting to Islam is easy. All you must do is to recite the Testimony of Faith (al-Shahada). And to please Allah, we do good deeds in life, for which He, through His grace, rewards us by granting us entry to paradise. 'Allah said, 'Behold! This is the Paradise which you are made to inherit as a reward for your deeds'" (al-Arafa 7:43[72])."

June said, "So, Anwar, wouldn't you say that the good deeds you do are the underlying conditions or mandates for you to go to paradise?" Anwar quietly wobbled his head. When he did not reply, June continued explaining that the verses are pointing to Jesus as "He." God gives us the right to become His child when we receive Jesus, who represents the kingdom of God. The disciple Mark wrote in 10:13–15:

> People were bringing little children to Jesus for him to place his hands on them, but the disciples rebuked them. When Jesus saw this, he was indignant. He said to them, "Let the little children come to me, and do not hinder them, for the Kingdom of God belongs to such as these. Truly I tell you, *anyone who will not receive the Kingdom of God like a little child will never enter it.* (emphasis added)

When it was my turn, I agreed with June that the verses in John 1:12–13 are pointing to the second person in the Trinity, Jesus. I believe that the moment God regenerated me as born again and I received Jesus, God gave me the right to become a child of God in the kingdom of God.

I shared with the group that John 1:12–13 and Mark 10:15 laid down the principles to follow for receiving God's eternal gift of becoming His child. Suddenly, the room echoed "How?" in one voice.

"I want to get baptized in water!" I exclaimed.

The group received my announcement with mixed feelings. Anwar was the first to caution me about baptism. Anwar's

---

[72] Ibid., 200.

comment reminded me of my sister's warning to skip baptism because it would seal my conversion.

I kept my baptismal date a secret; I wanted to focus on God and the process without any distractions. Two weeks before my baptism day, I went shopping to buy my baptism outfit, all in white. In my heart, I wanted my baptism to be like what is described in Psalm 51:7.[73] I spent the days before my baptism in quiet time, meditating on the Word and repenting. I recall I was unusually quiet and at peace both at work and at home.

On March 9, 1997, the day of my baptism, I met with the six other people scheduled to be baptized. Dr. Kendall and Bill Reynolds joined us to give us last-minute instructions. Bill handed us each a certificate of baptism, and I asked if I could put down my new Christian name. "Yes, you may," he responded, So, I put "Marie Christine," the name I'd always wanted to have since my childhood! Praise God!

I was baptized by full immersion at Westminster Chapel. I was excited beyond words. I was ready to make a public confession that I was not ashamed of becoming Jesus's follower. I realized that water baptism was only a symbolic, external act to declare my faith publicly. Dr. D. Prince (1993) wrote, "The act of baptism was an outward seal and confirmation of an inward spiritual condition." I wanted to profess publicly my conscious decision and commitment to dedicate my life to Jesus Christ. I was eager to be baptized because I wanted to publicly declare my faith in Jesus, the Son of God, and in His sacrificial death to free me from my sins. I was excited to be baptized because I wanted to restore my relationship with God ASAP and be united symbolically with Christ in His death, burial, and resurrection.

The water baptism was for me a unique experience. For example, before being immersed in the water, I identified with

---

[73] "Cleanse me with hyssop, and I will be clean; wash me, and I will be whiter than snow."

Jesus on the cross, thanking God for forgiving me, as I did not know what I was doing. In front of the congregation and guests who attended the baptism ceremony, I reiterated my confession in Christ and my belief in the new covenant and thanked God for saving me "from the dominion of darkness and [for bringing me] into the kingdom of the Son he loves, in whom we have redemption, the forgiveness of sins" (Colossians 1:13–14).

While immersed in the water, I symbolically buried my sins—a representation of Jesus's death and burial. I put my old self to death. As I rose from the water, I identified with Jesus's resurrection and coming alive anew. I came out with a new beginning, clothed with Jesus, dedicated to Christ, forgiven, freed from being a slave to sin (Romans 6:1–4).[74] What a glorious moment! On that day, God, through His grace, handed me the baton to run my race to witness about Jesus, proclaiming to all "The kingdom of God is here!" and the gospel of salvation. For this, I rejoice for having passed from spiritual death into life through the Spirit of God. I rejoice for having been transported from the dominion of darkness into the Kingdom of Light and Hope (Colossians 1:13).

I wish I could say that after my conversion, everything in my life became smooth and rosy, but such was not the case. Far from it. Soon after my conversion, I experienced what the Bible calls Satan's attacks on believers. I warn you: they are ferocious and vicious. When the word got out that I had converted, I received angry and threatening phone calls. People who objected to my conversion stalked me and chased me, intending to hurt me. People's hostility led them to report me to the police, falsely accusing me of fabricating bombs in my flat. Sure enough, the

---

[74] "Or don't you know that all of us who were baptized into Christ Jesus were baptized into his death? We were therefore buried with him through baptism into death in order that, just as Christ was raised from the dead through the glory of the Father, we too may live a new life."

day after I had been reported, at five o'clock in the morning, the police closed off the surrounding streets with yellow tape and raided my flat. They found nothing and left with apologies. For a couple of hours, the police interrogated me. In the end, they asked me if I had any enemies, knowing I was a victim of a terrible hoax. I shared with the police that I had converted, adding that the incident was retaliation for my conversion. The police agreed with me and asked me to stay the next few days at an undisclosed location. I left the police station shaken and stayed away from home until the security company Banham installed a security system in my flat. According to police protocol, the police did not disclose to me the names of the perpetrators. While I forgave the people responsible, I will never forget the incident. God alone knows who did it, and He will bring those responsible ones to His judgment (if not already done).

I put all hate-related incidents behind me, and I moved on to change myself, mold myself, and train myself to fulfill the mission He had commissioned me to do.

Following my baptism, I felt as if I were going through endless cleansing cycles. O the never-ending cleansing of the Holy Spirit! Like peeling an onion one layer at a time, the Holy Spirit worked in me. Repentance became my daily workout. Gradually, I noticed a change within me. One day, my dad complimented me for the radical change in my behavior. "You have changed," he said. "You have become softer and gentler." My priorities had changed; my focus in life had shifted. I put Jesus first; I became last. The knowledge that Christ lives in me changed my life. I yielded entirely to the Holy Spirit to change me from the inside out, so those with eyes to see and ears to hear would notice God's glory and His presence in my life.

PART VIII
HE REGENERATED ME

And you *He made alive*, who were dead in trespasses and sins.
—Ephesians 2:1 (NKJV; emphasis added)

29
AND HE REGENERATED ME

How God Changed Me
My friend June told me that when God regenerates us, He revives our spiritual heart, removes the scales of blindness from our spiritual eyes, and opens our blocked spiritual ears. That was the first time I had heard about spiritual eyes and ears. June's comment reminded me of the verse God spoke through the prophet Ezekiel, saying, "Son of man, you are living among a rebellious people. They have eyes to see but do not see and ears to hear but do not hear, for they are a rebellious people" (Ezekiel 12:1–2).

What June was saying was that to seek the kingdom of God, that is, Jesus and His righteousness, I must change. The thought of change terrified me. I never imagined I could change, let alone change my destiny. I believed that my past had already shaped my future, while anger and rebellion molded my personality. I had grown accustomed to living in my foxhole; getting myself out of it seemed impossible. Besides, I did not want to change. Change to what? I was comfortable in my own skin.

Until my conversion, the horrific experience of my childhood abuse had turned my heart to stone. I hated everyone for letting me down; I distrusted everyone and everything, including Allah. I turned my pain into a promise to get revenge on those who had hurt me. I concealed my emotional struggle with rejection, distrust, and depression behind a thick wall of bricks in my heart, determined to keep the abuse completely secret. I applied the lessons I had learned from my dad on how to look tough and pretend I was happy even during my darkest hours. So, I wore a happy face mask and moved on with my life. I tried my luck with marriage, hoping to taste a bit of happiness, coveting my friends. Little did I know that my husband did not love me. The marriage ended in divorce. The divorce crushed my spirit. I channeled my anger into focusing on my career and aiming for success. I drowned my sorrow in workaholism; I loved my work despite the job stress, and quickly it became my identity and my god. Unfortunately, the bottled grief and anxiety caught up with me and started attacking my health. I fell prey to endometriosis, which poisoned my female organs; I ended up having a hysterectomy. New waves of depression and deep sadness engulfed me. An intense bonfire of anger raged inside me. I blamed Allah for my misfortune and cursed those toxic people who had caused the stress-related condition for which I had to have surgery. There is not a single day I don't think of and grieve the loss of the possibility of being a mother.

    I moved to London for a fresh start. Unfortunately, disasters didn't stop raiding my life at every turn. You name it, I've had it. Three crises struck me at the same time: (1) cancer threatened my health, (2) my boyfriend's extravagant spending had left me with considerable debt, and (3) bullying had endangered my reputation and career. All three problems came in like a wrecking ball and crushed me, plunging me into the worst suffering and frustration I have ever experienced. I became an absolute train wreck! I reached the end of my strength and gave up on the last thread of hope. My pride and ego kept me from calling on my dad for help. Did I contemplate suicide? You bet, but I was too afraid to do it. So, as a last resort, I called on Allah for help. Instead, Jesus responded.

It was around that time when Jesus showed up in my life. Someone told me that God has perfect timing: never early, never late, He is always on time. Also, Dr. R. T. Kendall wrote in *When God Shows Up* (1998), "There is no question that God shows up in our lives in unexpected ways and at unexpected times—and always when we need Him most."

Indeed, the Lord Jesus showed up at the time when I needed Him most. I candidly say that when Jesus called me to follow Him, I did not think of my physical and financial crises. My mind was focused on his calling. I answered Jesus's calling for who He was, my God. Period. I learned later that the Holy Spirit had prepared my heart to receive Jesus and accept His calling. Ezekiel 12:1–2 describes my spiritual condition before my conversion. I was rebellious living with rebellious people. By His grace and mercy, God, through the Holy Spirit, revived my spiritual heart, removed the scales of blindness from my spiritual eyes, and opened my blocked spiritual ears. I had no clue what the calling was about or why Jesus had called me. But I can say that since that encounter, my journey of healing unexpectedly started. I am thankful that Jesus called me.

From the genesis of my Christian walk, I learned about sin, the devil, and demons. I got scared when I learned that according to the scriptures I am a sinner deserving of God's wrath. What? How can I be a sinner when I was a victim of horrific abuse that left me emotionally disabled with permanent scars? Had I not suffered enough? How could I be a sinner when I had committed no crimes? I did not kill anyone (okay, I did wish death to those who abused me). I did not lie except white and innocent lies. I did not steal, etc. Okay, so I hated with passion those who abused me and the fact that child sexual abuse is a taboo subject to disclose and acknowledge due to the shame and stigma. Overall, I thought I was a decent person with morals and ethical values (at least humanly speaking and from worldly standards). But when the scriptures showed me that my habits and morals fell short of what the holy God demanded, I tried to justify my shortcomings before God in prayer. I blamed the abuse, saying that it had made me the rebellious person I had become. *So you see, God, I had valid reasons, right?* I was dead wrong! The knowledge of God's stance toward sin filled me with fear, deep sorrow, and regret. On the one hand, I did not want to perish, and on the other hand, I was eager to please God and become His child.

At the time I discovered God's position on sin and Satan, I learned about God's grace. God's grace made a significant difference to my heart. God's grace filled my heart with humbleness and meekness, as I found that God does not deal with me according to my sins and inequities. In other words, God does not punish me or retaliate against me for my unfaithfulness to Him. What a relief! Indeed, God's grace is undeserved favor.

Soon after my conversion, I listened to a sermon by Pastor J. Piper (1986), "Preparing to Receive Christ: Willing to Do the Will of God." The pastor made me think of what I should do to prepare my heart to follow Jesus when he said, "Something has to happen deep down in the root of our will to remove the rebellion against God that we all have by nature … to take away our antagonism against the authority of God."

I understood from Pastor Piper that I needed to cleanse myself of my rebellion and trespasses against God (Romans 6:23) so I could move under His authority and will. While my head registered what I needed to do, my heart lagged considerably behind, not because I lacked faith, but because the changes were easier said than done.

Being an anxious and doubtful person, I was afraid to change; character and behavioral changes are big things. Because my heart had gone through a constant beating, it had grown frail and sensitive, especially to change. Change threatened some areas in me that I was too embarrassed to expose before God. Change scared me because I was skeptical of the unknown outcome. What type of person would I become? The adjustments I might need to make and the things I might need to let go of frightened me. Besides, I did not want to change everything about me. There were some character traits I was comfortable with that formed my identity. Above all, I resisted God's change because it meant I would no longer be in control of my life.

Relinquishing my self-control was not natural to me. But the pain from the three recent disasters that struck me all at once had brought me to my knees. I came to the end of myself. Losing hope grieved me more than any pain; it was the worst suffering.

It is one thing to want God to change me, and it is another to *allow* Him to change me. I came to face the reality that unless I allowed God to change me (i.e., unless I submitted my will to God and invited the Holy Spirit to effect the change), God's plans for my life wouldn't happen.

I tried to get rid of my self-will myself. But I found it almost impossible to do alone as I was stuck in an inner emotional prison. So, I cried out of my depth: "God, have mercy on me, a sinner" (Luke 18:13).

Out of His love for me (and to you), God responded and poured His grace onto me. I felt loved and secure. God's grace filled me with new hopes and desires. I longed to receive His promises that He has for me, one of which is about His plans for my life, "plans to prosper [me] and not to harm [me], plans to give [me] hope and a future" (Jeremiah 29:11).

How Did I Receive the Change?

How did God change me? When I received Jesus in my heart, He bestowed on me a type of love I had never experienced before. His peace, which surpasses all understanding, helped me to learn to trust for the first time in my life. I took refuge in Him, and He became my fortress in which, gradually, I let my guard down. I allowed God to change me, and the Holy Spirit slowly started to work on me. The Holy Spirit brought Jesus's teaching alive in my life. I learned that when I turned against God and His authority, I unconsciously allowed evil and rebellious spiritual forces that are against God into my spirit and soul. They controlled my mind and heart, which were under their influence and will. By doing so, I had walked onto wrong paths with sharp turns and made wrong decisions that ended in painful consequences. It was a chilling discovery!

The more I read the scriptures, the more I found a God contrary to what I believed (as well as contrary to popular belief). I found a gentle and loving God, not a God of fear, eternal wrath, and destruction. Before conversion, I thought God was harsh, pouring onto me and the world His calamities. Then, I found out through His Word that it was my obedience to ungodly spirits that had led me into disaster, not the almighty God! I was shortsighted with thick scales on my eyes, unable to consider my problems as trials aimed to get my attention and turn me to God. Instead, I ran from them and missed the growth and transformation they otherwise would have brought.

Because God knew of my inability to accept and receive love, He waited for my move toward Him, for He is such a gentle and patient God. He does not impose Himself on us. Psalm 103 and Zephaniah 3:17 gave me a glimpse of God. Truly, God is love!

In short, by studying the scriptures, I recognized that I had built my life on a heap of sins and rebellion, away from God. Sorrow choked me. But no greater sorrow dwelled within me than that which arose when I discovered that my sins grieved God. For days I mourned with deep regret for my sins.

God Started Changing Me
By God's grace and love, the wheels of my life started slowly to move in a different direction. Changes in my behavior, character, and values began to crystalize and manifest in adjustments in my personal and professional life. Some were more radical than others, and some were instantaneous rather than planned or premeditated. One of the most significant changes was the

opening of my spiritual eyes to see visions and of my spiritual ears to hear God's voice. From the first vision I had, I knew that I had become spiritually alive! A flowing stream of inner joy gushed through me and watered my hope with the living water (the Holy Spirit dwelling in me). That was the first time I had had a taste of inner joy and peace!

Another awe-striking change that I noticed was my unexpected love and forgiveness toward my family. My conversion transformed my relationship with every member of my family, including those who had hurt me. Deep wells of anger and blame that had poisoned my mind for decades had suddenly dried up. In place, new geysers of love erupted, broke the walls of bricks, behind which I had jailed myself, and ushered me to freedom. I admit that forgiveness did not happen instantaneously. There were times I resisted forgiving certain people with the excuses "God, do You not know what they did to me?" and "You don't know how painful it was." God did not force me to forgive; He gave me the free will and the mind to *choose* to forgive.

While forgiveness did not erase the bad memories, it did heal the sting. I wondered why God did not permanently uproot the horrific events from my mind. Perhaps God wanted to teach me a lesson: every time I recall painful memories, I develop a hatred for my sins. The lesson learned is never to repeat the same mistake. I marveled at God's transformation of my heart as if I'd had a heart transplant!

I noticed that it was the spiritual changes that first took effect and, in turn, influenced changes in the physical aspects of my life. This is what is meant by regeneration.

The *Holman Bible Dictionary* defines *regeneration* as follows: "the radical spiritual change in which God brings an individual from a condition of spiritual defeat and death to a renewed condition of holiness and life. The biblical doctrine of Regeneration emphasizes God's role in making this spiritual change possible."

M. G. Easton (1989) defined *regeneration* in his *The Illustrated Bible Dictionary*:

> This word literally means "new birth." ... In Matthew 19:28 the word is equivalent to the "restitution of all things" (Acts 3:21 KJV). In Titus 3:5 it denotes that change of heart elsewhere spoken of a passing from death to life (1 John 3:14); becoming a new creature in Christ Jesus (2 Corinthians 5:17); being born again (John 3:3–5); a renewal of the mind (Romans 12:2); a resurrection from the dead (Ephesians 2:6). [...] This change is ascribed to the Holy Spirit. It originates not with man but with God (John 1:12, 13; 1 John 2:29, 5:1, 4). As to the nature of the change, it consists in the implanting of a new principle or disposition in the soul. When God created Adam, the disposition of his heart was created holy. Regeneration is the recreating of the governing disposition; The impartation of spiritual life to those who are by nature "dead in trespasses and sins" (Ephesians 2:1, NKJV). The necessity of such a change is emphatically affirmed in scriptures (John 3:3; Romans 7:18, 8:7–9; 1 Corinthians 2:14; Ephesians 2:1 [NKJV], 4:21–24). (577)

In other words, to be born again, I have to overcome my sinful nature that does not please God. To do that, I have to rely on discernment through the Holy Spirit, who lives in me.

I noticed that my firm commitment to follow Jesus led me to open my heart to repentance. Repentance became my daily exercise. Sometimes, it was hard. But the Holy Spirit helped me to press on. I noticed that the more my knowledge in the Word about the Godhead deepened, the more my faith grew, the more I repented, and the more the *grace of God changed me* (it is an ongoing process). Faith and repentance are the wheels that led me to change. I stress that regeneration is not my doing. Regeneration is a gift offered by God's grace to create a new me and you, a new creature as per 2 Corinthians 5:17. Hallelujah!

Being free from the sting of sin doesn't mean that I have stopped sinning. God, through the Holy Spirit, corrects me in two ways: by convicting me whenever I sin, and by reminding me of the ungodly actions I've done in the past. All I have to do in these situations is repent. Dr. R. T. Kendall (1998[75]) wrote, "There are two kinds of repentance. One is being sorry because you got caught. … The second kind of repentance is a real change of mind." These words helped me to evaluate the sincerity of my repentance. The book *God Meant It for Good* also helped me to divert my mind from the thought *God is punishing me.*

It is worth mentioning that while God gave me the free will to choose my actions, the power of the Holy Spirit dwelling in me empowers me now with the will to resist sin and choose God's ways. I followed King David's example by asking God to create in me a pure heart. I made Psalm 51 my personal daily prayer.

I admit that I still struggle to this day with forgiveness. I struggle with forgiving myself and those who abused me and destroyed my childhood. I thought that by not forgiving them, I was displaying power over them and holding off God's blessing over them. I was dead wrong! One of my aha moments was when I learned that *I* am the beneficiary of forgiving others! By forgiving others, I experience freedom from the power of sin, resentment, and hatred. It removes a massive weight off my shoulders. I discovered that only by forgiving others, I receive God's forgiveness and His blessings of peace and joy. Jesus said,

---

[75] R. T. Kendall, *God Meant It for Good* (Carlisle, Cumbria: Paternoster Press, 1995), 169.

"But if you do not forgive others their sins, your Father will not forgive your sins" (Matthew 6:15). Reading and meditating on the psalms and the book of Job helped me a lot in healing my emotions and releasing resentment. Next to the Bible, Dr. Kendall's book *God Meant It for Good* helped me tremendously (and still does) in learning about helpless and hopeless trials, God's position in trials, and the victory of forgiveness. It is a book I highly recommend that you read! You will not regret it!

I thank God for regenerating me into the person He created me to be, to do the work He assigned for me since the genesis of the world. You may ask what proof I have that the Holy Spirit changed me. Well, my family, friends, and colleagues noticed many changes in me. For example, my worldview changed from my perspective to God's viewpoint. The arrogant spirit behind which I had displayed a show-off superiority to hide my lack of self-esteem fled. Instead, the Lord filled me with a humble spirit. My priorities changed; I put my relationship with God first, even before my family.

Becoming a follower of Jesus was an exciting journey. Do I regret the changes, some of which were radical? Absolutely *not*! The good news is that I did not go through the transformation alone (nor will you), because the power of the Holy Spirit within me guided me and strengthened me. I never doubted my conversion, and I never looked back. Daily, I thank Jesus for saving me and transforming my lifestyle and behavior. I feel a shift in my spiritual atmosphere with a new sense of being a child of God. As a result, changes became more natural to me, and obeying God becomes more comfortable, because of my love for and gratitude to Him.

Life's trials left me stranded with nowhere to go but to God. The closer I got to God, the more I came to know Him. Falling in love with God was inevitable. C. S. Lewis, in *The Problem of Pain* (1940), wrote, "God whispers to us in our pleasures, speaks in our conscience, but shouts in our pains: it is His megaphone to rouse a deaf world."

In summary, becoming a follower of Jesus led me to change completely the way I think, speak, behave, and live. I am no longer the same. I allowed God to let my old self die while I rose with Jesus as a new person to a new life in Him. The apostle Paul said, "I have been crucified with Christ and I no longer live, but Christ lives in me. The life I now live in the body, I live by faith in the Son of God, who loved me and gave himself for me" (Galatians 2:20).

I thank God for regenerating me and loving me first. I thank God for saving me and choosing me to serve Him and glorify Him in everything I do, giving Him all the glory and praise. I welcome God's work in me for His glory until the end of my life. Until then, the work is in progress.

I thought I was doing well until I found that I was not living life to its fullest. But now, in Him, I am!

SOURCES

"#108: Athanasius on Christ Athanasius." Christian History Institute. Accessed January 4, 2021, https://christianhistoryinstitute.org/study/module/athanasius.

"356 Prophecies Fulfilled in Jesus Christ." According to the Scriptures. Accessed January 4, 2021, https://www.accordingtothescriptures.org/prophecy/353prophecies.html.

Bullinger, E. W. *Figures of Speech Used in the Bible.* New York: Cosimo Classics, 2012.

Cummings, C. K. *Covenant of Grace: A Key to an Understanding of the Bible for Young Christians.* Suwanee: Great Commission Publications, 1987.

Easton, M. G. *Illustrated Bible Dictionary.* New York: Crescent, 1989, 577.

Erickson, M. J. *Christian Theology*, 2nd ed. Grand Rapids, MI: Baker Book House, 1998, 517.

Grigg, R. "Made in the Image of God." *Creation* 16, no. 4: 42–45. https://creation.com/made-in-the-image-of-god.

Henry, M. *Concise Commentary on the Whole Bible.* Nashville, TN: Thomas Nelson, 1997, 116.

Hodge, C. *Systematic Theology*, vol. 1. Peabody, MA: Hendrickson, 2020. First published 1871, 485.

Kendall. R. T. *Understanding Theology*, vol. II. Ross-shire, Christian Focus Publications, 2000, 75.

———. *God Meant It for Good*. Carlisle, Cumbria: Paternoster Press, 1998, pp. 54, 169.

———. *Understanding Theology*, vol. I. Ross-shire: Christian Focus Publications, 1998, pp. 28, 52, 116.

Lallier. J. "What Makes an Idol?" Life Hope & Truth. https://lifehopeandtruth.com/bible/blog/what-makes-an-idol.

Lewis, C. S. *Mere Christianity*. New York: HarperCollins, 2002, 130.

Lloyds-Jones. M. *Why Does God Allow War?* Bryntirion, Bridgend, Wales: Bryntirion Press, 1939, pp. 79–80.

MacArthur, J. *Worship: The Ultimate Priority*. Chicago: Moody, 1983, 166.

Morris. H. *The Genesis Record*. Grand Rapids, MI: Baker Book House, and El Cajon, CA: Master Books, 1990, 74.

Nilsen. B. "Why God Has to Be a Jealous God." Active Christianity. https://activechristianity.org/why-god-has-to-be-a-jealous-god-be-a-jealous-god.

Phillips, J. B. *J. B. Phillips' the New Testament in Modern English*. New York: Scribner, 1972, pp. 412–13.

Piper, J. "Preparing to Receive Christ: Willing to Do the Will of God" (sermon), 1986. Desiring God. https://www.

desiringgod.org/messages/preparing-to-receive-christ-willing-to-do-the-will-of-god.

Prince, D. *The Spirit-Filled Believer's Handbook.* Eastbourne: Bookprint Creative Services, 1994, pp. 253–54.

The Qur'an: Arabic Text with Corresponding English Meanings. Singapore: Abul-Qasim, 1997. Saheeh International Translation.

    al-Baqara 2:256, p. 53.
    Ali'Imran 3:45, p. 69.
    Ali'Imran 3:64, p. 72.
    al-Arafa 7:43, p. 200.
    al-Anbiya 21:91, p. 448.
    al-Waqi'ah 56:79, p. 773.
    al-Kafirun 109:26, p. 910.

Schaff, Philip. "ANF01. The Apostolic Fathers with Justin Martyr and Irenaeus." Edited by A. Roberts and J. Donaldson. Grand Rapids, MI: Christian Classics Ethereal Library, 2002. https://www.holybooks.com/wp-content/uploads/Ante-Nicene-Fathers-Vol-1.pdf, 777.

"Examples of Figures of Speech Used in the Bible: What Are They, Their Purpose, Recognizing Them …" August 7, 2013. https://www.truthortradition.com/articles/examples-of-figure-of-speech-used-in-the-bible.

Von Schlegel, K. A. D. "Be Still, My Soul." Translated by Jane Laurie Borthwick. 1752.

Wesley, J. *Sermons of John Wesley: The Complete Collection of 141 Sermons.* Edited by Michael R. Martin. Cedar Eden Books, Kindle Edition, 1708.

APPENDICES

Appendix A. Diversity-in-Unity within the Godhead

Appendix B. Three Hundred Fifty-Six Prophecies Fulfilled by Jesus Christ

APPENDIX A

DIVERSITY-IN-UNITY WITHIN THE GODHEAD

Deuteronomy 6:4
Hear, O Israel: The Lord our God, the Lord is one.

Isaiah 61:1
The Spirit of the Sovereign Lord is on me, because the Lord has anointed me to proclaim good news to the poor. He has sent me to bind up the brokenhearted, to proclaim freedom for the captives and release from darkness for the prisoner.

Isaiah 48:16–17
Come near me and listen to this: "From the first announcement I have not spoken in secret; at the time it happens, I am there." And now the Sovereign Lord has sent me, endowed with his Spirit.

Matthew 3:16
As soon as Jesus was baptized, he went up out of the water. At that moment heaven was opened, and he saw the Spirit of God descending like a dove and alighting on him.

Matthew 28:19
Go and make disciples of all the nations, baptizing them in the name of the Father and the Son and the Holy Spirit.

John 1:1
In the beginning was the Word, and the Word was with God, and the Word was God.

John 15:26
When the Advocate comes, whom I will send to you from the Father—the Spirit of truth who goes out from the Father—He will testify about Me.

John 1:32–34
Then John gave this testimony: "I saw the Spirit come down from heaven as a dove and remain on him. And I myself did not know him, but the one who sent me to baptize with water told me, 'The man on whom you see the Spirit come down and remain is the one who will baptize with the Holy Spirit.' I have seen and I testify that this is God's Chosen One."

John 10:30
I and the Father are one.

Hebrews 4:12–13
For the word of God is alive and active. Sharper than any double-edged sword, it penetrates even to dividing soul and spirit, joints, and marrow; it judges the thoughts and attitudes of the heart.

1 John 5:6
This is the one who came by water and blood—Jesus Christ. He did not come by water only, but by water and blood. And it is the Spirit who testifies, because the Spirit is the truth.

1 John 5:7–9
For there are three that testify: the Spirit, the water, and the blood; and the three are in agreement. We accept human testimony, but God's testimony is greater because it is the testimony of God, which he has given about his Son.

1 John 5:10–11
Whoever believes in the Son of God accepts this testimony. Whoever does not believe God has made him out to be a liar, because they have not believed the testimony God has given about his Son.

Luke 3:22
And the Holy Spirit descended on him in bodily form like a dove. And a voice came from heaven: "You are my Son, whom I love; with you I am well pleased."

John 14:26
But the Advocate, the Holy Spirit, whom the Father will send in my name, will teach you all things and will remind you of everything I have said to you.

John 15:26
When the Advocate comes, whom I will send to you from the Father—the Spirit of truth who goes out from the Father—he will testify about me.

Acts 1:4
On one occasion, while he was eating with them, he gave them this command: "Do not leave Jerusalem, but wait for the gift my Father promised, which you have heard me speak about."

Acts 2:33
Exalted to the right hand of God, he has received from the Father the promised Holy Spirit and has poured out what you now see and hear.

Acts 10:38
How God anointed Jesus of Nazareth with the Holy Spirit and power, and how he went around doing good and healing all who were under the power of the devil, because God was with him.

Romans 1:4
And who through the Spirit of holiness was appointed the Son of God in power by his resurrection from the dead: Jesus Christ our Lord.

Romans 8:9
You, however, are not in the realm of the flesh but are in the realm of the Spirit, if indeed the Spirit of God lives in you. And if anyone does not have the Spirit of Christ, they do not belong to Christ.

1 Corinthians 6:11
And that is what some of you were. But you were washed, you were sanctified, you were justified in the name of the Lord Jesus Christ and by the Spirit of our God.

2 Corinthians 13:14
May the grace of the Lord Jesus Christ, and the love of God, and the fellowship of the Holy Spirit be with you all.

Galatians 4:6
Because you are his sons, God sent the Spirit of his Son into our hearts, the Spirit who calls out, "*Abba*, Father."

Ephesians 1:17
I keep asking that the God of our Lord Jesus Christ, the glorious Father, may give you the Spirit of wisdom and revelation, so that you may know him better.

Ephesians 2:18
For through him we both have access to the Father by one Spirit.

Ephesians 2:22
And in him you too are being built together to become a dwelling in which God lives by his Spirit.

Titus 3:6
Whom he [the Holy Spirit] poured out on us generously through Jesus Christ our Savior.

Hebrews 9:14
How much more, then, will the blood of Christ, who through the eternal Spirit offered himself unblemished to God, cleanse our consciences from acts that lead to death, so that we may serve the living God!

1 Peter 1:2
Who have been chosen according to the foreknowledge of God the Father, through the sanctifying work of the Spirit, to be obedient to Jesus Christ and sprinkled with his blood: Grace and peace be yours in abundance.

APPENDIX B

THREE HUNDRED FIFTY-SIX PROPHECIES FULFILLED BY JESUS CHRIST

Scripture Prophecy Fulfillment

1. Gen. 3:15	Seed of a woman (Virgin Birth)	Gal. 4:4–5; Matt. 1:18
2. Gen. 3:15	He will bruise Satan's head	Heb. 2:14; 1 John 3:8
3. Gen. 3:15	Christ's heel would be bruised with nails on the cross	Matt. 27:35; Luke 24:39–40
4. Gen. 5:24	The bodily ascension to heaven illustrated	Mark 16:19; Rev. 12:5
5. Gen. 9:26–27	The God of Shem will be the son of Shem	Luke 3:23–36
6. Gen. 12:3	Seed of Abraham will bless all nations	Gal. 3:8; Acts 3:25–26
7. Gen. 12:7	The promise made to Abraham's Seed	Gal. 3:16
8. Gen. 14:18	A priest after the Order of Melchizedek	Heb. 6:20
9. Gen. 14:18	King of peace and righteousness	Heb. 7:2
10. Gen. 14:18	The Last Supper foreshadowed	Matt. 26:26–29
11. Gen. 17:19	Seed of Isaac (Gen. 21:12)	Rom. 9:7
12. Gen. 22:8	The Lamb of God promised	John 1:29
13. Gen. 22:18	As Isaac's Seed, will bless all nations	Gal. 3:16
14. Gen. 26:2–5	The Seed of Isaac promised as the Redeemer	Heb. 11:18
15. Gen. 28:12	The Bridge to heaven	John 1:51
16. Gen. 28:14	The Seed of Jacob	Luke 3:34

17. Gen. 49:10	The time of His coming	Luke 2:1–7; Gal. 4:4
18. Gen. 49:10	The Seed of Judah	Luke 3:33
19. Gen. 49:10	Called Shiloh or One Sent	John 17:3
20. Gen. 49:10	Messiah to come before Judah loses identity	John 11:47–52
21. Gen. 49:10	Unto Him shall the obedience of the people be	John 10:16
22. Exod. 3:13–15	The great I Am	John 4:26; 8:58
23. Exod. 12:3–6	The Lamb presented to Israel four days before Passover	Mark 11:7–11
24. Exod. 12:5	A Lamb without blemish	Heb. 9:14; 1 Pet. 1:19
25. Exod. 12:13	The blood of the Lamb saves from wrath	Rom. 5:8
26. Exod. 12:21–27	Christ is our Passover	1 Cor. 5:7
27. Exod. 12:46	Not a bone of the Lamb to be broken	John 19:31–36
28. Exod. 15:2	His exaltation predicted as Yeshua	Acts 7:55–56
29. Exod. 15:11	His character—holiness	Luke 1:35; Acts 4:27
30. Exod. 17:6	The spiritual Rock of Israel	1 Cor. 10:4
31. Exod. 33:19	His character—merciful	Luke 1:72
32. Lev. 1:2–9	His sacrifice a sweet-smelling savor unto God	Eph. 5:2
33. Lev. 14:11	The leper cleansed—sign to priesthood	Luke 5:12–14; Acts 6:7
34. Lev. 16:15–17	Prefigures Christ's once-for-all death	Heb. 9:7–14
35. Lev. 16:27	Suffering outside the camp	Matt. 27:33; Heb. 13:11–12
36. Lev. 17:11	The blood—the life of the flesh	Matt. 26:28; Mark 10:45
37. Lev. 17:11	It is the blood that makes atonement	Rom. 3:23–24; 1 John 1:7
38. Lev. 23:36–37	The drink offering: "If any man thirst"	John 7:37
39. Num. 9:12	Not a bone of Him broken	John 19:31–36
40. Num. 21:9	The serpent on a pole; Christ lifted up	John 3:14–18; 12:32
41. Num. 24:17	Time: "I shall see him, but not now."	John 1:14; Gal. 4:4
42. Deut. 18:15	"This is of a truth that prophet."	John 6:14
43. Deut. 18:15–16	"Had ye believed Moses, ye would believe me,"	John 5:45–47
44. Deut. 18:18	Sent by the Father to speak His Word	John 8:28–29

45. Deut. 18:19	Whoever will not hear must bear his sin	Acts 3:22–23	
46. Deut. 21:23	Cursed is he that hangs on a tree	Gal. 3:10–13	
47. Josh. 5:14–15	The captain of our salvation	Heb. 2:10	
48. Ruth 4:4–10	Christ, our kinsman, has redeemed us	Eph. 1:3–7	
49. 1 Sam. 2:35	A faithful priest	Heb. 2:17; 3:1–3, 6; 7:24–25	
50. 1 Sam. 2:10	Shall be an anointed King to the Lord	Matt. 28:18; John 12:15	
51. 2 Sam. 7:12	David's Seed	Matt. 1:1	
52. 2 Sam. 7:13	His kingdom is everlasting	2 Pet. 1:11	
53. 2 Sam. 7:14	The Son of God	Luke 1:32; Rom. 1:3–4	
54. 2 Sam. 7:16	David's house established forever	Luke 3:31; Rev. 22:16	
55. 2 Kings 2:11	The bodily ascension to heaven illustrated	Luke 24:51	
56. 1 Chron. 17:11	David's Seed	Matt. 1:1; 9:27	
57. 1 Chron. 17:12–13	To reign on David's throne forever	Luke 1:32–33	
58. 1 Chron. 17:13	"I will be His Father, He … my Son."	Heb. 1:5	
59. Job 9:32–33	Mediator between humankind and God	1 Tim. 2:5	
60. Job 19:23–27	The resurrection predicted	John 5:24–29	
61. Ps. 2:1–3	The enmity of kings foreordained	Acts 4:25–28	
62. Ps. 2:2	To own the title "Anointed" ("Christ")	John 1:41; Acts 2:36	
63. Ps. 2:6	His character—holiness	John 8:46; Rev. 3:7	
64. Ps. 2:6	To own the title "King"	Matt. 2:2	
65. Ps. 2:7	Declared the Beloved Son	Matt. 3:17; Rom. 1:4	
66. Ps. 2:7–8	The Crucifixion and resurrection intimated	Acts 13:29–33	
67. Ps. 2:8–9	Rules the nations with a rod of iron	Rev. 2:27; 12:5; 19:15	
68. Ps. 2:12	Life comes through faith in Him	John 20:31	
69. Ps. 8:2	The mouths of babes perfect His praise	Matt. 21:16	
70. Ps. 8:5, 6	His humiliation and exaltation	Heb. 2:5–9	
71. Ps. 9:7–10	Judge the world in righteousness	Acts 17:31	
72. Ps. 16:10	Was not to see corruption	Acts 2:31; 13:35	
73. Ps. 16:9–11	Was to rise from the dead	John 20:9	
74. Ps. 17:15	The resurrection predicted	Luke 24:6	

75.	Ps. 18:2–3	The horn of salvation	Luke 1:69–71
76.	Ps. 22:1	Forsaken because of sins of others	2 Cor. 5:21
77.	Ps. 22:1	"My God, my God, why hast thou forsaken me?"	Matt. 27:46
78.	Ps. 22:2	Darkness upon Calvary for three hours	Matt. 27:45
79.	Ps. 22:7	They shoot out the lip and shake the head	Matt. 27:39–44
80.	Ps. 22:8	"He trusted in God. Let Him deliver him."	Matt. 27:43
81.	Ps. 22:9–10	Born the Savior	Luke 2:7
82.	Ps. 22:12–13	They seek His death	John 19:6
83.	Ps. 22:14	His blood poured out when they pierced His side	John 19:34
84.	Ps. 22:14–15	Suffered agony on Calvary	Mark 15:34–37
85.	Ps. 22:15	He thirsted	John 19:28
86.	Ps. 22:16	They pierced His hands and His feet	John 19:34, 37; 20:27
87.	Ps. 22:17–18	They stripped Him before the stares of men	Luke 23:34–35
88.	Ps. 22:18	They parted His garments	John 19:23–24
89.	Ps. 22:20–21	He committed Himself to God	Luke 23:46
90.	Ps. 22:20–21	Satanic power bruising the Redeemer's heel	Heb. 2:14
91.	Ps. 22:22	His resurrection declared	John 20:17
92.	Ps. 22:27–28	He shall be the governor of the nations	Col. 1:16
93.	Ps. 22:31	"It is finished."	John 19:30; Heb. 10:10, 12, 14, 18
94.	Ps. 23:1	"I am the Good Shepherd."	John 10:11; 1 Pet. 2:25
95.	Ps. 24:3	His exaltation predicted	Acts 1:11; Phil. 2:9
96.	Ps. 30:3	His resurrection predicted	Acts 2:32
97.	Ps. 31:5	"Into thy hands I commit my spirit."	Luke 23:46
98.	Ps. 31:11	His acquaintances fled from Him	Mark 14:50
99.	Ps. 31:13	They took counsel to put Him to death	Matt. 27:1; John 11:53
100.	Ps. 31:14–15	"He trusted in God, let Him deliver him."	Matt. 27:43
101.	Ps. 34:20	Not a bone of His broken	John 19:31–36
102.	Ps. 35:11	False witnesses rose up against Him	Matt. 26:59
103.	Ps. 35:19	He was hated without cause	John 15:25
104.	Ps. 38:11	His friends stood far off	Luke 23:49
105.	Ps. 38:12	Enemies try to entangle Him by craft	Mark 14:1; Matt. 22:15

106.	Ps. 38:12–13	Silent before His accusers	Matt. 27:12–14
107.	Ps. 38:20	He went about doing good	Acts 10:38
108.	Ps. 40:2–5	The joy of His resurrection predicted	John 20:20
109.	Ps. 40:6–8	His delight—the will of the Father	John 4:34; Heb. 10:5–10
110.	Ps. 40:9	He was to preach the righteousness in Israel	Matt. 4:17
111.	Ps. 40:14	Confronted by adversaries in the garden	John 18:4–6
112.	Ps. 41:9	Betrayed by a familiar friend	John 13:18
113.	Ps. 45:2	Words of grace come from His lips	John 1:17; Luke 4:22
114.	Ps. 45:6	To own the title "God" or "Elohim"	Heb. 1:8
115.	Ps. 45:7	A special anointing by the Holy Spirit	Matt. 3:16; Heb. 1:9
116.	Ps. 45:7–8	Called the Christ (Messiah or Anointed)	Luke 2:11
117.	Ps. 45:17	His name remembered forever	Eph. 1:20–21; Heb. 1:8
118.	Ps. 55:12–14	Betrayed by a friend, not an enemy	John 13:18
119.	Ps. 55:15	Unrepentant death of the betrayer	Matt. 27:3–5; Acts 1:16–19
120.	Ps. 68:18	To give gifts to humankind	Eph. 4:7–16
121.	Ps. 68:18	Ascended into heaven	Luke 24:51
122.	Ps. 69:4	Hated without a cause	John 15:25
123.	Ps. 69:8	A stranger to own brethren	John 1:11; 7:5
124.	Ps. 69:9	Zealous for the Lord's house	John 2:17
125.	Ps. 69:14–20	Messiah's anguish of soul before crucifixion	Matt. 26:36–45
126.	Ps. 69:20	"My soul is exceeding sorrowful."	Matt. 26:38
127.	Ps. 69:21	Given vinegar in thirst	Matt. 27:34
128.	Ps. 69:26	The Savior given and smitten by God	John 17:4; 18:11
129.	Ps. 72:10–11	Great persons were to visit Him	Matt. 2:1–11
130.	Ps. 72:16	The corn of wheat to fall into the ground	John 12:24–25
131.	Ps. 72:17	Belief on His name will produce offspring	John 1:12–13
132.	Ps. 72:17	All nations shall be blessed by Him	Gal. 3:8
133.	Ps. 72:17	All nations shall call Him blessed	John 12:13; Rev. 5:8–12
134.	Ps. 78:1–2	He would teach in parables	Matt. 13:34–35
135.	Ps. 78:2	To speak the wisdom of God with authority	Matt. 7:29
136.	Ps. 80:17	The man of God's right hand	Mark 14:61–62
137.	Ps. 88	The suffering and reproach of Calvary	Matt. 27:26–50
138.	Ps. 88:8	They stood far off and watched	Luke 23:49

139. Ps. 89:9	He calms the wind and the sea	Matt. 8:26
140. Ps. 89:27	Firstborn	Col. 1:15, 18
141. Ps. 89:27	Emmanuel to be higher than earthly kings	Luke 1:32–33
142. Ps. 89:35–37	David's Seed, throne, kingdom, endure forever	Luke 1:32–33
143. Ps. 89:36–37	His character—faithfulness	Rev. 1:5; 19:11
144. Ps. 90:2	He is from everlasting (Mic. 5:2)	John 1:1
145. Ps. 91:11–12	Identified as messianic; used to tempt Christ	Luke 4:10–11
146. Ps. 97:9	His exaltation predicted	Acts 1:11; Eph. 1:20
147. Ps. 100:5	His character—goodness	Matt. 19:16–17
148. Ps. 102:1–11	The suffering and reproach of Calvary	John 19:16–30
149. Ps. 102:25–27	Messiah is the preexistent Son	Heb. 1:10–12
150. Ps. 109:25	Ridiculed	Matt. 27:39
151. Ps. 110:1	Son of David	Matt. 22:42–43
152. Ps. 110:1	To ascend to the right hand of the Father	Mark 16:19
153. Ps. 110:1	David's son called Lord	Matt. 22:44–45
154. Ps. 110:4	A priest after Melchizedek's order	Heb. 6:20
155. Ps. 112:4	His character—compassionate, gracious, etc.	Matt. 9:36
156. Ps. 118:17–18	Messiah's resurrection assured	Luke 24:5–7; 1 Cor. 15:20
157. Ps. 118:22–23	The rejected stone is Head of the corner	Matt. 21:42–43
158. Ps. 118:26	The Blessed One presented to Israel	Matt. 21:9
159. Ps. 118:26	To come while Temple standing	Matt. 21:12–15
160. Ps. 132:11	The Seed of David (the fruit of His body)	Luke 1:32; Acts 2:30
161. Ps. 129:3	He was scourged	Matt. 27:26
162. Ps. 138:1–6	The supremacy of David's Seed amazes kings	Matt. 2:2–6
163. Ps. 147:3, 6	The earthly ministry of Christ described	Luke 4:18
164. Prov. 1:23	He will send the Spirit of God	John 16:7
165. Prov. 8:23	Foreordained from everlasting	Rev. 13:8; 1 Pet. 1:19–20
166. Song of Sol. 5:16	The altogether lovely one	John 1:17
167. Isa. 2:3	He shall teach all nations	John 4:25
168. Isa. 2:4	He shall judge among the nations	John 5:22
169. Isa. 6:1	When Isaiah saw His glory	John 12:40–41

170.	Isa. 6:8	The One sent by God	John 12:38–45
171.	Isa. 6:9–10	Parables fall on deaf ears	Matt. 13:13–15
172.	Isa. 6:9–12	Blind to Christ and deaf to His words	Acts 28:23–29
173.	Isa. 7:14	To be born of a virgin	Luke 1:35
174.	Isa. 7:14	To be Emmanuel—God with us	Matt. 1:18–23; 1 Tim. 3:16
175.	Isa. 8:8	Called Emmanuel	Matt. 1:23
176.	Isa. 8:14	A stone of stumbling, a Rock of offense	1 Pet. 2:8
177.	Isa. 9:1–2	His ministry to begin in Galilee	Matt. 4:12–17
178.	Isa. 9:6	A child born—humanity	Luke 1:31
179.	Isa. 9:6	A Son given—Deity	Luke 1:32; John 1:14; 1 Tim. 3:16
180.	Isa. 9:6	Declared to be the Son of God with power	Rom. 1:3–4
181.	Isa. 9:6	The Wonderful One, Peleh	Luke 4:22
182.	Isa. 9:6	The Counsellor, Yaatz	Matt. 13:54
183.	Isa. 9:6	The Mighty God, El Gibor	1 Cor. 1:24; Titus 2:13
184.	Isa. 9:6	The Everlasting Father, Avi Adth	John 8:58; 10:30
185.	Isa. 9:6	The Prince of Peace, Sar Shalom	John 16:33
186.	Isa. 9:7	Inherits the throne of David	Luke 1:32
187.	Isa. 9:7	His character—just	John 5:30
188.	Isa. 9:7	No end to his government, throne, and kingdom	Luke 1:33
189.	Isa. 11:1	Called a Nazarene—the Branch, Netzer	Matt. 2:23
190.	Isa. 11:1	A rod out of Jesse—son of Jesse	Luke 3:23, 32
191.	Isa. 11:2	Anointed One by the Spirit	Matt. 3:16, 17; Acts 10:38
192.	Isa. 11:2	His character—wisdom, knowledge, etc.	Col. 2:3
193.	Isa. 11:3	He would know their thoughts	Luke 6:8; John 2:25
194.	Isa. 11:4	Judge in righteousness	Acts 17:31
195.	Isa. 11:4	Judges with the sword of His mouth	Rev. 2:16; 19:11, 15
196.	Isa. 11:5	Character: righteous and faithful	Rev. 19:11
197.	Isa. 11:10	The Gentiles seek Him	John 12:18–21
198.	Isa. 12:2	Called Jesus—Yeshua	Matt. 1:21
199.	Isa. 22:22	The One given all authority to govern	Rev. 3:7
200.	Isa. 25:8	The resurrection predicted	1 Cor. 15:54
201.	Isa. 26:19	His power of resurrection predicted	Matt. 27:50–54
202.	Isa. 28:16	The Messiah is the precious cornerstone	Acts 4:11–12
203.	Isa. 28:16	The sure foundation	1 Cor. 3:11; Matt. 16:18

204. Isa. 29:13	He indicated hypocritical obedience to His Word	Matt. 15:7–9
205. Isa. 29:14	The wise are confounded by the Word	1 Cor. 1:18–31
206. Isa. 32:2	A refuge—a man shall be a hiding place	Matt. 23:37
207. Isa. 35:4	He will come and save you	Matt. 1:21
208. Isa. 35:5–6	To have a ministry of miracles	Matt. 11:2–6
209. Isa. 40:3–4	Preceded by forerunner	John 1:23
210. Isa. 40:9	"Behold your God."	John 1:36; 19:14
211. Isa. 40:10	He will come to reward	Rev. 22:12
212. Isa. 40:11	A shepherd—compassionate life-giver	John 10:10–18
213. Isa. 42:1–4	The Servant as a faithful, patient Redeemer	Matt. 12:18–21
214. Isa. 42:2	Meek and lowly	Matt. 11:28–30
215. Isa. 42:3	He brings hope for the hopeless	Matt. 12:14–21; John 4:1–54
216. Isa. 42:4	The nations shall wait on His teachings	John 12:20–26
217. Isa. 42:6	The Light (salvation) of the Gentiles	Luke 2:32
218. Isa. 42:1, 6	His is a worldwide compassion	Matt. 28:19–20
219. Isa. 42:7	Eyes opened	John 9:25–38
220. Isa. 43:11	He is the only Savior	Acts 4:12
221. Isa. 44:3	He will send the Spirit of God	John 16:7, 13
222. Isa. 45:21–25	He is Lord and Savior	Phil. 3:20; Titus 2:13
223. Isa. 45:23	He will be the Judge	John 5:22; Rom. 14:11
224. Isa. 46:9–10	Declares things not yet done	John 13:19
225. Isa. 48:12	The First and the Last	John 1:30; Rev. 1:8–17
226. Isa. 48:16–17	He came as a Teacher	John 3:2
227. Isa. 49:1	Called from the womb—His humanity	Matt. 1:18
228. Isa. 49:5	A Servant from the womb	Luke 1:31; Phil. 2:7
229. Isa. 49:6	He will restore Israel	Acts 3:19–21; 15:16–17
230. Isa. 49:6	He is salvation for Israel	Luke 2:29–32
231. Isa. 49:6	He is the Light of the Gentiles	John 8:12; Acts 13:47
232. Isa. 49:6	He is salvation unto the ends of the earth	Acts 15:7–18
233. Isa. 49:7	He is despised of the nations	John 1:11; 8:48–49; 19:14–15
234. Isa. 50:3	Heaven is clothed in black at His humiliation	Luke 23:44–45

235.	Isa. 50:4	He is a learned Counselor for the weary	Matt. 7:29; 11:28–29
236.	Isa. 50:5	The Servant bound willingly to obedience	Matt. 26:39
237.	Isa. 50:6	"I gave my back to the smiters."	Matt. 27:26
238.	Isa. 50:6	He was smitten on the cheeks	Matt. 26:67
239.	Isa. 50:6	He was spat upon	Matt. 27:30
240.	Isa. 52:7	Published good tidings upon mountains	Matt. 5:12; 15:29; 28:16
241.	Isa. 52:13	The Servant exalted	Acts 1:8–11; Eph. 1:19–22; Phil. 2:5–9
242.	Isa. 52:14	The Servant shockingly abused	Luke 18:31–34; Matt. 26:67–68
243.	Isa. 52:15	Nations startled by message of the Servant	Luke 18:31–34; Matt. 26:67–68
244.	Isa. 52:15	His bloodshed sprinkles nations	Heb. 9:13–14; Rev. 1:5
245.	Isa. 53:1	His people would not believe Him	John 12:37–38
246.	Isa. 53:2	Appearance of an ordinary man	Phil. 2:6–8
247.	Isa. 53:3	Despised	Luke 4:28–29
248.	Isa. 53:3	Rejected	Matt. 27:21–23
249.	Isa. 53:3	Great sorrow and grief	Matt. 26:37–38; Luke 19:41; Heb. 4:15
250.	Isa. 53:3	People hide from being associated with Him	Mark 14:50–52
251.	Isa. 53:4	He would have a healing ministry	Matt. 8:16–17
252.	Isa. 53:4	Thought to be cursed by God	Matt. 26:66; 27:41–43
253.	Isa. 53:5	Bears penalty for humankind's iniquities	2 Cor. 5:21; Heb. 2:9
254.	Isa. 53:5	His sacrifice provides peace between humankind and God	Col. 1:20
255.	Isa. 53:5	His sacrifice would heal humankind of sin	1 Pet. 2:24
256.	Isa. 53:6	He would be the sin-bearer for all humankind	1 John 2:2; 4:10
257.	Isa. 53:6	God's will that He bear sin for all humankind	Gal. 1:4
258.	Isa. 53:7	Oppressed and afflicted	Matt. 27:27–31
259.	Isa. 53:7	Silent before His accusers	Matt. 27:12–14
260.	Isa. 53:7	Sacrificial Lamb	John 1:29; 1 Pet. 1:18–19

261. Isa. 53:8	Confined and persecuted	Matt. 26:47–75; 27:1–31
262. Isa. 53:8	He would be judged	John 18:13–22
263. Isa. 53:8	He would be killed	Matt. 27:35
264. Isa. 53:8	Dies for the sins of the world	1 John 2:2
265. Isa. 53:9	Buried in a rich man's grave	Matt. 27:57
266. Isa. 53:9	Innocent and had done no violence	Luke 23:41; John 18:38
267. Isa. 53:9	No deceit in His mouth	1 Pet. 2:22
268. Isa. 53:10	God's will that He die for humankind	John 18:11
269. Isa. 53:10	An offering for sin	Matt. 20:28; Gal. 3:13
270. Isa. 53:10	Resurrected to live forever	Rom. 6:9
271. Isa. 53:10	He would prosper	John 17:1–5
272. Isa. 53:11	God fully satisfied with His suffering	John 12:27
273. Isa. 53:11	God's Servant would justify humankind	Rom. 5:8–9; 18–19
274. Isa. 53:11	The sin-bearer for all humankind	Heb. 9:28
275. Isa. 53:12	Exalted by God because of His sacrifice	Matt. 28:18
276. Isa. 53:12	He would give up His life to save humankind	Luke 23:46
277. Isa. 53:12	Numbered with the transgressors	Mark 15:27–28; Luke 22:37
278. Isa. 53:12	Sin-bearer for all humankind	1 Pet. 2:24
279. Isa. 53:12	Intercede to God on behalf of humankind	Luke 23:34, Rom. 8:34
280. Isa. 55:3	Resurrected by God	Acts 13:34
281. Isa. 55:4	A witness	John 18:37
282. Isa. 55:4	He is a leader and commander	Heb. 2:10
283. Isa. 55:5	God would glorify Him	Acts 3:13
284. Isa. 59:16	Intercessor between humankind and God	Matt. 10:32
285. Isa. 59:16	He would come to provide salvation	John 6:40
286. Isa. 59:20	He would come to Zion as their Redeemer	Luke 2:38
287. Isa. 60:1–3	He would show light to the Gentiles	Acts 26:23
288. Isa. 61:1	The Spirit of God upon Him	Matt. 3:16–17
289. Isa. 61:1	The Messiah would preach the good news	Luke 4:16–21
290. Isa. 61:1	Provide freedom from the bondage of sin	John 8:31–36
291. Isa. 61:1–2	Proclaim a period of grace	Gal. 4:4–5
292. Jer. 11:21	Conspiracy to kill Jesus	John 7:1; Matt. 21:38
293. Jer. 23:5–6	Descendant of David	Luke 3:23–31

294. Jer. 23:5–6	The Messiah would be both God and man	John 13:13; 1 Tim. 3:16
295. Jer. 31:22	Born of a virgin	Matt. 1:18–20
296. Jer. 31:31	The Messiah would be the new covenant	Matt. 26:28
297. Jer. 33:14–15	Descendant of David	Luke 3:23–31
298. Ezek. 34:23–24	Descendant of David	Matt. 1:1
299. Ezek. 37:24–25	Descendant of David	Luke 1:31–33
300. Dan. 2:44–45	The Stone that shall break the kingdoms	Matt. 21:44
301. Dan. 7:13–14	He would ascend into heaven	Acts 1:9–11
302. Dan. 7:13–14	Highly exalted	Eph. 1:20–22
303. Dan. 7:13–14	His dominion would be everlasting	Luke 1:31–33
304. Dan. 9:24	To make an end to sins	Gal. 1:3–5
305. Dan. 9:24	To make reconciliation for iniquity	Rom. 5:10; 2 Cor. 5:18–21
306. Dan. 9:24	He would be holy	Luke 1:35
307. Dan. 9:25	His announcement	John 12:12–13
308. Dan. 9:26	Cut off	Matt. 16:21; 21:38–39
309. Dan. 9:26	Die for the sins of the world	Heb. 2:9
310. Dan. 9:26	Killed before the destruction of the Temple	Matt. 27:50–51
311. Dan. 10:5–6	Messiah in a glorified state	Rev. 1:13–16
312. Hosea 11:1	He would be called out of Egypt	Matt. 2:15
313. Hosea 13:14	He would defeat death	1 Cor. 15:55–57
314. Joel 2:32	Offer salvation to all humankind	Rom. 10:9–13
315. Jon. 1:17	Death and resurrection of Christ	Matt. 12:40; 16:4
316. Mic. 5:2	Born in Bethlehem	Matt. 2:1–6
317. Mic. 5:2	Ruler in Israel	Luke 1:33
318. Mic. 5:2	From everlasting	John 8:58
319. Hag. 2:6–9	He would visit the Second Temple	Luke 2:27–32
320. Hag. 2:23	Descendant of Zerubbabel	Luke 2:27–32
321. Zech. 3:8	God's Servant	John 17:4
322. Zech. 6:12–13	Priest and King	Heb. 8:1
323. Zech. 9:9	Greeted with rejoicing in JeruRita	Matt. 21:8–10
324. Zech. 9:9	Beheld as King	John 12:12–13
325. Zech. 9:9	The Messiah would be just	John 5:30
326. Zech. 9:9	The Messiah would bring salvation	Luke 19:10
327. Zech. 9:9	The Messiah would be humble	Matt. 11:29

328.	Zech. 9:9	Presented to JeruRita riding on a donkey	Matt. 21:6–9
329.	Zech. 10:4	The cornerstone	Eph. 2:20
330.	Zech. 11:4–6	At His coming, Israel to have unfit leaders	Matt. 23:1–4
331.	Zech. 11:4–6	Rejection causes God to remove His protection	Luke 19:41–44
332.	Zech. 11:4–6	Rejected in favor of another king	John 19:13–15
333.	Zech. 11:7	Ministry to "poor," the believing remnant	Matt. 9:35–36
334.	Zech. 11:8	Unbelief forces Messiah to reject them	Matt. 23:33
335.	Zech. 11:8	Despised	Matt. 27:20
336.	Zech. 11:9	Stops ministering to those who rejected Him	Matt. 13:10–11
337.	Zech. 11:10–11	Rejection causes God to remove protection	Luke 19:41–44
338.	Zech. 11:10–11	The Messiah would be God	John 14:7
339.	Zech. 11:12–13	Betrayed for thirty pieces of silver	Matt. 26:14–15
340.	Zech. 11:12–13	Rejected	Matt. 26:14–15
341.	Zech. 11:12–13	Thirty pieces of silver cast in the house of the Lord	Matt. 27:3–5
342.	Zech. 11:12–13	The Messiah would be God	John 12:45
343.	Zech. 12:10	The Messiah's body would be pierced	John 19:34–37
344.	Zech. 12:10	The Messiah would be both God and man	John 10:30
345.	Zech. 12:10	The Messiah would be rejected	John 1:11
346.	Zech. 13:7	God's will that He die for humankind	John 18:11
347.	Zech. 13:7	A violent death	Mark 14:27
348.	Zech. 13:7	Both God and man	John 14:9
349.	Zech. 13:7	Israel scattered as a result of rejecting Him	Matt. 26:31–56
350.	Zech. 14:4	He would return to the Mount of Olives	Acts 1:11–12
351.	Mal. 3:1	Messenger to prepare the way for the Messiah	Mark 1:1–8
352.	Mal. 3:1	Sudden appearance at the Temple	Mark 11:15–16
353.	Mal. 3:1	Messenger of the new covenant	Luke 4:43
354.	Mal. 3:6	The God who changes not	Heb. 13:8
355.	Mal. 4:5	Forerunner in spirit of Elijah	Matt. 3:1–3; 11:10–14; 17:11–13
356.	Mal. 4:6	Forerunner would turn many to righteousness	Luke 1:16–17

Lightning Source UK Ltd.
Milton Keynes UK
UKHW020907121021
392079UK00011B/1014